CW00921985

Theories of Mind

Theories of Mind

An Introductory Reader

Edited by
Maureen Eckert

ROWMAN & LITTLEFIELD PUBLISHERS, INC.
Lanham • Boulder • New York • Toronto • Oxford

ROWMAN & LITTLEFIELD PUBLISHERS, INC.

Published in the United States of America
by Rowman & Littlefield Publishers, Inc.
A wholly owned subsidary of The Rowman & Littlefield Publishing Group, Inc.
4501 Forbes Boulevard, Suite 200, Lanham, Maryland 20706
www.rowmanlittlefield.com

PO Box 317, Oxford
OX2 9RU, UK

Copyright © 2006 by Rowman & Littlefield Publishers, Inc.

All rights reserved. No part of this publication may be reproduced,
stored in a retrieval system, or transmitted in any form or by any
means, electronic, mechanical, photocopying, recording, or otherwise,
without the prior permission of the publisher.

British Library Cataloguing in Publication Information Available

Library of Congress Cataloging-in-Publication Data

Theories of mind : an introductory reader / edited by Maureen Eckert.
   p.   cm.
   Includes bibliographical references and index.
   ISBN-13: 978-0-7425-5062-9 (cloth : alk. paper)
   ISBN-10: 0-7425-5062-1 (cloth : alk. paper)
   ISBN-13: 978-0-7425-5063-6 (pbk. : alk. paper)
   ISBN-10: 0-7425-5063-X (pbk. : alk. paper)
   1. Philosophy of mind.   I. Eckert, Maureen, 1966–   .
BD418.3.T43   2006
128'.2—dc22   2006007947

Printed in the United States of America

♾ ™ The paper used in this publication meets the
minimum requirements of American National Standard for
Information Sciences—Permanence of Paper for Printed
Library Materials, ANSI/NISO Z39.48-1992.

Contents

Acknowledgments

I am grateful to the Office of the Provost, University of Massachusetts at Dartmouth, for support of this project. Colleagues lent their ideas and support throughout various stages, especially Pete Mandik, Steven Cahn, Eric Steinhart, and Catherine Villanueva Gardner. I wish to thank my editor, Eve DeVaro, and her assistants, Tessa Fallon and Emily Ross, for their constant, invaluable assistance, and my mom, Agnes, for her generous help in typing readings for the manuscript.

Maureen Eckert
University of Massachusetts, Dartmouth

Introduction

Philosophy of mind is an area of inquiry seeking to answer fundamental questions about the nature of the human mind: What is a mind? How is it structured? What is the relationship between the mind and the brain? Do other things besides human beings have minds? In one sense, philosophers in the Western tradition have engaged in philosophical inquiry about the mind for more than two thousand years, since Plato (c. 428–347 B.C.) and Aristotle (384–322 B.C.) each theorized about the nature of the "soul" (*psyche*). However, the discipline of philosophy of mind has changed dramatically over time, especially as the sciences developed and independent disciplines such as psychology, neuroscience, and cognitive science were established. This anthology of readings aims to provide the background to the more recent twentieth and twenty-first century history of philosophy of mind, focusing on theories of mind that have shaped contemporary debates and research in the field. It will become clear that philosophy of mind has become an interdisciplinary endeavor in which philosophers often utilize discoveries about the mind from the sciences and sometimes even participate in scientific research themselves. What makes philosophy of mind "philosophical" is the manner in which questions concerning our assumptions about the mind and our mental states are explored and debated rigorously. As theories of the mind are fundamentally theories about ourselves, it is not surprising that philosophers seek a firm understanding of what we can truly know about the mind. Our place in the world and how we understand ourselves in relation to it is at stake.

The overall theme explored by the philosophers in this anthology is the Mind-Body problem—the relationship between the mind and the brain. This problem is, arguably, less of a "problem" presently, as research on the mind and cognitive processes continues to grow; yet the problem provides us with an opportunity to learn significant strands of thought regarding the mind—

the motivations behind the most viable theories of mind to date—and how these views are defended. The Mind-Body problem helps us learn about philosophical argument itself when we explore it.

The twenty-one selections in this anthology are tailored to suit an undergraduate course introducing the philosophy of mind. It is an intellectually challenging discipline, and few papers are written to be accessible to the general public or beginning student. I have tried to include essential readings, and I have tried to include a sampling of the most vivid and elucidating arguments whenever possible. In the introductions to the reading selections, technical terms in **bold face type** are explained in a glossary at the end of this anthology. I provide a list of well-known resource sites on the Internet that can assist readers on general philosophical terminology, viewpoints within the discipline of philosophy of mind and related disciplines, as well as key thinkers. Reference books are also listed. I also provide the websites of authors at the end of each reading selection, many of which include online papers and full lists of publications by some of the individual authors.

PHILOSOPHY AND PHILOSOPHY OF MIND RESOURCES

Internet Sites

Stanford Encyclopedia of Philosophy
http://plato.stanford.edu/contents.html

The Internet Encyclopedia of Philosophy
www.utm.edu/research/iep/

Dictionary of Philosophy of Mind
www.artsci.wustl.edu/~philos/MindDict/main.html

Guide to the Philosophy of Mind: Compiled by David Chalmers
http://consc.net/guide.html

City University of New York: Cognitive Science Web Resources (Includes
   Philosophy, Psychology, and Cognitive Science)
http://web.gc.cuny.edu/cogsci/re.htm

A Field Guide to the Philosophy of Mind
http://host.uniroma3.it/progetti/kant/field/

Books

LIBRARY REFERENCES

Craig, E. (ed.). 1998. *Routledge Encyclopedia of Philosophy*. New York: Routledge. On-line version is available through subscription.
Edwards, P. (ed.). 1996. *The Encyclopedia of Philosophy*. New York: Macmillan.

GENERAL REFERENCES

Audi, R. (ed.). 1999. *The Cambridge Dictionary of Philosophy*, 2nd ed. New York: Cambridge University Press.
Blackburn, S. 1992. *Oxford Dictionary of Philosophy*, 2nd ed. New York: Oxford University Press.
Craig, E. (ed.). 2005. *The Shorter Routledge Encyclopedia of Philosophy*, 2nd ed. New York: Routledge.

MIND AND COGNITIVE SCIENCE

Bechtel, W., Graham, G. (eds.). 1999. *A Companion to Cognitive Science*. London: Blackwell.
Guttenplan, S. (ed.). 1996. *A Companion to the Philosophy of Mind*. London: Blackwell.
Stich, S. 2003. *The Blackwell Guide to Philosophy of Mind*. London: Blackwell.
Wilson, R., Kell, F. (eds.). 2001. *MIT Encyclopedia of the Cognitive Sciences*. Cambridge: MIT Press.

I

SUBSTANCE DUALISM AND ITS CONTEMPORARY CRITICS

Selections from Rene Descartes' *Principles of Philosophy* (1644) are presented in this section to provide a concise account of Descartes' views on the mind and the body, a view known as "**Substance Dualism**." This view generally holds that the mind and body are two wholly distinct kinds of substances, the body being comprised of matter, extended in space, and observable and measurable through the sciences, while the mind cannot be so described, investigated, and "quantified." It is a different kind of substance marked by the activity of thinking. Descartes finds that bodies are "**extended things**" and the mind is a "**thinking thing**." This thesis about the nature of minds and bodies derives from Descartes' systematic philosophical intention to place knowledge on a firm and lasting foundation, one that cannot be shaken. This intention is clarified at the start of the *Principles of Philosophy*, where Descartes describes the search for truth through the demolition of his former beliefs, since these beliefs often come from the sense and may be unreliable. He suggests a test for discovering indubitable beliefs: if we find any reason to doubt a belief, we should treat this belief as though it were false (**hyperbolic doubt**). Such doubt, he notes, does not apply to ordinary life and to our decisions there but rather to the philosophical quest for absolute certainty. It turns out that most all of our beliefs can be doubted. We cannot be certain that we are not dreaming at any given moment or that we are not being systematically fooled by an all-powerful malevolent being (whom he called the **Evil Genius** in his *Meditations on First Philosophy*) into believing that the world around us exists when it does not. These possibilities lead us to doubt practically every belief we have—except one, the famous

1

"**Cogito, ergo sum**": "*I am thinking, therefore I exist.*" This belief is indubitable, since even if one is dreaming or is being fooled by an all-powerful evil being and must philosophically doubt all one's beliefs—even if one doubts that one is thinking, one must be thinking in order to do this!

The "Cogito" permits Descartes to find that all of our mental activities, such as thinking, doubting, willing, perceiving, and desiring, insofar as they regard the mind alone, are indubitable to the thinker, while what is thought about (perceived, desired, doubted) is much less certain. For instance, you perceive a chair. The chair that you are perceiving may or may not exist, as you *could* be dreaming it. Yet you, insofar as you are perceiving it, *you* must exist. The *you* in question is not to be confused with your physical body, since you could also be dreaming about the body you normally find "real" in everyday life. The *you* that Descartes finds indubitable is your mind alone that engages in this perceptual activity. Descartes finds that thinking, in this broad sense, is our awareness of everything happening within us "insofar as we are aware of it" (Section 9). Descartes' idea that our mental activities must be those of which we are self-aware has lasting and controversial significance in the philosophy of mind. Are mental states only mental states by virtue of our being aware of them? Are there certain mental states, such as pain or perceptions, for which we must be aware of if we are in these states? How does such awareness factor into an explanation of the mind?

Since Descartes was also a scientist who studied the body, selections from the *Principles of Philosophy* concerning his view on the relationship between the mind and the brain are included. Although he held that the mind and body must be two fundamentally different substances, these passages demonstrate that even a dualist, like Descartes, believed that the mind and the brain are connected in an important way. In the excerpts 189 and 196, Descartes relates that the soul (mind) has sensory awareness only insofar as it is in the brain. The nervous system must transmit sensory information to the mind, and cases of brain damage as well as the phantom limb syndrome show that interferences with the nervous system affect the mind's ability to have sensations. Sensations are mental states, not simply states of the parts of the body. We apprehend our environment through the nervous system, which transmits information to the brain and then to the mind. The question that this assessment of the relationship between the brain and mind raises is: how does the physical substance of the body affect the non-physical substance of the mind or soul? If they are truly two different kinds of substances, it cannot be the case that they stand in a causal relationship in the way that physical bodies collide and affect each other. There is a mystery, then, about how the brain and the mind affect each other (and vice versa), given Descartes' understanding of the mind and body. In everyday life, we tend to believe that physical events cause us to have mental reactions—and our mental states cause physical events. When someone drops a couch on your foot, you feel pain. You feel pain, and move the couch. "Mental causation" is an important feature of how we explain human behavior, and we assume that the mind can be affected by the body and that the body can be affected by the mind. Yet, a substance dualist cannot explain mental causation.

In the twentieth century, Gilbert Ryle, the author of *The Concept of Mind*, from which the selection discussed here is taken, has problems such as this in mind when he raises criticisms of Descartes' "Official Doctrine." His critique of Descartes' **substance dualism** questions how this theory of mind can explain the way in which a non-physical substance can interact with a physical substance—the body—and how we can understand anything about this "ghost in the machine." How can the mind, as Descartes construes it, be said to be located "inside" anything, given that non-physical substances cannot be said to have any location at all. Ryle identifies the main mistake of the "Official Doctrine" as a "**Category Mistake**." He illustrates this philosophical concept through examples. Someone is watching a winning team playing and is told that this team has "team spirit." In response, the person looks for the player on the team who is identifiable as "team spirit." This person will not, of course, find this player on the team. "Team spirit" is a quality of the entire team and the way they are playing. This person has made a "**category mistake**" in looking to find some physical person, "team spirit," that is just like the rest of the team. The person has confused the kind of category a phenomenon like team spirit belongs to, thinking this "ghostly" player belongs to the same category as all the players on the team. Ryle believes the "Official Doctrine" makes a category mistake when it holds that the mind is a substance like the body. Since one cannot find this "mind," just like "team spirit," the mind is assumed to be a substance, but a non-physical one. Ryle asks, why believe that the mind is a substance at all? We can correct this category mistake and reject the "Official Doctrine."

Ryle's own view is known as "**logical behaviorism**," a view that holds that the mind is not a ghostly entity, but a feature of our behaviors. Like "team spirit," the mind is a quality of the whole of our physical selves. The language that we use to refer to our mental states, such as "sadness," "pain," and "intelligence," does not refer to unobservable internal states of the mind but must be understood as referring to observable behaviors and to our **dispositions** to behave in certain ways under certain circumstances. An example of a disposition is solubility. Salt has this quality, it dissolves when placed in a liquid. It has this quality whether or not it actually is placed in water—its disposition to dissolve is a quality it has if it *were* to be placed in liquid. Thus, sadness is a disposition one has to behave in certain ways, to cry, frown, mope under particular circumstances, when someone said something mean, a pet died, etc. The selections from Ryle's work include his explanation of a term we typically take to be one of the most "mental" of mental states—"intelligence." In this selection, Ryle discusses the distinction between "**knowing how**" and "**knowing that**." "Knowing how" regards skills and abilities that we learn, which become second nature to us once we acquire them. "Knowing that" regards items of knowledge that we possess. Ryle maintains that we must not confuse cases of "knowing how" with "knowing that," and we are inclined to misunderstand both cases when it comes to ascribing "intelligence" to someone—applying the "Official Doctrine's" idea that a mysterious "internal" mind is responsible for all of our intelligent behavior. Intelligent cases of "knowing that" are our dispositions to provide certain answers under certain circumstances. Ryle uses an example of a clever clown to illustrate the way that we might mistakenly think that the clown's clever performance is due to thoughts "in his mind" that are put into action. The clown's clever performance is not a matter of the clown referring back "in his mind" to a set of directions located there but is a quality of the performance itself. The clown "knows how" to perform cleverly, and the public performance of his tricks is what determines the cleverness of the performance. As Ryle notes, the clown's trippings and jokes are the workings of his mind—they themselves *are* these workings and are not attributable to a different mental substance.

The reading from Jerry A. Fodor's *Language of Thought* discusses Ryle's **Logical Behaviorism** and provides a lively critique of this view. He begins his discussion with Ryle's example of the clown's clever pratfalls. For Ryle, the cleverness of the clown is not due to mental operations that cause this behavior, and Fodor notes that in Ryle's view any psychologist who would want to explain the clown's behavior in this "**mentalist**" manner (believing in the existence of the mind) would be mistaken. The psychologist may not be mistaken, according to Fodor. There may be more options available to the psychologist wishing to investigate mental operations than Cartesian dualism and behaviorism.

Fodor's selection is quite helpful in providing an illustration of what makes Ryle's behaviorism "logical behaviorism." He asks us to consider the question, "What makes Wheaties the Breakfast of Champions?" There are two kinds of answers to this question. The first is a "causal story" in which we find that the vitamins, minerals, carbohydrates, etc., make Wheaties the Breakfast of Champions. The second is a "conceptual story" in which we find that Wheaties is the Breakfast of Champions because champions eat it. This answer is logically true. A conceptual story might define mental states, much like Ryle believes, but it is not a causal explanation. Both kinds of explanations can be true at the same time. Even *if* Ryle was correct about the meanings of mental state words, this would not affect the mentalist's view that internal mental states cause behavior and can be investigated. Another reading from Fodor, "The Mind-Body Problem," is presented in the **Functionalist** view of mind section of this anthology.

1

Principles of Philosophy

René Descartes

1. *THE SEEKER AFTER TRUTH MUST, ONCE IN THE COURSE OF HIS LIFE, DOUBT EVERYTHING, AS FAR AS IS POSSIBLE.*

Since we began life as infants, and made various judgments concerning the things that can be perceived by the senses before we had the full use of our reason, there are many preconceived opinions that keep us from knowledge of the truth.[1] It seems that the only way of freeing ourselves from these opinions is to make the effort, once in the course of our life, to doubt everything which we find to contain even the smallest suspicion of uncertainty.

2. *WHAT IS DOUBTFUL SHOULD EVEN BE CONSIDERED AS FALSE.*

Indeed, it will even prove useful, once we have doubted these things, to consider them as false, so that our discovery of what is most certain and easy to know may be all the clearer.

3. *THIS DOUBT SHOULD NOT MEANWHILE BE APPLIED TO ORDINARY LIFE.*

This doubt, while it continues, should be kept in check and employed solely in connection with the contemplation of the truth. As far as ordinary life is concerned, the chance for action would frequently pass us by if we waited until we could free ourselves from our doubts, and so we are often compelled to accept what is merely probable. From time to time we may even have to make a choice between two alternatives, even though it is not apparent that one of the two is more probable than the other.

4. *THE REASONS FOR DOUBT CONCERNING THE THINGS THAT CAN BE PERCEIVED BY THE SENSES.*

Given, then, that our efforts are directed solely to the search for truth, our initial doubts will be about the existence of the objects of sense-perception and imagination. The first reason for such doubts is that from time to time we have caught out the senses when they were in error, and it is prudent never to place too much trust in those who have deceived us even once. The second reason is that in our sleep we regularly seem to have sensory perception of, or to imagine, countless things which do not exist anywhere; and if our doubts are on the scale just outlined, there seem to be no marks by means of which we can with certainty distinguish being asleep from being awake.

5. *THE REASONS FOR DOUBTING EVEN MATHEMATICAL DEMONSTRATIONS.*

Our doubt will also apply to other matters which we previously regarded as most certain—even the demonstrations of mathematics and even the principles which we hitherto considered to be self-evident. One reason for this is that we have sometimes seen people make mistakes in such matters and accept as most certain and self-evident things which seemed false to us. Secondly, and most importantly, we have been told that there is an omnipotent God who created us. Now we do not know whether he may have wished to make us beings of the sort who are always deceived even in those matters which seem to us supremely evident; for such constant deception seems no less a possibility than the occasional deception which, as we have noticed on previous occasions, does occur. We may of course suppose that our existence derives not from a supremely powerful God but either from ourselves or from some other source; but in that case, the less powerful we make the author of our coming into being, the more likely it will be that we are so imperfect as to be deceived all the time.

6. WE HAVE FREE WILL, ENABLING US TO WITHHOLD OUR ASSENT IN DOUBTFUL MATTERS AND HENCE AVOID ERROR.

But whoever turns out to have created us, and however powerful and however deceitful he may be, in the meantime we nonetheless experience within us the kind of freedom which enables us always to refrain from believing things which are not completely certain and thoroughly examined. Hence we are able to take precautions against going wrong on any occasion.

7. IT IS NOT POSSIBLE FOR US TO DOUBT THAT WE EXIST WHILE WE ARE DOUBTING; AND THIS IS THE FIRST THING WE COME TO KNOW WHEN WE PHILOSOPHIZE IN AN ORDERLY WAY.

In rejecting—and even imagining to be false—everything which we can in any way doubt, it is easy for us to suppose that there is no God and no heaven, and that there are no bodies, and even that we ourselves have no hands or feet, or indeed any body at all. But we cannot for all that suppose that we, who are having such thoughts, are nothing. For it is a contradiction to suppose that what thinks does not, at the very time when it is thinking, exist. Accordingly, this piece of knowledge[2]—*I am thinking, therefore I exist*—is the first and most certain of all to occur to anyone who philosophizes in an orderly way.

8. IN THIS WAY WE DISCOVER THE DISTINCTION BETWEEN SOUL AND BODY, OR BETWEEN A THINKING THING AND A CORPOREAL THING.

This is the best way to discover the nature of the mind and the distinction between the mind and the body. For if we, who are supposing that everything which is distinct from us is false,[3] examine what we are, we see very clearly that neither extension nor shape nor local motion, nor anything of this kind which is attributable to a body, belongs to our nature, but that thought alone belongs to it. So our knowledge of our thought is prior to, and more certain than, our knowledge of any corporeal thing; for we have already perceived it, although we are still in doubt about other things.

9. WHAT IS MEANT BY "THOUGHT".

By the term 'thought', I understand everything which we are aware of as happening within us, in so far as we have awareness of it. Hence, *thinking* is to be identified here not merely with understanding, willing and imagining, but also with sensory awareness. For if I say 'I am seeing, or I am walking, therefore I exist', and take this as applying to vision or walking as bodily activities, then the conclusion is not absolutely certain. This is because, as often happens during sleep, it is possible for me to think I am seeing or walking, though my eyes are closed and I am not moving about; such thoughts might even be possible if I had no body at all. But if I take 'seeing' or 'walking' to apply to the actual sense or awareness of seeing or walking, then the conclusion is quite certain, since it relates to the mind, which alone has the sensation or thought that it is seeing or walking.

10. MATTERS WHICH ARE VERY SIMPLE AND SELF-EVIDENT ARE ONLY RENDERED MORE OBSCURE BY LOGICAL DEFINITIONS, AND SHOULD NOT BE COUNTED AS ITEMS OF KNOWLEDGE WHICH IT TAKES EFFORT TO ACQUIRE.

I shall not here explain many of the other terms which I have already used or will use in what follows, because they seem to me to be sufficiently self-evident. I have often noticed that philosophers make the mistake of employing logical definitions in an attempt to explain what was already very simple and self-evident; the result is that they only make matters more obscure. And when I said that the proposition *I am thinking, therefore I exist* is the first and most certain of all to occur to anyone who philosophizes in an orderly way, I did not in saying that deny that one must first know what thought, existence and certainty are, and that it is impossible that that which thinks should not exist, and so forth. But because these are very simple notions, and ones which on their own provide us with no knowledge of anything that exists, I did not think they needed to be listed.

11. HOW OUR MIND IS BETTER KNOWN THAN OUR BODY.

In order to realize that the knowledge of our mind is not simply prior to and more certain than the knowledge of our body, but also more evident, we should notice something very well known by the natural light: nothingness possesses no attributes or qualities. It follows that, wherever we find some attributes or qualities, there is necessarily some thing or substance to be found for them to belong to; and the more attributes we discover in the same thing or substance, the clearer is our knowledge of that substance. Now we find more attributes in our mind than in anything else, as is manifest from the fact that whatever enables us to know anything else cannot but lead us to a much surer knowledge of our own mind. For example; if I judge that the earth exists from the fact that I touch it or see it, this very fact undoubtedly gives even greater support for the judgment that my mind exists. For it may perhaps be the case that I judge that I am touching the earth even though the earth does not exist at all; but it cannot be that, when I make this judgment, my mind which is making the judgment does not exist. And the same applies in other cases.

12. *WHY THIS FACT DOES NOT COME TO BE KNOWN TO ALL ALIKE.*

Disagreement on this point has come from those who have not done their philosophizing in an orderly way; and the reason for it is simply that they have never taken sufficient care to distinguish the mind from the body. Although they may have put the certainty of their own existence before that of anything else, they failed to realize that they should have taken 'themselves' in this context to mean their minds alone. They were inclined instead to take 'themselves' to mean only their bodies—the bodies which they saw with their eyes and touched with their hands, and to which they incorrectly attributed the power of sense-perception; and this is what prevented them from perceiving the nature of the mind.

189. *WHAT SENSATION IS AND HOW IT OPERATES.*

It must be realized that the human soul, while informing[4] the entire body, nevertheless has its principal seat in the brain; it is here alone that the soul not only understands and imagines but also has sensory awareness. Sensory awareness comes about by means of nerves, which stretch like threads from the brain to all the limbs, and are joined together in such a way that hardly any part of the human body can be touched without producing movement in several of the nerve-ends that are scattered around in that area. This movement is then transmitted to the other ends of the nerves which are all grouped together in the brain around the seat of the soul, as I explained very fully in Discourse Four of the *Optics*.[5] The result of these movements being set up in the brain by the nerves is that the soul or mind that is closely joined to the brain is affected in various ways, corresponding to the various different sorts of movements. And the various different states of mind, or thoughts, which are the immediate result of these movements are called sensory perceptions, or in ordinary speech, sensations . . .

196. *THE SOUL HAS SENSORY AWARENESS ONLY IN SO FAR AS IT IS IN THE BRAIN.*

There is clear proof that the soul's sensory awareness, via the nerves, of what happens to the individual limbs of the body does not come about in virtue of the soul's presence in the individual limbs, but simply in virtue of its presence in the brain or because the nerves by their motions transmit to it the actions of external objects which touch the parts of the body where the nerves are embedded. Firstly, there are various diseases which affect only the brain but remove or interfere with all sensation. Again, sleep occurs only in the brain, yet every day it deprives us of a great part of our sensory faculties, though these are afterwards restored on waking. Next, when the brain is undamaged, if there is an obstruction in the paths by which the nerves reach the brain from the external limbs, this alone is enough to destroy sensation in those limbs. Lastly, we sometimes feel pain in certain limbs even though there is nothing to cause pain in the limbs themselves; the cause of the pain lies in the other areas through which the nerves travel in their journey from the limbs to the brain. This last point can be proved by countless observations, but it will suffice to mention one here. A girl with a seriously infected hand used to have her eyes bandaged whenever the surgeon visited her, to prevent her being upset by the surgical instruments. After a few days her arm was amputated at the elbow because of a creeping gangrene, and wads of bandages were put in its place so that she was quite unaware that she had lost her arm. However she continued to complain of pains, now in one then in another finger of the amputated hand. The only possible reason for this is that the nerves which used to go from the brain down to the hand now terminated in the arm near the elbow, and were being agitated by the same sorts of motion as must previously have been set up in the hand, so as to produce in the soul, residing in the brain, the sensation of pain in this or that finger.

NOTES

©Cambridge University Press 1988. Reprinted with the permission of Cambridge University Press.
    1. Some examples of such preconceived opinions are given in art. 71, pp. 185f below. [This note refers to section and page number in the Cambridge University Press edition from which the reprinted material comes.]

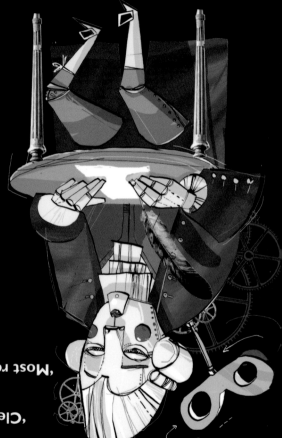

INTRODUCING

'Often imitated ... seldom equalled'
John Gribbin

'Clever and witty'
Guardian

'Most recommended'
Time Out

The highly acclaimed series of graphic guides
to the most challenging subjects around

introducingbooks.com

INTRODUCING

introducingbooks.com

WIN THE ENTIRE INTRODUCING SERIES!

Send your name, address and email to: introducing@iconbooks.co.uk

You will be signed up to join the Icon e-newsletter and, with each newsletter sent, ten lucky subscribers will win every book in the series!

  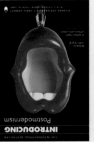 

INTRODUCING Hindu... | INTRODUCING Kant | INTRODUCING Postmodernism | INTRODUCING Logic | ...UCING Islam

Each book: UK £9.99 * Can $17.00 * USA $12.95 * 210 x 140 paperback * 176 pp

Anthropology	Existentialism	Melanie Klein
Barthes	Foucault	Mind and Brain
Buddha	Fractal Geometry	Modernism
Chaos	Freud	Nietzsche
Chomsky	Genetics	Philosophy
Consciousness	Heidegger	Plato
Critical Theory	Hinduism	Postmodernism
Cultural Studies	Islam	Psychology
Darwin	Jung	Quantum Theory
Derrida	Kant	Romanticism
Descartes	Lacan	Sartre
Einstein	Linguistics	Semiotics
Empiricism	Logic	Sociology
The Enlightenment	Marx	Stephen Hawking
Ethics	Marxism	Time
Evolution	Mathematics	Wittgenstein
Evolutionary Psychology	Media Studies	

INTRODUCING is the brilliant series of illustrated guides to the big thinkers and subjects from the history of ideas.

Written by experienced academics in collaboration with leading graphic artists, INTRODUCING is famous for being one of the best – and most enjoyable – ways to get your head around the most challenging ideas there are.

2. 'this inference' (French version).

3. Lat. *falsum*. Descartes uses this term to refer not only to propositions which are false, but also to objects which are unreal, spurious or non-existent. The French version here reads: 'we who are now thinking that there is nothing outside of our thought which truly is or exists . . .'

4. Lat. *informare*. Descartes occasionally employs this standard scholastic term, though of course he rejects the Aristotelian account of the soul as the 'form' of the body. The French version has simply 'while being united to the entire body'.

5. *Optics*, pp. 62ff; cf. *Passions*, pp. 22ff.

Online resources:

Descartes
Meditations
www.wright.edu/cola/descartes/
Meditations and Discourse on the Method of Rightly Conducting the Reason and seeking Truth in the Sciences
www.classicallibrary.org/descartes/

2

The Concept of Mind

Gilbert Ryle

1. THE OFFICIAL DOCTRINE [SELECTIONS FROM CHAPTER 1 OF *CONCEPT OF MIND*]

There is a doctrine about the nature and place of minds which is so prevalent among theorists and even among laymen that it deserves to be described as the official theory. Most philosophers, psychologists and religious teachers subscribe, with minor reservations, to its main articles and, although they admit certain theoretical difficulties in it, they tend to assume that these can be overcome without serious modifications being made to the architecture of the theory. It will be argued here that the central principles of the doctrine are unsound and conflict with the whole body of what we know about minds when we are not speculating about them.

The official doctrine, which hails chiefly from Descartes, is something like this. With the doubtful exceptions of idiots and infants in arms every human being has both a body and a mind. Some would prefer to say that every human being is both a body and a mind. His body and his mind are ordinarily harnessed together, but after the death of the body his mind may continue to exist and function.

Human bodies are in space and are subject to the mechanical laws which govern all other bodies in space. Bodily processes and states can be inspected by external observers. So a man's bodily life is as much a public affair as are the lives of animals and reptiles and even as the careers of trees, crystals and planets.

But minds are not in space, nor are their operations subject to mechanical laws. The workings of one mind are not witnessable by other observers; its career is private. Only I can take direct cognisance of the states and processes of my own mind. A person therefore lives through two collateral histories, one consisting of what happens in and to his body, the other consisting of what happens in and to his mind. The first is public, the second private. The events in the first history are events in the physical world, those in the second are events in the mental world.

It has been disputed whether a person does or can directly monitor all or only some of the episodes of his own private history; but, according to the official doctrine, of at least some of these episodes he has direct and unchallengeable cognisance. In consciousness, self-consciousness and introspection he is directly and authentically apprised of the present states and operations of his mind. He may have great or small uncertainties about concurrent and adjacent episodes in the physical world, but he can have none about at least part of what is momentarily occupying his mind.

It is customary to express this bifurcation of his two lives and of his two worlds by saying that the things and events which belong to the physical world, including his own body, are external, while the workings of his own mind are internal. This antithesis of outer and inner is of course meant to be construed as a metaphor, since minds, not being in space, could not be described as being spatially inside anything else, or as having things going on spatially inside themselves. But relapses from this good intention are common and theorists are found speculating how stimuli, the physical sources of which are yards or miles outside a person's skin, can generate mental responses inside his skull, or how decisions framed inside his cranium can set going movements of his extremities.

Even when 'inner' and 'outer' are construed as metaphors, the problem of how a person's mind and body influence one another is notoriously charged with theoretical difficulties. What the mind wills, the legs, arms and the tongue execute; what affects the ear and the eye has something to do with what the mind perceives; grimaces and smiles betray the mind's moods and bodily castigations lead, it is hoped, to moral improvement. But the actual transactions between the episodes of the private history and those of the public history remain mysterious, since by definition they can belong to neither series. They could not be reported among the happenings described in a person's autobiography of his inner life, but nor could they be reported among those described in some one else's biography of that person's overt career. They can be inspected neither by introspection nor by laboratory experiment. They are theoretical shuttlecocks which are forever being bandied from the physiologist back to the psychologist and from the psychologist back to the physiologist.

Underlying this partly metaphorical representation of the bifurcation of a person's two lives there is a seemingly more profound and philosophical assumption. It is assumed that there are two different kinds of existence or status. What exists or happens may have the status of physical existence, or it may have the status of mental existence. Somewhat as the faces of coins are either heads or tails, or somewhat as living creatures are either male or female, so, it is supposed, some existing is physical existing, other existing is mental existing. It is a necessary feature of what has physical existence that it is in space and time, it is a necessary feature of what has mental existence that it is in time but not in space. What has physical existence is composed of matter, or else is a function of matter; what has mental existence consists of consciousness, or else is a function of consciousness.

There is thus a polar opposition between mind and matter, an opposition which is often brought out as follows. Material objects are situated in a common field, known as 'space', and what happens to one body in one part of space is mechanically connected with what happens to other bodies in other parts of space. But mental happenings occur in insulated fields, known as 'minds', and there is, apart maybe from telepathy, no direct causal connection between what happens in one mind and what happens in another. Only through the medium of the public physical world can the mind of one person make a difference to the mind of another. The mind is its own place and in his inner life each of us lives the life of a ghostly Robinson Crusoe. People can see, hear and jolt one another's bodies, but they are irremediably blind and deaf to the workings of one another's minds and inoperative upon them.

What sort of knowledge can be secured of the workings of a mind? On the one side, according to the official theory, a person has direct knowledge of the best imaginable kind of the workings of his own mind. Mental states and processes are (or are normally) conscious states and processes, and the consciousness which irradiates them can engender no illusions and leaves the door open for no doubts. A person's present thinkings, feelings and willings, his perceivings, rememberings and imaginings are intrinsically 'phosphorescent'; their existence and their nature are inevitably betrayed to their owner. The inner life is a stream of consciousness of such a sort that it would be absurd to suggest that the mind whose life is that stream might be unaware of what is passing down it.

True, the evidence adduced recently by Freud seems to show that there exist channels tributary to this stream, which run hidden from their owner. People are actuated by impulses the existence of which they vigorously disavow; some of their thoughts differ from the thoughts which they acknowledge; and some of the actions which they think they will to perform they do not really will. They are thoroughly gulled by some of their own hypocrisies and they successfully ignore facts about their mental lives which on the official theory ought to be patent to them. Holders of the official theory tend, however, to maintain that anyhow in normal circumstances a person must be directly and authentically seized of the present state and workings of his own mind.

Besides being currently supplied with these alleged immediate data of consciousness, a person is also generally supposed to be able to exercise from time to time a special kind of perception, namely inner perception, or introspection. He can take a (non-optical) 'look' at what is passing in his mind. Not only can he view and scrutinize a flower through his sense of sight and listen to and discriminate the notes of a bell through his sense of hearing; he can also reflectively or introspectively watch, without any bodily organ of sense, the current episodes of his inner life. This self-observation is also commonly supposed to be immune from illusion, confusion or doubt. A mind's reports of its own affairs have a certainty superior to the best that is possessed by its reports of matters in the physical world. Sense-perceptions can, but consciousness and introspection cannot, be mistaken or confused.

On the other side, one person has no direct access of any sort to the events of the inner life of another. He cannot do better than make problematic inferences from the observed behavior of the other persons's body to the states of mind which, by analogy from his own conduct, he supposes to be signalised by that behaviour. Direct access to the workings of a mind is the privilege of that mind itself; in default of such privileged access, the workings of one mind are inevitably occult to everyone else. For the supposed arguments from bodily movements similar to their own to mental workings similar to their own would lack any possibility of observational corroboration. Not unnaturally, therefore, an adherent of the official theory finds it difficult to resist this consequence of his premises, that he had no good reason to believe that there do exist minds other than his own. Even if he prefers to believe that to other human bodies there are harnessed minds not unlike his own, he cannot claim to be able to discover their individual characteristics, or the particular things that they undergo and do. Absolute solitude is on this showing the ineluctable destiny of the soul. Only our bodies can meet.

As a necessary corollary of this general scheme there is implicitly prescribed a special way of construing our ordinary concepts of mental powers and operations. The verbs, nouns and adjectives, with which in ordinary life we describe the wits, characters and higher-grade performances of the people with whom we have do, are required to be construed as signifying special episodes in their secret histories, or else as signifying tendencies for such episodes to occur. When someone is described as knowing, believing or guessing something, as hoping, dreading, intending or shirking something, as designing this or being amused at that, these verbs are supposed to denote the occurrence of specific modifications in his (to us) occult stream of consciousness. Only his own privileged access to this stream in direct awareness and introspection could provide authentic testimony that these mental-conduct verbs were correctly or incorrectly applied. The onlooker, be he teacher, critic, biographer or friend, can never assure himself that his comments have any vestige of truth. Yet it was just because we do in fact all know how to make such comments, make them with general correctness and correct them when they turn out to be confused or mistaken, that philosophers found it necessary to construct their theories of the nature and place of minds. Finding mental-conduct concepts being regularly and effectively used, they properly sought to fix their logical geography. But the logical geography officially recommended would entail that there could be no regular or effective use of these mental-conduct concepts in our descriptions of, and prescriptions for, other people's minds.

2. THE ABSURDITY OF
THE OFFICIAL DOCTRINE

Such in outline is the official theory. I shall often speak of it, with deliberate abusiveness, as 'the dogma of the Ghost in the Machine'. I hope to prove that it is entirely false, and false not in detail but in principle. It is not merely an assemblage of particular mistakes. It is one big mistake and a mistake of a special kind. It is, namely, a category-mistake. It represents the facts of mental life as if they belonged to one logical type or category (or range of types or categories), when they actually belong to another. The dogma is therefore a philosopher's myth. In attempting to explode the myth I shall probably be taken to be denying well-known facts about the mental life of human beings, and my plea that I aim at doing nothing more than rectify the logic of mental-conduct concepts will probably be disallowed as mere subterfuge.

I must first indicate what is meant by the phrase 'Category-mistake.' This I do in a series of illustrations.

A foreigner visiting Oxford or Cambridge for the first time is shown a number of colleges, libraries, playing fields, museums, scientific departments and administrative offices. He then asks 'But where is the University? I have seen where the members of the Colleges live, where the Registrar works, where the scientists experiment and the rest. But I have not yet seen the University in which reside and work the members of your University.' It has then to be explained to him that the University is not another collateral institution, some ulterior counterpart to the colleges, laboratories and offices which he has seen. The University is just the way in which all that he has already seen is organized. When they are seen and when their coordination is understood, the University has been seen. His mistake lay in his innocent assumption that it was correct to speak of Christ Church, the Bodleian Library, the Ashmolean Museum *and* the University, to speak, that is, as if 'the University' stood for an extra member of the class of which these other units are members. He was mistakenly allocating the University to the same category as that to which the other institutions belong.

The same mistake would be made by a child witnessing the march-past of a division, who, having had pointed out to him such and such battalions, batteries, squadrons, etc., asked when the division was going to appear. He would be supposing that a division was a counterpart to the units already seen, partly similar to them and partly unlike them. He would be shown his mistake by being told that in watching the battalions, batteries and squadrons marching past he had been watching the division marching past. The march-past was not a parade of battalions, batteries, squadrons *and* a division; it was a parade of the battalions, batteries and squadrons *of* a division.

One more illustration. A foreigner watching his first game of cricket learns what are the functions of the bowlers, the batsmen, the fielders, the umpires and the scorers. He then says 'But there is no one left on the field to contribute the famous element of team-spirit. I see who does the bowling, the batting and the wicket-keeping; but I do not see whose role it is to exercise *esprit de corps*.' Once more, it would have to be explained that he was looking for the wrong type of thing. Team-spirit is not another cricketing-operation supplementary to all of the other special tasks. It is, roughly, the keenness with which each of the special tasks is performed, and performing a task keenly is not performing two tasks. Certainly exhibiting team spirit is not the same thing as bowling or catching, but nor is it a third thing such that we can say that the bowler first bowls *and* then exhibits team-spirit or that a fielder is at a given moment *either* catching *or* displaying *esprit de corps*.

These illustrations of category-mistakes have a common feature which must be noticed. The mistakes were made by people who did not know how to wield the concepts *University, division,* and *team-spirit.* Their puzzles arose from inability to use certain items in the English vocabulary.

The theoretically interesting category-mistakes are those made by people who are perfectly competent to apply concepts, at least in the situations with which they are familiar, but are still liable in their abstract thinking to allocate those concepts to logical types to which they do not belong. An instance of a mistake of this sort would be the following story. A student of politics has learned the main differences between the British, the French and the American Constitutions, and has learned also the differences and connections between the Cabinet, Parliament, the various Ministries, the Judicature and the Church of England. But he still becomes embarrassed when asked questions about the connections between the Church of England, the Home Office and the British Constitution. For while the Church and the Home Office are institutions, the British Constitution is not another institution in the same sense of that noun. So inter-institutional relations which can be asserted or denied to hold between the Church and the Home Office cannot be asserted or denied to hold between either of them and the British Constitution. 'The British Constitution' is not a term of the same logical type as 'the Home Office' and 'the Church of England'. In a partially similar way, John Doe may be a relative, a friend, an enemy or a stranger to Richard Roe; but he cannot be any of these things to the Average Taxpayer. He knows how to talk sense in certain sorts of discussions about the Average Taxpayer, but he is baffled to say why he could not come across him in the street as he can come across Richard Roe.

It is pertinent to our main subject to notice that, so long as the student of politics continues to think of the British Constitution as a counterpart to the other institutions, he will tend to describe it as a mysteriously occult institution; and so long as John Doe continues to think of the Average Taxpayer as a fellow-citizen, he will tend to think of him as an elusive insubstantial man, a ghost who is everywhere yet nowhere.

My destructive purpose is to show that a family of radical category-mistakes is the source of the double-life theory. The representation of a person as a ghost mysteriously ensconced in a machine derives from this argument. Because, as is true, a person's thinking, feeling and purposive doing cannot be described solely in the idioms of physics, chemistry and physiology, therefore they must be described in counterpart idioms. As the human body is a complex organised unit, so the human mind must be another complex organised unit, though one made of a different sort of stuff and with a different sort of structure. Or, again, as the human body, like any other parcel of matter, is a field of causes and effects, so the mind must be another field of causes and effects, though not (Heaven be praised) mechanical causes and effects.

3. THE ORIGIN OF THE CATEGORY-MISTAKE

One of the chief intellectual origins of what I have yet to prove to be the Cartesian category-mistake seems to be this. When Galileo showed that his methods of scientific discovery were competent to provide a mechanical theory which should cover every occupant of space, Descartes found in himself two conflicting motives. As a man of scientific genius he could not but endorse the claims of mechanics, yet as a religious and moral man he could not accept, as Hobbes accepted, the discouraging rider to those claims, namely that human nature differs only in degree of complexity from clockwork. The mental could not be just a variety of the mechanical.

He and subsequent philosophers naturally but erroneously availed themselves of the following escape-route. Since mental-conduct words are not to be construed as signifying the occurrence of mechanical processes, they must be construed as signifying the occurrence of non-mechanical processes; since mechanical laws explain movements in space as the effects of other movements in space, other laws must explain some of the non-spatial workings of minds as the effects of other non-spatial workings of minds. The difference between the human behaviours which we describe as intelligent and those which we describe as unintelligent must be a difference in their causation; so, while some movements of human tongues and limbs are the effects of mechanical causes, others must be the effects of non-mechanical causes, i.e. some issue from movements of particles of matter, others from workings of the mind.

The differences between the physical and the mental were thus represented as differences inside the common framework of the categories of 'thing,' 'stuff,' 'attribute,' 'state,' 'process,' 'change,' 'cause' and 'effect.' Minds are things, but different sorts of things from bodies; mental processes are causes and effects, but different sorts of causes and effects from bodily movements. And so on. Somewhat as the foreigner expected the University to be an extra edifice, rather like a college but also considerably different, so the repudiators of mechanism represented minds as extra centres of causal processes, rather like machines but also considerably different from them. Their theory was a para-mechanical hypothesis.

That this assumption was at the heart of the doctrine is shown by the fact that there was from the beginning felt to be a major theoretical difficulty in explaining how minds can influence and be influenced by bodies. How can a mental process, such as willing, cause spatial movements like the movements of the tongue? How can a physical change in the optic nerve have among its effects a mind's perception of a flash of light? This notorious crux by itself shows the logical mould into which Descartes pressed his theory of the mind. It was the self-same mould into which he and Galileo set their mechanics. Still unwittingly adhering to the grammar of mechanics, he tried to avert disaster by describing minds in what was merely an obverse vocabulary. The workings of minds had to be described by the mere negatives of the specific descriptions given to bodies; they are not in space, they are not motions, they are not modifications of matter, they are not accessible to public observation. Minds are not bits of clockwork, they are just bits of not-clockwork.

As thus represented, minds are not merely ghosts harnessed to machines, they are themselves just spectral machines. Though the human body is an engine, it is not quite an ordinary engine, since some of its workings are governed by another engine inside it—this interior governor-engine being one of a very special sort. It is invisible, inaudible and it has no size or weight. It cannot be taken to bits and the laws it obeys are not those known to ordinary engineers. Nothing is known of how it governs the bodily engine.

A second major crux points the same moral. Since, according to the doctrine, minds belong to the same category as bodies and since bodies are rigidly governed by mechanical laws, it seemed to many theorists to follow that minds must be similarly governed by rigid non-mechanical laws. The physical world is a deterministic system, so the mental world must be a deterministic system. Bodies cannot help the modifications that they undergo, so minds cannot help pursuing the careers fixed for them. *Responsibility, choice, merit* and *demerit* are therefore inapplicable concepts—unless the compromise solution is adopted of saying that the laws governing mental processes, unlike those governing physical processes, have the congenial attribute of being only rather rigid. The problem of the Freedom of the Will was the problem how to reconcile the hypothesis that minds are to be described in terms drawn from the categories of mechanics with the knowledge that higher-grade human conduct is not of a piece with the behaviour of machines.

It is an historical curiosity that it was not noticed that the entire argument was broken-backed. Theorists correctly assumed that any sane man could already recognise the differences between, say, rational and non-rational utterances or between purposive and automatic behaviour. Else there would have been nothing requiring to be salved from mechanism. Yet the explanation given presupposed that one person could in principle never recognise the difference between the rational and the irrational utterances issuing from other human bodies, since he could never get access to the postulated immaterial causes of some of their utterances. Save for the doubtful exception of himself, he could never tell the difference between a man and a Robot. It would have to be conceded, for example, that, for all that we can tell, the inner lives of persons who are classed as idiots or lunatics are as rational as those of anyone else. Perhaps only their overt behaviour is disappointing; that is to say, perhaps 'idiots' are not really idiotic, or 'lunatics' lunatic. Perhaps, too, some of those who are classed as sane are really idiots. According to the theory, external observers could never know how the overt behaviour of others is correlated with their mental powers and processes and so they could never know or even plausibly conjecture whether their applications of mental-conduct concepts to these people were correct or incorrect. It would then be hazardous or impossible for a man to claim sanity or logical consistency even for himself, since he would be debarred from comparing his own performances with those of others. In short, our characterisations of persons and their performances as intelligent, prudent and virtuous or as stupid, hypocritical and cowardly could never have been made, so the problem of providing a special causal hypothesis to serve as the basis of such diagnoses would never have arisen. The question, 'How do persons differ from machines?' arose just because everyone already knew how to apply mental-conduct concepts before the new causal hypothesis was introduced. This causal hypothesis could not therefore be the source of the criteria used in those applications. Nor, of course, has the causal hypothesis in any degree improved our handling of those criteria. We still distinguish good from bad arithmetic, politic from impolitic conduct and fertile from infertile imaginations in the ways in which Descartes himself distinguished them before and after he speculated how the applicability of these criteria was compatible with the principle of mechanical causation.

He had mistaken the logic of his problem. Instead of asking by what criteria intelligent behaviour is actually distinguished from non-intelligent behaviour, he asked 'Given that the principle of mechanical causation does not tell us the difference, what other causal principle will tell it us?' He realized that the problem was not one of mechanics and assumed that it must therefore be one of some counterpart to mechanics. Not unnaturally psychology is often cast for just this role.

When two terms belong to the same category, it is proper to construct conjunctive propositions embodying them. Thus a purchaser may say that he bought a left-hand glove and a right-hand glove, but not that he bought a left-hand glove, a right-hand glove and a pair of gloves. 'She came home in a flood of tears and a sedan-chair' is a well-known joke based on the absurdity of conjoining terms of different types. It would have been equally ridiculous to construct the disjunction 'She came home either in a flood of tears or else in a sedan-chair'. Now the dogma of the Ghost in the Machine does just this. It maintains that there exist both bodies and minds: that there occur physical processes and mental processes: that there are mechanical causes of corporeal movements and mental causes of corporeal movements. I shall argue that these and other analogous conjunctions are absurd: but, it must be noticed, the argument will not show that either of the illegitimately conjoined propositions is absurd in itself. I am not, for example, denying that there occur mental processes. Doing long division is a mental process and so is making a joke. But I am saying that the phrase 'there occur mental processes' does not mean the same sort of thing as 'there occur physical processes,' and, therefore, that it makes no sense to conjoin or disjoin the two.

If my argument is successful, there will follow some interesting consequences. First, the hallowed contrast between Mind and Matter will be dissipated, but dissipated not by either of the equally hallowed absorptions of Mind by Matter or of Matter by Mind, but in quite a different way. For the seeming contrast of the two will be shown to be as illegitimate as would be the contrast of 'she came home in a flood of tears' and 'she came home in a sedan-chair'. The belief that there is a polar opposition between Mind and Matter is the belief that they are terms of the same logical type.

It will also follow that both Idealism and Materialism are answers to an improper question. The 'reduction' of the material world to mental states and processes, as well as the 'reduction' of mental states and processes to physical states and processes, presuppose the legitimacy of the disjunction 'Either there exist minds or there exist bodies (but not both).' It would be like saying, 'Either she bought a left-hand and a right-hand glove or she bought a pair of gloves (but not both).'

It is perfectly proper to say, in one logical tone of voice, that there exist minds and to say, in another logical tone of voice, that there exist bodies. But these expressions do not indicate two different species of existence, for 'existence' is not a generic word like 'colored' or 'sexed.' They indicate two different senses of 'exist,' somewhat as 'rising' has different senses in 'the tide is rising,' 'hopes are rising,' and 'the average age of death is rising.' A man would be thought to be making a poor joke who said that three things are now rising, namely the tide, hopes and the average age of death. It would he just as good or bad a joke to say that there exist prime numbers and Wednesdays and public opinions and navies; or that there exist both minds and bodies.

4. HISTORICAL NOTE

It would not be true to say that the official theory derives solely from Descartes' theories, or even from a more widespread anxiety about the implications of seventeenth century mechanics. Scholastic and Reformation theology had schooled the intellects of the scientists as well as of the laymen, philosophers and clerics of that age. Stoic-Augustinian theories of the will were embedded in the Calvinist doctrines of sin and grace; Platonic and Aristotelian theories of the intellect shaped the orthodox doctrines of the immortality of the soul. Descartes was reformulating already prevalent theological doctrines of the soul in the new syntax of Galileo. The theologian's privacy of conscience became the philosopher's privacy of consciousness, and what had been the bogy of Predestination reappeared as the bogy of Determinism.

It would also not be true to say that the two-worlds myth did no theoretical good. Myths often do a lot of theoretical good, while they are still new. One benefit bestowed by the para-mechanical myth was that it partly superannuated the then prevalent para-political myth. Minds and their Faculties had previously been described by analogies with political superiors and political subordinates. The idioms used were those of ruling, obeying, collaborating and rebelling. They survived and still survive in many ethical and some epistemological discussions. As, in physics, the new myth of occult Forces was a scientific improvement on the old myth of Final Causes, so, in anthropological and psychological theory, the new myth of hidden operations, impulses and agencies was an improvement on the old myth of dictations, deferences and disobediences.

3. KNOWING HOW AND KNOWING THAT
[SELECTION FROM CHAPTER 2
OF *CONCEPT OF MIND*]

When a person is described by one or other of the intelligence-epithets such as 'shrewd' or 'silly,' 'prudent' or 'imprudent,' the description imputes to him not the knowledge, or ignorance, of this or that truth, but the ability, or inability, to do certain sorts of things. Theorists have been so preoccupied with the task of investigating the nature, the source and the credentials of the theories that we adopt that they have for the most part ignored the question what it is for someone to know how to perform tasks. In ordinary life, on the contrary, as well as in the special business of teaching, we are much more concerned with people's competences than with their cognitive repertoires, with the operations than with the truths that they learn. Indeed even when we are concerned with their intellectual excellences and deficiencies, we are interested less in the stocks of truths that they acquire and retain than in their capacities to find out truths for themselves and their ability to organize and exploit them, when discovered. Often we deplore a person's ignorance of some fact only because we deplore the stupidity of which his ignorance is a consequence.

There are certain parallelisms between knowing *how* and knowing *that*, as well as certain divergences. We speak of learning how to play an instrument as well as of learning that something is the case; of finding out how to prune trees as well as of finding out that the Romans had a camp in a certain place; of forgetting how to tie a reef-knot as well as of forgetting that the German for 'knife' is '*Messer.*' We can wonder *how* as well as wonder *whether*.

On the other hand we never speak of a person believing or opining *how*, and though it is proper to ask for the grounds or reasons for someone's acceptance of a proposition, this question cannot be asked of someone's skill at cards or prudence in investments.

What is involved in our descriptions of people as knowing how to make and appreciate jokes, to talk grammatically, to play chess, to fish, or to argue? Part of what is meant is that, when they perform these operations, they tend to perform them well, i.e. correctly or efficiently or successfully. Their performances come up to certain standards, or satisfy certain criteria. But this is not enough. The well-regulated clock keeps good time and the well-drilled circus seal performs its tricks flawlessly, yet we do not call them 'intelligent'. We reserve this title for the persons responsible for their performances. To be intelligent is not merely to satisfy criteria, but to apply them; to regulate one's actions and not merely to be well-regulated. A person's performance is described as careful or skilful, if in his operations he is ready to detect and correct lapses, to repeat and improve upon successes, to profit from the examples of others and so forth. He applies criteria in performing critically, that is, in trying to get things right.

This point is commonly expressed in the vernacular by saying that an action exhibits intelligence, if, and only if, the agent is thinking what he is doing while he is doing it, and thinking what he is doing in such a manner that he would not do the action so well if he were not thinking what he is doing. This popular idiom is sometimes appealed to as evidence in favor of the intellectualist legend. Champions of this legend are apt to try to reassimilate knowing *how* to knowing *that* by arguing that intelligent performance involves the observance of rules, or the application of criteria. It follows that the operation which is characterized as intelligent must be preceded by an intellectual acknowledgment of these rules or criteria; that is, the agent must first go through the internal process of avowing to himself certain propositions about what is to be done ('maxims,' 'imperatives' or 'regulative propositions' as they are sometimes called); only then can he execute his performance in accordance with those dictates. He must preach to himself before he can practice. The chef must recite his recipes to himself before he can cook according to them; the hero must lend his inner ear to some appropriate moral imperative before swimming out to save the drowning man; the chess-player must run over in his head all the relevant rules and tactical maxims of the game before he can make correct and skilful moves. To do something thinking what one is doing is, according to this legend, always to do two things; namely, to consider certain appropriate propositions, or prescriptions, and to put into practice what these propositions or prescriptions enjoin. It is to do a bit of theory and then to do a bit of practice.

Certainly we often do not only reflect before we act but reflect in order to act properly. The chess-player may require some time in which to plan his moves before he makes them. Yet the general assertion that all intelligent performance requires to be prefaced by the consideration of appropriate propositions rings unplausibly, even when it is apologetically conceded that the required consideration is often very swift and may go quite unmarked by the agent. I shall argue that the intellectualist legend is false and that when we describe a performance as intelligent, this does not entail the double operation of considering and executing . . .

4. THE MOTIVES OF THE INTELLECTUALIST LEGEND [SELECTION FROM CHAPTER 2 OF *CONCEPT OF MIND*]

Why are people so strongly drawn to believe, in the face of their own daily experience, that the intelligent execution of an operation must embody two processes, one of doing and another of theorizing? Part of the answer is that they are wedded to the dogma of the ghost in the machine. Since doing is often an overt muscular affair, it is written off as a merely physical process. On the assumption of the antithesis between 'physical' and 'mental,' it follows that muscular doing cannot itself be a mental operation. To earn the title 'skilful,' 'cunning,' or 'humorous,' it must therefore get it by transfer from another counterpart act occurring not 'in the machine' but 'in the ghost'; for 'skilful,' 'cunning' and 'humorous' are certainly mental predicates.

It is, of course, perfectly true that when we characterize as witty or tactful some piece of overt behaviour, we are not considering only the muscular movements which we witness. A parrot might have made the same remark in the same situation without our crediting it with a sense of humor, or a lout might have done precisely what the tactful man did, without our thinking him tactful. But if one and the same vocal utterance is a stroke of humor from the humorist, but a mere noise-response, when issuing from the parrot, it is tempting to say that we are ascribing it not to something that we hear but to something else that we do not hear. We are accordingly tempted to say that what makes one audible or visible action witty, while another audibly or visibly similar action was not, is that the former was attended by another inaudible and invisible action which was the real exercise of wit. But to admit, as we must, that there may be no visible or audible difference between a tactful or witty act and a tactless or humorless one is not to admit that the difference is constituted by the performance or non-performance of some extra secret acts.

The cleverness of the clown may be exhibited in his tripping and tumbling. He trips and tumbles just as clumsy people do, except that he trips and tumbles on purpose and after much rehearsal and at the golden moment and where the children can see him and so as not to hurt himself. The spectators applaud his skill at seeming clumsy, but what they applaud is not some extra hidden performance executed 'in his head'. It is his visible performance that they admire, but they admire it not for being an effect of any hidden internal causes but for being an exercise of a skill. Now a skill is not an act. It is therefore neither a witnessable nor an unwitnessable act. To recognize that a performance is an exercise of a skill is indeed to appreciate it in the light of a factor which could not be separately recorded by a camera. But the reason why the skill exercised in a performance cannot be separately recorded by a camera is not that it is an occult or ghostly happening, but that it is not a happening at all. It is a disposition, or complex of dispositions, and a disposition is a factor of the wrong logical type to be seen or unseen, recorded or unrecorded. Just as the habit of talking loudly is not itself loud or quiet, since it is not the sort of term of which 'loud' and 'quiet' can be predicated, or just as a susceptibility to headaches is for the same reason not itself unendurable or endurable, so the skills, tastes and bents which are exercised in overt or internal operations are not themselves overt or internal, witnessable or unwitnessable. The traditional theory of the mind has misconstrued the type-distinction between disposition and exercise into its mythical bifurcation of unwitnessable mental causes and their witnessable physical effects.

The clown's trippings and tumblings are the workings of his mind, for they are his jokes; but the visibly similar trippings and rumblings of a clumsy man are not the workings of that man's mind. For he does not trip on purpose. Tripping on purpose is both a bodily and a mental process, but it is not two processes, such as one process of purposing to trip and, as an effect, another process of tripping. Yet the old myth dies hard . . .

NOTES

The Concept of Mind, Gilbert Ryle, 1949, Routledge, reprinted with the permission of the Principal, Fellows and Scholars of Hertford College in the University of Oxford.

Online resources:

Gilbert Ryle

The Electronic Journal of Analytic Philosophy, The Philosophy of Gilbert Ryle
  Issue 7, 2002

http://ejap.louisiana.edu/EJAP/2002/contents.html

3

Logical Behaviorism [Selection from *Language of Thought*]

Jerry A. Fodor

Among the many passages in Ryle's *Concept of Mind* (1949) that repay close attention, there is one (around p. 33) in which the cards are more than usually on the table. Ryle is discussing the question: 'What makes a clown's clowning intelligent (witty, clever, ingenious, etc.)?' The doctrine he is disapproving goes as follows: What makes the clowning intelligent is the fact that it is the consequence of certain mental operations (computations, calculations) privy to the clown and causally responsible for the production of the clown's behavior. Had these operations been other than they were, then (the doctrine claims) either the clowning would have been witless or at least it would have been witty clowning of some different kind. In short, the clown's clowning was clever in the way that it was because the mental operations upon which the clowning was causally contingent had whatever character they did have. And, though Ryle doesn't say so, it is presumably implied by this doctrine that a psychologist interested in explaining the success of the clown's performance would ipso facto be in the business of saying what those operations were and how, precisely, they were related to the overt pratfalls that the crowd saw.

Strictly speaking, this is not a single theory but a batch of closely connected ones. In particular, one can distinguish at least three claims about the character of the events upon which the clown's behavior is said to be causally contingent:

1. That some of them are mental events;
2. That some (or all) of the mental events are privy to the clown in at least

the sense that they are normally unobserved by someone who observes the clown's performance, and, perhaps, also in the stronger sense that they are in principle unobservable by anyone except the clown;

3. That it is the fact that the behavior was caused by such events that makes it the kind of behavior it is; that intelligent behavior *is* intelligent because it has the kind of etiology it has.

I want to distinguish these doctrines because a psychologist might accept the sorts of theories that Ryle doesn't like without wanting to commit himself to the full implications of what Ryle calls 'Cartesianism'. For example, Ryle assumes (as most psychologists who take a Realistic view of the designata of mental terms in psychological theories would not) that a mentalist must be a dualist; in particular, that mentalism and materialism are mutually exclusive. Suffice it to remark here that one result of this confusion is the tendency to see the options of dualism and behaviorism as exhaustive in the philosophy of mind.

Similarly, it seems to me, one might accept some such view as that of item 3 without embracing a doctrinaire reading of item 2. It may be that some of the mental processes that are causally responsible for the clown's behavior are de facto unobservable by the crowd. It may be, for that matter, that some of these processes are de facto unobservable by the clown. But there would seem to be nothing in the project of explaining behavior by reference to mental processes which requires a commitment to epistemological privacy in the traditional sense of that notion. Indeed, for better or for worse, a materialist *cannot* accept such a commitment since his view is that mental events are species of physical events, and physical events are publicly observable at least in principle.[1,2]

It is notorious that, even granting these caveats, Ryle doesn't think this kind of account could possibly be true. For this theory says that what makes the clown's clowning clever is the fact that it is the effect of a certain kind of cause. But what, in Ryle's view, actually does make the clowning clever is something quite else: For example, the fact that it happens out where the audience can see it; the fact that the things that the clown does are not the things that the audience expected him to do; the fact that the man he hit with the pie was dressed in evening clothes, etc.

There are two points to notice. First, none of these facts are in any sense private to the clown. They are not even de facto private in the sense of being facts about things going on in the clown's nervous system. On the contrary, what makes the clown's clowning clever is precisely the *public* aspects of his performance; precisely the things that the audience *can* see. The second point is that what makes the clowning clever is not the character of the *causes* of the clown's behavior, but rather the character of the behavior itself. It counts for the pratfall being clever that it occurred when it wasn't expected, but its occurring when it wasn't expected surely wasn't one of its causes on any conceivable construal of 'cause.' In short, what makes the clowning clever is not some event distinct from, and causally responsible for, the behavior that the clown produces. A fortiori, it is not a mental event prior to the pratfall. Surely, then, if the mentalist program involves the identification and characterization of such an event, that program is doomed from the start.

Alas for the psychology of clever clowning. We had assumed that psychologists would identify the (mental) causes upon which clever clowning is contingent and *thereby* answer the question: 'What makes the clowning clever?' Now all that appears to be left of the enterprise is the alliterations. Nor does Ryle restrict his use of this pattern of argument to undermining the psychology of clowns. Precisely similar moves are made to show that the psychology of perception is a muddle since what makes something (e.g.) the recognition of a robin or a tune is not the occurrence of some or other mental event, but rather the fact that what was claimed to be a robin was in fact a robin, and what was taken to be a rendition of "Lillibullero" was one. It is, in fact, hard to think of an area of cognitive psychology in which this sort of argument would not apply or where Ryle does not apply it. Indeed, it is perhaps Ryle's *central* point that 'Cartesian' (i.e., mentalistic) psychological theories treat what is really a *logical* relation between aspects of a single event as though it were a causal relation between pairs of distinct events. It is this tendency to give mechanistic answers to conceptual questions which, according to Ryle, leads the mentalist to orgies of regrettable hypostasis: i.e., to attempting to explain behavior by reference to underlying psychological mechanisms.[3]

If this *is* a mistake I am in trouble. For it will be the pervasive assumption of my discussion that such explanations, however often they may prove to be empirically unsound, are, in principle, methodologically impeccable. What I propose to do is to take such explanations absolutely seriously and try to sketch at least the outlines of the general picture of mental life to which they lead. So something will have to be done to meet Ryle's argument. Let's, to begin with, vary the example.

Consider the question: 'What makes Wheaties the breakfast of champions?' (Wheaties, in case anyone hasn't heard, is, or are, a sort of packaged cereal. The details are very inessential.) There are, it will be noticed, at least two kinds of answers that one might give.[4] A sketch of one answer, which belongs to what I shall call the 'causal story' might be: 'What make Wheaties the breakfast of champions are the health-giving vitamins and minerals that it contains'; or 'It's the carbohydrates in Wheaties, which give one the energy one needs for hard days on the high hurdle'; or 'It's the special springiness of all the little molecules in Wheaties, which gives Wheaties eaters their unusually high coefficient or restitution', etc.

It's not important to my point that any of these specimen answers should be true. What *is* essential is that some causal story or other must be true if

Wheaties really *are* the breakfast of champions as they are claimed to be. Answers propose causal stories insofar as they seek to specify properties of Wheaties which may be causally implicated in the processes that make champions of Wheaties eaters. Very roughly, such answers suggest provisional values of P in the explanation schema: 'P causes (x eats Wheaties) brings about (x becomes a champion) for significantly many values of x.' I assume that, if Wheaties do make champions of those who eat them, then there must be at least one value of P which makes this schema true. Since that assumption is simply the denial of the miracle theory of Wheaties, it ought not be in dispute.

I suggested that there is another kind of answer that 'What makes Wheaties the breakfast of champions?' may appropriately receive. I will say that answers of this second kind belong to the 'conceptual story'. In the present case, we can tell the conceptual story with some precision: What makes Wheaties the breakfast of champions is the fact that it is eaten (for breakfast) by nonnegligible numbers of champions. This is, I take it, a conceptually necessary and sufficient condition for *anything* to be the breakfast of champions;[5] as such, it pretty much exhausts the conceptual story about Wheaties.

The point to notice is that answers that belong to the conceptual story typically do not belong to the causal story and vice versa.[6] In particular, its being eaten by nonnegligible numbers of champions does not *cause* Wheaties to be the breakfast of champions; no more than its occurring unexpectedly causes the clown's pratfall to be witty. Rather, what we have in both cases are instances of (more or less rigorous) conceptual connections. Being eaten by nonnegligible numbers of champions and being unexpected belong, respectively, to the analyses of 'being the breakfast of champions' and 'being witty', with the exception that, in the former case, we have something that approaches a logically necessary and sufficient condition and, in the latter case, we very clearly do not.[7]

The notion of conceptual connection is notoriously a philosophical miasma; all the more so if one holds that there are species of conceptual connections which cannot, even in principle, be explicated in terms of the notions of logically necessary and/or sufficient conditions. The present point, however, is that on *any* reasonable construal of conceptual connectedness, Wheaties prove that *both* the causal *and* the conceptual story can be simultaneously true, distinct answers to questions of the form: 'What makes (an) x (an) F?' To put it succinctly, the dietitian who appears on television to explain that Wheaties is the breakfast of champions because it contains vitamins is not refuted by the philosopher who observes (though not, usually, on television) that Wheaties is the breakfast of champions because champions eat it for breakfast. The dietitian, in saying what he says, does not suppose that his remarks express, or can replace, the relevant conceptual truths. The philosopher, in saying what *he* says, ought not suppose that his remarks express, or can replace, the relevant causal explanations.

To put this point as generally as I know how, even if the behaviorists were right in supposing that logically necessary and sufficient conditions for behavior being of a certain kind can be given (just) in terms of stimulus and response variables, that fact would not in the least prejudice the mentalist's claim that the *causation* of behavior is determined by, and explicable in terms of, the organism's internal states. So far as I know, the philosophical school of 'logical' behaviorism offers not a shadow of an argument for believing that this claim is false. And the failure of behavioristic psychology to provide even a first approximation to a plausible theory of cognition suggests that the mentalist's claim may very well be true.

NOTES

Excerpts from *The Language of Thought* by Jerry A. Fodor. Copyright © 1975 by Thomas Y. Crowell Company, Inc. Reprinted by permission of Pearson Education, Inc.

1. The purist will note that this last point depends on the (reasonable) assumption that the context 'is publicly observable at least in principle' is transparent to substitutivity of identicals.

2. It might be replied that if we allow the possibility that mental events might be physical events, that some mental events might be unconscious, and that no mental event is essentially private, we will have so attenuated the term 'mental' as to deprive it of all force. It is, of course, true that the very notion of a mental event is often specified in ways that presuppose dualism and/or a strong doctrine of epistemological privacy. What is unclear, however, is what we want a definition of 'mental event' *for* in the first place.

Surely not, in any event, in order that it should be possible to do psychology in a methodologically respectable way. *Pre*-theoretically we identify mental events by reference to clear cases. *Post*-theoretically it is sufficient to identify them as the ones which fall under psychological laws. This characterization is, of course, question-begging since it rests upon an unexplained distinction between psychological laws and all the others. The present point, however, is that we are in no better position vis-á-vis such notions as chemical event (or meteorological event, or geological event . . . , etc.), a state of affairs which does not prejudice the rational pursuit of chemistry. A chemical event is one that falls under chemical laws; chemical laws are those which follow from (ideally completed) chemical theories; chemical theories are theories in chemistry; and chemistry, like all other special sciences, is individualated large post facto and by reference to its typical problems and predicates. (For example, chemistry is that science which concerns itself with such matters as the combinatorial properties of elements, the analysis and synthesis of compounds, etc.) Why, precisely, is this not good enough?

3. 'Criterion' isn't one of Ryle's words: Nevertheless, the line of argument just reviewed relates Ryle's work closely to the criteriological tradition in post-Wittgensteinian philosophy of mind. Roughly, what in Ryle's terms "makes" *a* be *F* is *a*'s possession of those properties which are criterial for the application of '*F*' to *xs*.

4. I am reading 'What makes Wheaties the breakfast of champions?' as asking 'What about Wheaties makes champions of (some, many, so many) Wheaties eaters?' rather than 'What about Wheaties makes (some, many, so many) champions eat them?' The latter question invites the reasons that champions give for eating Wheaties; and though these *may* include reference to properties Wheaties have by virtue of which its eaters become champions, they need not do so. Thus, a plausible answer to the second question which is *not* plausibly an answer to the first might be: 'They taste good'.

I am uncertain which of these questions the Wheaties people have in mind when they ask 'What makes Wheaties the breakfast of champions?' rhetorically, as, I believe, they are wont to do. Much of their advertising consists of publicizing statements by champions to the effect that they (the champions) do, in fact, eat Wheaties. If, as may be the case, such statements are offered as arguments for the truth of the presupposition of the question on its *first* reading (viz., that there *is* something about Wheaties that makes champions of those who eat them), then it would appear that General Mills has either misused the method of differences or committed the fallacy of affirmation of the consequent.

Philosophy can be made out of anything. Or less.

5. This is not quite right. Being eaten for breakfast by nonnegligible numbers of champions is a conceptually necessary and sufficient condition for something being a breakfast of champions (cf. Russell, 1905). Henceforth I shall resist this sort of pedantry whenever I can bring myself to do so.

6. The exceptions are interesting. They involve cases where the conceptual conditions for something being a thing of a certain kind include the requirement that it have, or be, a certain kind of cause. I suppose, for example, that it is a conceptual truth that nothing counts as a drunken brawl unless the drunkenness of the brawlers contributed causally to bringing about the brawling. See also: flu viruses, tears of rage, suicides, nervous stammers, etc. Indeed, one can imagine an analysis of 'the breakfast of champions' which would make it one of these cases too; viz, an analysis which says that it is logically necessary that the breakfast of champions is (not only what champions eat for breakfast but also) what champions eat for breakfast that is causally responsible for their being champions. But enough!

7. It is, by the way, no accident that the latter analysis is incomplete. The usual situation is that the logically necessary and sufficient conditions for the ascription of a mental state to an organism refer not just to environmental variables but to other mental states of that organism. (For example, to *know* that *P* is to *believe* that *P* and to satisfy certain further conditions; to be *greedy* is to be disposed *to feel pleasure* at getting, or at the prospect of getting, more than one's share, etc.) The faith that there *must* be a way out of this network of interdependent mental terms—that one will surely get to pure behavioral ascriptions if only one pursues the analysis far enough—is, so far as I know, unsupported by either argument or example.

Online resources:

Jerry A. Fodor
http://ruccs.rutgers.edu/faculty/Fodor/cv.html

II

THREE VIEWS OF
THE MIND

This section presents three theories of views of the mind: (1) **Type Identity**, which holds that the general kinds of mental states we possess are identical to types of brain states; (2) **Functionalism** (also known as **Token Identity**), which holds that our mental states can be understood as the causal relations between typical environmental causes or stimuli, their behavioral effects and, most importantly, their causal relations with other mental states; and (3) **Eliminative Materialism**, a more radical view that our commonsense conceptions of mental states, like being in pain, tasting an apple, or thinking about Descartes, will one day no longer be useful to us at all and can be eliminated and replaced by more precise, neuro-scientific terminology.

Each of these views contrasts with our previous readings on **Substance Dualism** and **Logical Behaviorism** as well as with each other. The Type Identity theory of the mind is a **materialist** or **physicalist** view of the mind since it holds that our mental states, being identical to brain states, must be physical states. The Type Identity view thus seems immune to the kinds of criticisms Gilbert Ryle raises against the Cartesian view of Substance Dualism. At the same time, the Type Identity theorist does not agree with Ryle that our mental state language (terms) is explained solely on the basis of observable behavioral descriptions. The "Official Doctrine" misleads us into believing that there is an entity, "the mind," that is a distinct, unobservable entity that is the cause of our behavior. For the Type Identity Theorist, there is a "mind" and it is the brain. The types of mental states we have are identical to types of brain states. Our first selection of this section, J. J. C. Smart's "Sensations and Brain Processes," presents his view of the way in which mental states, such as a sensation of pain, are identical to a kind of brain state, "C-Fibers firing." These brain states are completely physical. **Ockham's**

Razor, the principle that advises us not to multiply entities beyond necessity, has inspired Smart to defend a materialist view of the mind that does
not merely correlate mental states like sensations with brain states, for this
would leave us with an extra feature of the world that would need explanation. At the same time, Smart wants to avoid a position that denies that our
claims to be in mental states (our mental state terms) refer to a "ghostly"
entity "the mind," or have no meaning at all, or are terms that can be eliminated—simply translated into a description of a type of brain state and done
away with. Whenever we report being in a mental state, Smart believes that
this kind of report refers to the brain process that it is, but it does so "neu-
trally." As stated in his paper, Smart's example in his reply to Objection 3 is
that when a person reports "I see a yellowish-orange after-image," what this
person means is that there is "something going on which is like what is going
one when I have my eyes open, am awake, and there is an orange illuminated
in good light in front of me, that is, when I really see an orange." The person's report of the after-image, her mental state, is not itself committed to
dualism or materialism. It simply tells us how the state relates analogically
to other mental states and their qualities. Thus, when we speak of our mental
states, we are not committed to the idea that there are non-physical mental
properties or physical properties. Sensations and all mental states are strictly
identical to physical states, but our reports about them are neutral. Our
mental state terms and reports about our mental life, in short, do not need
to be rejected, even though these are identical to brain states.

Smart's adherence to **"strict identity"** certainly helps him maintain
adherence to Ockham's Razor: Mental states are nothing over and above
types of physical brain states, yet we might question how a strict identity
can truly be maintained. A common criticism of Type Identity is that our
mental states could not be strictly identical to brain states given **"Leibniz'
Law,"** that strictly identical entities share all properties in common. Granting Smart that our reports of mental states refer to types of brain states, how
are the qualities of a sensation like seeing a red apple—the qualities of this
experience—identical to a type of brain state, a particular stimulation of the
visual cortex? The qualities that a neuro-scientist would use to describe the
latter do not appear to be identical to those of the former. This sort of criticism will appear frequently against materialist and materialist-friendly views
of the mind (like functionalism). It may remind us of Descartes in that these
critics will wonder how the qualities of our mental states can be at the same
time wholly identical to the qualities of physical states, but we should notice
a significant change to **Property Dualism.** This sort of criticism does not
hold that the mind is necessarily a completely different substance than that
of physical bodies, rather it holds that mental qualities must be substantially
different from physical qualities.

Type Identity

4

Sensations and Brain Processes

J. J. C. Smart

This paper[1] takes its departure from arguments to be found in U. T. Place's "Is Consciousness a Brain process."[2] I have had the benefit of discussing Place's thesis in a good many universities in the United States and Australia, and I hope that the present paper answers objections to his thesis which Place has not considered and that it presents his thesis in a more nearly unobjectionable form. This paper is meant also to supplement the paper, "The 'Mental' and the 'Physical,'" by H. Feigel,[3] which in part argues for a similar thesis to Place's.

Suppose that I report that I have at this moment a roundish, blurry-eyed after-image which is yellowish towards its edge and is orange towards its center. What is it that I am reporting? One answer to this question might be that I am not reporting anything, that when I say that it looks to me as though there is a roundish yellowy orange patch of light on the wall I am expressing some sort of *temptation*, the temptation to say that there *is* a roundish yellow orange patch of light on the wall (though I may know that there is not such a patch on the wall). This is perhaps Wittgenstein's view in the *Philosophical Investigations* (see paragraph 367, 370). Similarly, when I "report" a pain, I am not really reporting anything (or, if you like, I am reporting in a queer sense of "reporting"), but am doing a sophisticated sort of wince. (See paragraph 244: "The verbal expression of pain replaces the crying and does not describe it." Nor does it describe anything else?)[4] I prefer most of the time to discuss an after-image rather than a pain, because the word "pain" brings in something which is irrelevant to my purpose: the notion of "distress." I think that "he is in pain" entails "he is in distress," that is, that he is in a certain agitation-condition.[5] Similarly, to say that "I am in pain" may be to do more than "replace pain behavior": it may be partly to report something, though this something is quite nonmysterious, being an agitation-condition, and so susceptible of behavioristic analysis. The suggestion I wish if possible to avoid is a different one, namely that "I am in pain" is a genuine report, and that what it reports is an irreducibly physical something. And similarly the suggestion I wish to resist is also to say "I have a yellowish orange after-image" is to report something irreducibly physical.

Why do I wish to resist this suggestion? Mainly because of Ockham's razor. It seems to me that science is increasingly giving us a viewpoint whereby organisms are able to be seen as physico-chemical mechanisms:[6] it seems that even the behavior of man himself will one day be explicable in mechanistic terms. There does seem to be, so far as science is concerned, nothing in the world but increasingly complex arrangements of physical constituents. All except for one place: in consciousness. That is, for a full description of what is going on in a man you would have to mention not only the physical process in his tissue, glands, nervous system, and so forth, but also in his states of consciousness: his visual, auditory, and tactile sensations, his aches and pains. That these should be _correlated_ with the brain process does not help, for to say that they are _correlated_ is to say that they are something "over and above." You cannot correlate something with itself. You correlate footprints with burglars, but not Bill Sikes the burglar with Bill Sykes the burglar. So sensations, states of consciousness, do seem to be the one sort of thing left outside the physicalist picture, and for various reasons I just cannot believe that this can be so. That everything should be explicable in terms of physics (together of course with descriptions of the ways in which parts are put together—roughly, biology is to physics as radio-engineering is to electro-magnetism) except the occurrence of sensations seems to me to be frankly unbelievable. Such sensations would be "nomological danglers," to use Feigl's expression.[7] It is not often realized how odd would be the laws whereby these nomological danglers would dangle. It is sometimes asked, "Why can't there just be psycho-physical laws which are of a novel sort, just as the laws of electricity and magnetism were novelties from the standpoint of Newtonian mechanics?" Certainly we are pretty sure in the future to come across new ultimate laws of a novel type, but I expect them to relate simple constituents: for example, whatever ultimate particles are then in vogue. I cannot believe that ultimate laws of nature could relate simple constituents to configurations consisting of perhaps billions of neurons (and goodness knows how many billion billions of ultimate particles) all put together for all the world as though their main purpose in life was to be a negative feedback mechanism of a complicated sort. Such ultimate laws would be like nothing so far known in science. They have a queer "smell" to them. I am just unable to believe in the nomological danglers themselves, or in the laws whereby they would dangle. If any philosophical arguments seemed to compel us to believe in such things, I would suspect a catch in the argument. In any case it is the object of this paper to show that there are no philosophical arguments which compel us to be dualists.

The above is largely a confession of faith, but it explains why I find Wittgenstein's position (as I construe it) so congenial. For on this view there are, in a sense, no sensations. A man is a vast arrangement of physical particles, but there are just behavioral facts about this vast mechanism, such as that it expresses a temptation (behavioral disposition) to say, "there is a yellowish-red patch on the wall" or that it goes through a sophisticated sort of winch, that is, says "I am in pain." Admittedly Wittgenstein says that though the sensation "is not a something," it is nevertheless "not a nothing either" (paragraph 304), but this need only mean that the word "ache" has a use. An ache is a thing, but only in an innocuous sense in which the plain man, in the first paragraph of Frege's *Foundation of Arithmetic*, answers the question "what is the number one?" by "a thing." It should be noted that when I assert that to say "I have a yellowish-orange after-image" is to express a temptation to assert the physical-object statement "there is a yellowish-orange patch on the wall," I mean that saying "I have a yellowish-orange after-image" is (partly) the exercise of the disposition[8] which is the temptation. It is not to *report* that I have a temptation, any more than is "I love you" normally a report that I love someone. Saying "I love you" is just part of a behavior which is the exercise of the disposition of loving someone.

Though, for the reasons given above, I am very receptive to the above "expressive" account of sensation statements, I do not feel that it will quite do the trick. Maybe this is because I have not thought it out sufficiently, but it does seem to me as though, when a person says "I have an after-image," he *is* making a genuine report, and that when he says "I have a pain," he *is* doing more than "replace pain-behavior," and that "this more" is not just to say that he is in distress. I am not so sure, however, that to admit this is to admit that there are nonphysical correlates of brain processes, but I shall try to argue that these arguments are by no means as cogent as is commonly thought to be the case.

Let me first try to state more accurately the thesis that sensations are brain processes. It is not the thesis that, for example, "after-image" or "ache" means the same as "brain process of sort X" (where "X" is replaced by a description of a certain sort of brain process). It is that, in so far as "after-image" or "ache" is a report of a process, it is a report of a process that *happens to be* a brain process. It follows that the thesis does not claim that sensation statements can be translated into statements about brain processes.[9] Nor does it claim that the logic of a sensation statement is the same as that of a brain-process statement. All it claims is that in so far as a sensation statement is a report of something, that something is in fact a brain process. Sensations are nothing over and above brain processes. Nations are nothing "over and above" citizens, but this does not seem to prevent the logic of nation statements being very different from the logic of citizen statements, nor does it insure the translatability of nation statements into citizen statements. (I do not, however, wish to assert that the relation of sensation statements to brain-process statements is very like that of nation statements to citizen statements. Nations do not just *happen to be* nothing over and above citizens, for example. I bring in the "nations" example merely to make a negative point: that the fact that the logic of A-statements is different from that of B-statements does not insure that A's are anything over and above B's.)

Remarks on identity. When I say that a sensation is a brain process or that lightning is an electric discharge, I am using "is" in the sense of strict identity. (Just as in the—in this case necessary—proposition "7 is identical with the smallest prime number greater than 5.") When I say that a sensation is a brain process or that lightning is an electric discharge I do not mean just that the sensation is somehow spatially or temporally continuous with the brain process or that the lightning is just spatially or temporally continuous with the discharge. When on the other hand I say that the successful general is the same person as the small boy who stole the apples, I mean only that the successful general I see before me is a time slice[10] of the same four dimensional object of which the small boy stealing apples is an earlier time slice. However, the four dimensional object which has the general-I-see-before-me for its late time slice is identical in the strict sense with the four dimensional object which has the small-boy-who-stole-the-apples for an early time slice. I distinguish these two senses of "is identical with" because I wish to make it clear that the brain process doctrine asserts identity in the strict sense.

I shall now discuss various possible objections to the view that the processes reported in sensation statements are in fact processes in the brain. Most of us have met some of these objections in our first year as philosophy students. All the more reason to take a good look at them. Others of the objections will be more recondite and subtle.

Objection 1. Any illiterate peasant can talk perfectly well about his after-images, or how things look or feel to him, or about his aches and pains, and yet he may know nothing about neurophysiology. A man may, like Aristotle, believe that the brain is an organ for cooling the body without any impairment of his ability to make true statements about his sensations. Hence the things we are talking about when we describe our sensations cannot be processed in the brain.

Reply. You might as well say that a nation of slug-abeds, who never saw the morning star or who had never thought of the expression "the Morning Star," but who used the expression "the Evening Star" perfectly well, could not use this expression to refer to the same entity as we refer to (and describe as) "the Morning Star."[11]

You may object that the Morning Star is in a sense not the very same object as the Evening Star, but only something spatio-temporally continuous with it. That is, you may say that the Morning Star is not the Evening Star in the strict sense of "identity" that I distinguished earlier. I can perhaps forestall this objection by considering the slug-abeds to be New Zealanders and the early risers to be Englishmen. Then the thing the New Zealanders describe as "the Morning Star" could be the very same thing (in the strict sense) as the Englishmen describe "the Evening Star." And yet they could be ignorant of this fact.

There is, however, a more plausible example. Consider lightning.[12] Modern physical science tells us that lightning is a certain kind of electrical discharge due to ionization of clouds of water-vapor in the atmosphere. This, it is believed, is what the true nature of lightning is. Note that there are not two things: a flash of lightning and a physical discharge. There is one thing, a flash of lightning, which is described scientifically as an electrical discharge to the earth from a cloud of ionized water-molecules. The case is not at all like that of explaining a footprint by reference to a burglar. We say that what lightning really is, what its true nature as revealed by science is, is an electric discharge. (It is not the true nature of a footprint to be a burglar.)

To forestall irrelevant objections, I should make it clear that by "lightning" I mean the publicly observable physical object, lightning, not a visual sense-datum of lightning. I say that the publicly observable physical object lightning is in fact the electrical discharge, not just a correlate of it. The sense-datum, or at least the having of the sense-datum, the "look" of the lightning, may well in my view be a correlate of the electric discharge. For in my view it is a brain state *caused* by the lightning. But we should no more confuse sensations of lightning with lightning then we confuse sensations of a table with a table.

In short, the reply to Objection 1 is that there can be contingent statements of the form "A is identical with B," and a person may well know that something is an A without knowing that it is a B. An illiterate peasant might well be able to talk about his sensations without knowing about his brain processes, just as he can talk about lightning though he knows nothing about electricity.

Objection 2. It is only a contingent fact (if it is a fact) that when we have a certain kind of sensation there is a certain kind of process in the brain. Indeed it is possible, though perhaps in the highest degree unlikely, that our present psychological theories will be as out of date as the ancient theory connecting mental processes with goings on in the heart. It follows that when we report a sensation we are not reporting a brain-process.

Reply. The objection certainly proves that when we say "I have an after-image" we cannot *mean* something of the form "I have such and such a brain-process." But this does not show that what we report (having an after-image) is not *in fact* a brain process. "I see lightning" does not *mean* "I see an electrical discharge." Indeed, it is logically possible (though highly unlikely) that the electrical discharge account of lightning might one day be given up. Again, "I see the Evening Star" does not *mean* the same thing as "I see the Morning Star," and yet "the Evening Star and the Morning Star are one and the same thing" is a contingent proposition. Possibly Objection 2 derives some of its apparent strength from a "Fido"-Fido theory of meaning. If the meaning of an expression were what the expression named, then of course it would follow from the fact that "sensation" and "brain-process" have different meanings that they cannot name one and the same thing.

Objection 3.[13] Even if Objections 1 and 2 do not prove that sensations are something over and above brain-processes, they do prove that the qualities of sensations are something over and above the qualities of brain-processes. That is, it may be possible to get out of asserting the existence of irreducibly psychic processes, but not out of asserting the existence of irreducibly psychic *properties*. For suppose we identify the Morning Star with the Evening Star. Then there must be some properties which logically imply that of being the Morning Star, and quite distinct properties which entail that of being the Evening Star. Again, there must be some properties (for example, that of being a yellow flash) which are logically distinct from those in the physicalist story.

Reply. Indeed, it might be thought that the objection succeeds at one jump. For consider the property of "being a yellow flash." It might seem that this property lies inevitably outside the physicalist framework within which I am trying to work (either by "yellow," being an objective emergent property of physical objects, or else by being a power to produce yellow sense-data, where "yellow," in this second instantiation of the word, refers to a purely phenomenal or introspectible quality). I must therefore digress for a moment and indicate how I deal with secondary qualities. I shall concentrate on color.

First of all, let me introduce the concept of a normal percipient. One person is more a normal percipient than another if he can make color discriminations that the other cannot. For example, if A can pick a lettuce leaf out of a heap of cabbage leaves, whereas B cannot though he can pick a lettuce leaf out of a heap of beetroot leaves, then A is more normal than B. (I am assuming that A and B are not given time to distinguish the leaves by their slight difference in shape, and so forth.) From the concept of "more normal than" it is easy to see how we can introduce the concept of "normal." Of course, Eskimos may make the finest discriminations at the blue end of the spectrum, Hottentots at the red end. In this case the concept of a normal percipient is a slightly idealized one, rather like that of "the mean sum" in astronomical chronology. There is no need to go into such subtleties now. I say that "this is red" means something roughly like "A normal percipient would not easily pick this out of a clump of geranium petals though he would pick it out of a clump of lettuce leaves." Of course it does not exactly mean this: a person might know the meaning of "red" without knowing anything about geraniums, or even about normal percipients. But the point is that a person can be *trained* to say "This is red" of objects which would not easily be picked out of geranium petals by a normal percipient, and so on. (Note that even a color-blind person can reasonably assert that something is red, though of course he needs to use another human being, not just himself, as a "color meter.") This account of secondary qualities explains their unimportance in physics. For obviously the discriminations and lack of discriminations made by a very complex neurophysiological mechanism are hardly likely to correspond to simple and nonarbitrary distinctions in nature.

I therefore elucidate colors as powers, in Locke's sense, to evoke certain sorts of discriminatory responses in human beings. They are also, of course, powers to cause sensations in human beings (an account still nearer to Locke's). But these sensations, I am arguing, are identifiable with brain processes.

Now how do I get over the objection that a sensation can be identified with a brain process only if it has some phenomenal property, not possessed by brain processes, whereby one-half of the identification may be, so to speak, pinned down?

My suggestion is as follows. When a person says, "I see a yellowish-orange after-image," he is saying something like this: *"There is something going on which is like what is going on when* I have my eyes open, am awake, and there is an orange illuminated in good light in front of me, that is, when I really see an orange." (And there is no reason why a person should not say the same thing when he is having a veridical sense-datum, so long as we construe "like" in the last sentence in such a sense that something can be like itself.) Notice that the italicized words, namely "there is something going on which is like what is going on when," are all quasi-logical or topic-neutral words. This explains why the ancient Greek peasant's reports about his sensation can be neutral between dualistic metaphysics or my materialistic metaphysics. It explains how sensations can be brain-processes and yet how those who report them only need know nothing about brain-processes. For he reports them only very abstractly as "something going on which is like what is going on when . . ." Similarly, a person may say "someone is in the room," thus reporting truly that the doctor is in the room, even when he has never heard of doctors. (There are not two people in the room: "someone" *and* the doctor.) This account of sensation statements also explains the singular elusiveness of "raw feels"—why no one seems to be able to pin any properties on them.[14] Raw feels in my view, are colorless for the very same reason that *something* is colorless. This does not mean that sensations do not have properties, for if they are brain processes they certainly have properties. It only means that in speaking of them as being like or unlike one another we need not know or mention these properties.

This, then, is how I would reply to Objection 3. The strength of my reply depends on the possibility of our being able to report that one thing is like another without being able to state the respect in which it is like. I am not sure whether this is so or not, and that is why I regard Objection 3 as the strongest with which I have to deal.

Objection 4. The after-image is not in physical space. The brain-process is. So the after-image is not the brain process.

Reply. This is an *ignoratio elenchi.* I am not arguing that the after-image is a brain-process, but that the experience of having an after-image is a brain process. It is the *experience* which is reported in the introspective report. Similarly, if it is objected that the after-image is yellowy-orange but that a surgeon looking into your brain would see nothing yellowy-orange, my reply is that it is the experience of seeing yellowy-orange that is being described, and this experience is not a yellowy-orange something. So to say that a brain-process cannot be yellowy-orange is not to say that a brain process cannot in fact be the experience of having a yellowy-orange after-image. There is, in a sense, no such thing as an after-image or sense-datum, though there is such a thing as the experience of having an image, and this experience is described indirectly in material object language, not in phenomenal language, for there is no such thing.[15] We describe the experience by saying, in effect, that it is like the experience we have when, for example, we really see a yellowy-orange patch on the wall. Trees and wallpaper can be green, but not the experience of seeing or imagining a tree or wallpaper. (Or if they are described as green or yellow this can only be in a derived sense.)

Objection 5. It would make sense to say of a molecular movement in the brain that it is swift or slow, straight or circular, but it makes no sense to say this of the experience of seeing something yellow.

Reply. So far we have not given sense to talk of experiences as swift or slow, straight or circular. But I am not claiming that "experience" and "brain-processes" mean the same thing or even that they have the same logic. "Somebody" and "the doctor" do not have the same logic, but this does not lead us to suppose that talking about somebody telephoning is talking about someone over and above, say, the doctor. The ordinary man when he reports an experience is reporting that something is going on, but he leaves it open as to what sort of thing is going on, whether in a material or solid medium, or perhaps some sort of gaseous medium, or even perhaps in some sort of nonspatial medium (if this makes any sense). All that I am saying is that "experience" and "brain-process" may in fact refer to the same thing, and if so we may easily adopt a conversation (which is not in charge in our present rules for the use of experience words but an addition to them) whereby it would make sense to talk of an experience in terms of appropriate to physical process.

Objection 6. Sensations are private, brain-processes are public. If I sincerely say, "I see a yellowish-orange after-image" and I am not making a verbal mistake, then I cannot be wrong. But I can be wrong about a brain-process. The scientist looking into my brain might be having an illusion. Moreover, it makes sense to say that two or more people are observing the same brain-process but not that two or more people are reporting the same inner experience.

Reply. This shows that the language of introspective reports has a different logic from the language of material processes. It is obvious that until the brain-process theory is much improved and widely accepted there will be no *criteria* for saying, "Smith has an experience of such-and-such a sort" *except* Smith's introspective reports. So we have adopted a rule of language that (normally) what Smith says goes.

Objection 7. I can imagine myself turned to stone and yet having images, aches, pains, and so on.

Reply. I can imagine that the electrical theory of lightning is false, that lightning is some sort of purely optical phenomenon. I can imagine that the Evening Star is not the Morning Star. But it is. All the objection shows is that "experience" and "brain-process" do not have the same meaning. It does not show that experience is not in fact a brain process. . . .

I have now considered a number of objections to the brain-process thesis. I wish now to conclude by some remarks on the logical status of the thesis itself. U. T. Place seems to hold that it is a straight-out scientific hypothesis.[16] If so, he is partly right and partly wrong. If the issue is between (say) a brain-process thesis and a heart thesis, or a liver thesis, or a kidney thesis, the issue is a purely empirical one, and the verdict is overwhelmingly in favor of the brain. The right sorts of things don't go on in the heart, liver, or kidney, nor do these organs possess the right sort of complexity of structure. On the other hand if the issue is between a brain-or-heart-or-liver-or-kidney thesis (that is, some form of materialism) and epiphenomenalism, then the issue is not an empirical one. For there is no conceivable experiment which could decide between materialism and epiphenomenalism. This latter issue is not like the average straight-out empirical issue in science, but like the issue between the nineteenth-century English naturalist Phillip Gosse[17] and the orthodox geologists and paleontologists of his day. According to Gosse, the earth was created about 4004 B.C. exactly as described in *Genesis*, with twisted rock strata, "evidence" or erosion, and so forth, and all sorts of fossils, all in their appropriate strata, just as if the usual evolutionist story had been true. Clearly this theory is in a sense irrefutable: no evidence can possi-

bly tell against it. Let us ignore the theological setting in which Phillip
Gosse's hypothesis had been placed, thus ruling out objections of a theological kind, such as "what a queer God who would go to such elaborate lengths
to deceive us." Let us suppose that it is held that the universe just began in
4004 B.C. with the initial conditions just everywhere as they were in 4004
B.C., and in particular that our own planet began with the sediment in the
rivers, eroded cliffs, fossils in the rocks, and so on. No scientist would ever
entertain this as a serious hypothesis, consistent with all possible evidence.
This hypothesis offends against the principles of parsimony and simplicity.
There would be far too many brute and inexplicable facts. Why are pterodac-
tyl bones just as they are? No explanation in terms of the evolution of ptero-
dactyls from earlier forms of life would any longer be possible. We would
have millions of facts about the world as it was in 4004 B.C. that just have to
be *accepted*.

The issue between the brain-process theory and the epiphenomenalism
seems to be of the above sort. (Assuming that a behavioristic reduction of
introspective reports is not possible.) If it be agreed that there are no cogent
philosophical arguments which force us into accepting dualism, and if the
brain-process theory and dualism are equally consistent with the facts, then
the principles of parsimony and simplicity seem to me to decide overwhelmingly in favor of the brain-process theory. As I pointed out earlier, dualism
involves irreducibly psychophysical laws (whereby the "nomonlogical danglers" dangle) of a queer sort, that just have to be taken on trust, and are just
as difficult to swallow as the irreducible facts about the paleontology of the
earth with which we are faced on Phillip Gosse's theory.

NOTES

1. This is a very slightly revised version of a paper that was first published in the
Philosophical Review, LXVIII (1959), 141–56. Since that date there have been criticisms of my paper by J. T. Stevenson, *Philosophical Review*, LXIX (1960), 505–10, to
which I have replied in *Philosophical Review*, LXX (1961), 406–7, and by G. Pitcher
and by W. D. Jorke, *Australasian Journal of Philosophy*, XXXVIII (1960), to which I
have replied in the same volume of that journal, pp. 252–54.

2. *British Journal of Psychology*, XLVII (1956), pp. 44–50; reprinted in A. Flew
(ed.), *Body, Mind and Death* (New York: Macmillan, 1964).

3. *Minnesota Studies in the Philosophy of Science*, Vol. II (Minneapolis: University of Minnesota Press, 1958), pp. 370–497.

4. Some philosophers of my acquaintance, who have the advantage over me in
having known Wittgenstein, would say that this interpretation of him is too behavioristic. However, it seems to me a very natural interpretation of his printed words,
and whether or not it is Wittgenstein's real view is certainly an interesting and important one. I wish I could consider it here as a possible rival both to the "brain-process"
thesis and to straight-out old-fashioned dualism.

5. See Ryle, *The Concept of Mind* (London: Hutchinson's University Library, 1949), p. 93.

6. On this point see Paul Oppenheim and Hilary Putnam, "Unity of Science as a Working Hypothesis," in *Minnesota Studies in the Philosophy of Science*, Vol. II (Minneapolis: University of Minnesota Press, 1958), pp. 3–36.

7. Feigl, *op. cit.*, p. 428. Feigl uses the expression "nomological danglers" for the laws whereby the entities dangle: I have used the expression to refer to the dangling entities themselves.

8. Wittgenstein did not like the word "disposition." I am using it to put in a nutshell (and perhaps inaccurately) the view which I am attributing to Wittgenstein. I should like to repeat that I do not wish to claim that my interpretation of Wittgenstein is correct. Some of those who knew him do not interpret him in this way. It is merely a view which I find myself extracting from his printed words and which I think is important and worth discussion for its own sake.

9. See Place; and Feigl, *op. cit.*, p. 390, near top.

10. See J. H. Woodger, *Theory of Construction*, International Encyclopedia of Unified Science, II, No. 5 (Chicago: University of Chicago Press, 1939), p. 38. I here permit myself to speak loosely. For warnings against possible ways of going wrong with this sort of talk, see my note, "Spatialising Time," *Mind* (1955), pp. 239–41.

11. Cf. Feogl, *op. cit.*, p. 439.

12. See Place; also Feigl, *op. cit.*, p. 438.

13. I think this objection was first put to me by Professor Max Black. I think it is the most subtle of any of those I have considered, and the one which I am least confident of having satisfactorily met.

14. See B.A. Farrell, 'Experience,' *Mind*, LIX (1950), 170–98.

15. Dr. J. R. Smythies claims that a sense-datum language could be taught independently of the material object language ("A Note on the Fallacy of the 'Phenomenological Fallacy,'" *British Journal of Psychology*, XLVIII [1957], pp. 141–44). I am not so sure of this: there must be some public criteria for a person having got a rule wrong before we can teach him the rule. I suppose someone might accidentally learn color words by Dr. Smythies' procedure. I am not, of course, denying that we can learn a sense-datum language in the sense that we can learn to report our experience. Nor would Place deny it.

16. *Op. cit.* For a further discussion of this, in reply to the original version of the present paper, see Place's note "Materialism as a Scientific Hypothesis," *Philosophical Review* LXIX (1960), pp. 101–4.

17. See the entertaining account of Gosse's book *Omphalos* by Martin Gardner in Fads and Fallacies in the Name of Science, 2nd ed. (New York: Dover, 1957), pp. 124–7.

Online Resources:

J. J. C. Smart
www.arts.monash.edu.au/phil/department/smart/

Functionalism

In this section, three readings addressing the **Functionalist** theory of mind are provided. They are followed by two critical readings that pose difficulties for the position. As noted earlier, Functionalism is a theory of the mind that holds that mental states are causally describable. They are the typical (environmental) causes, the behavioral effects of these causes, and the effects upon other mental states. A mental state of pain, for example, is caused when you touch a hot stove and this causes you to react—to move your hand, wince, cry out—and also to yell "ouch" and think, "That was dumb!" What is crucial to notice is that, unlike Ryle's **Logical Behaviorism**, the Functionalist view maintains that there is something "inside" besides the behavioral responses you have or are disposed to have. The meaning of mental state terms is explained through causal relations that include other mental states, not only observable behaviors and our dispositions to behave in certain ways. The causal story, as Jerry Fodor has noted in an earlier selection in his criticism of Ryle, can be fleshed out to include mental processes. This theory advances on Ryle's in an important way and, as our readings will show, inspired great advances in ways that we currently research, model, and study mental processes.

An important feature of this view is that while functionalism is compatible with a **materialist** (physicalist) view of the mind, it holds that the identity between mental states and brain states is **contingent** (it could be otherwise). Smart's **Type Identity** thesis identifies types of mental states only with types of brain states, ruling out the possibility that other creatures besides human beings could have mental states just like ours. Functionalism is also known as the "**Token Identity Thesis**," maintaining that mental states are contingently associated with the material that instantiates them. This means that a **functional description** of a mental state—the typical causes and effects it has on behavior and other mental states—is a general description of that mental state, but any specific instance of a mental state—your particular mental state (a token of the general type of mental state) happens to be instantiated by a particular brain state in your brain (token of a general type of a brain state). These tokens are identical, but it could be otherwise. A computer, for example, that had a program describing the functional operations of the mental state type, if sufficiently powerful, could have a token mental state (a particular experience) of this state. The computer's hardware, correctly organized, would instantiate this token mental state and would (also) be contingently identical to it. In this way, Functionalism is said to offer "**Multiple Realization**." Other beings (aliens, possibly animals) and suitably organized machines, in principle, can realize (instantiate) mental states.

Alan Turing presents his version of functionalism in his classic paper, "Computing Machines and Intelligence." This paper inaugurated research on artificial intelligence. In the next section of this reader, papers devoted to this subject will be presented. At this point, our effort is to understand the **Functionalist** view of the mind and the arguments that support it. For Turing, the causal relations that describe mental states can be understood as a computer program with inputs (stimuli), outputs (behavioral effects), and changes in internal states (relations to other mental states). These inputs and outputs comprise a "machine table," a plan that describes a given mental state. The computer hardware is like the human brain in terms of instantiating an "intelligent" program. We find important and perhaps controversial ideas in Turing's paper, including not only the claim that a computer can implement a "mind program," but also a test, the "Imitation Game," also known as **"The Turing Test,"** through which we would determine if a computer (or potentially any being!) is intelligent. The Turing Test has us asking a battery of questions to which, if the computer provides a battery of convincing replies, we would have no choice but to ascribe intelligence to it. One thing to note about the "multiple realization" offered by Functionalism is that it would seem that if "it walks like a duck, talks like a duck, and acts like a duck, then it is a duck." This is a result of holding that mental states are contingently realized by whatever suitably organized material instantiates them. There is no "essential" connection between minds and brains such that there is *some other* feature besides the functional description of a mental state that makes it a mental state. In the criticisms of functionalism, as well as in the discussions of artificial intelligence, we will see that some philosophers find that Functionalism leaves something to be desired—leaves something essential out—in terms of wholly describing all there is to our mental states.

The reading on the Functionalist theory of mind is selected from David Lewis's "Psychophysical and Theoretical Identifications." This selection presents a version of Functionalism that does not rely so heavily on the idea of computer programs. Instead, holding a similar Functionalist view of mental states, Lewis first shows the way our mental state terms can be understood as theoretical terms within a larger theory—our commonsense "**folkpsychology**," an "unofficial" yet very real and useful theory that we acquire when we learn mental state words and their meanings. This theory helps us to explain and predict human behavior and has done so successfully for a very long time. And for Lewis, the mental state terms of our folk-psychology are understood functionally—in terms of their typical causal roles in relation to behavior and other mental states. Folk-psychology itself supports Functionalism. Lewis presents a story of a detective solving a crime by way of illustrating how the mental state terms of our folk-psychology and the roles they play in this theory will turn out to be identified with the terms in a neuro-scientific theory of the mind. The detective develops a theory of a crime by analyzing the behaviors of the different individuals involved in the crime. If the detective's theory is correct, he will know just who, exactly, the murderer is. Neuroscientists will likewise develop a physical theory of our mental states. The theoretical terms of our folk-psychology (our mental state terms) will turn out to be identical with those defined in the scientific theory. Of course, the theoretical terms in our folk-psychology could also be identified with the theoretical terms in another neuro-scientific theory of, say, Martian neuro-biology (very different from ours). His view allows for multiple realization, just as Turing-style functionalism does. The identification of a mental state term in our folk-psychology with a theoretical term in neuro-science could be otherwise (is **contingent**). We may wonder, though, if this means that our mental state terms would serve no purpose once neuro-scientists discover their identities. However, Lewis does not think this translation from one theory to the other means that we need to reject our commonsense folk-psychology. It is not wrong at all, and since it is not wrong, there is no need to get rid of it. In fact, it has helped us solve the mystery as to the physical identities of our mental states.

Jerry A. Fodor's "The Mind-Body Problem" provides a helpful review of the positions covered so far in this anthology—although from a Functionalist perspective. He reviews the positions of **Substance Dualism**, **Logical Behaviorism**, and the **Type (Central State) Identity Theory**, showing how **Functionalism** provides a solution to objections these positions confront. In Fodor's view, functionalism seems to capture the best features of the materialist alternatives to dualism, behaviorism, and identity theory. Any theory of psychology would need to provide a "robust" account of **mental causation**, and this is precisely the benefit of Functionalism. What Fodor means by this is that if we take the idea that we have minds and mental states and that these states affect the world around us (and are affected by it), Functionalism is a very promising theory. Clearly, functionalism emphasizes the causal relations between stimuli (inputs) and their effects on behavior and other mental states. Thus, the gnawing of one's empty stomach causes a sensation of hunger, the thought about making a sandwich, and a thought which also causes one to get up off the couch and look for food in the refrigerator. A series of causes and effects explains one's mental state of being hungry. Psychological explanations are more general than this particular illustration, but Fodor finds that Functionalism promises to provide the best explanation for how the mind causes our behaviors. Functionalism, Fodor notes, is especially promising for explaining **intentional states**, our thoughts, invigorating the "**representational theory of the mind**." This theory coheres well with functionalism since it holds that the mind operates upon mental representations—that thinking involves content that has a symbolic form that the mind manipulates in a rule-governed manner, much like spoken language.

Cognitive scientists and psychologists will be able to experimentally model and test their theories about the roles our intentional mental states have in psychological explanation.

This part concludes with two selections that are critical of Functionalism. The first is a section from Ned Block's paper, "Troubles with Functionalism." In this selection, Block poses a problem that he believes holds for Turing-style **"Machine Functionalism"** as well as **"Psychofunctionalism"** as presented by David Lewis. Both versions of Functionalism, he says, are guilty of "liberalism," attributing mentality to systems that lack it. He first invites us to entertain the possibility of a **homunculi**-headed robot. Supposing there was a functionalist description of you—a machine table that specified the inputs and outputs (changes in mental states and behavior). We could also suppose that tiny G-men were positioned inside your head so as to follow the functionalist specifications of your mental states *exactly*. This homunculi-headed robot would be functionally equivalent to you in every way. This homunculi-headed robot would not have mentality, but the functionalist would have to admit that it does. Making matters much worse, Block asks us to entertain that the entire nation of China could be organized to implement a functional description of a mental state. The functionalist would "liberally" have to admit that the entire nation of China is in a mental state—attribute mentality to a system that lacks it. Block explains that these examples serve to illustrate that Functionalism casts far too wide a net, including systems that lack qualitative states, ones that experience no "immediate **phenomenological** qualities." These are the mental qualities that we experience when we taste, see, touch, or hear—the feel of our sensations and perceptions. Systems may functionally specify mental states, but since there is nothing to the experience of being in the mental state for the systems, they actually cannot be in those states. The nation of China could (possibly) functionally implement the state of pain, but it does not feel pain. But if it does not actually feel pain, it cannot be in pain according to Block. He terms this the **"Absent Qualia** argument" against Functionalism.

Frank Jackson continues this discussion of **qualia** and the manner in which Functionalism fails as a theory to capture qualia—a feature of our mental life—in his paper, **"Epiphenomenal** Qualia." The failure of Functionalism to do so is a failure of the **Physicalist** view of the mind in general; Jackson finds that no amount of physical information, including that of functional explanations of our mental states, will capture qualia—physicalism about the mind will always leave something out, namely qualia. Jackson admits that he is a "qualia freak," someone who believes that these feels to our sensations and perceptions are a part of our mental lives that cannot be eliminated from an account of our minds, yet there is a question as to what kind of role they play. Jackson presents illustrations of the ways that qualia must exist but cannot be described in any physical and functional account of the world and mind—qualia are not describable with physical information. His examples of Fred, who has the ability to distinguish differences in colors that we cannot see, and Mary, a brilliant neuroscientist who is raised in a black-and-white room and who has never seen any colors, make the case that qualia must exist and make a difference of some kind in terms of experience, yet cannot be captured by any amount of physical information. But what sort of difference do qualia make in our experience? None, according to Jackson. Hence we come to the title of his paper, "Epiphenomenal Qualia." Jackson argues that qualia are effects of our brains, but that these qualities of our experiences make no difference—are inefficacious—with respect to the physical world. The thesis of **Physicalism** about the mind and the Functionalist view are overly optimistic with respect to what can be captured by physical information. They are the best we can do, but they cannot capture qualia.

5

Computing Machinery and Intelligence

Alan M. Turing

1. THE IMITATION GAME

I propose to consider the question, "Can machines think?" This should begin with definitions of the meaning of the terms "machine" and "think." The definitions might be framed so as to reflect so far as possible the normal use of the words, but this attitude is dangerous. If the meaning of the words "machine" and "think" are to be found by examining how they are commonly used it is difficult to escape the conclusion that the meaning and the answer to the question, "Can machines think?" is to be sought in a statistical survey such as a Gallup poll. But this is absurd. Instead of attempting such a definition I shall replace the question by another, which is closely related to it and is expressed in relatively unambiguous words.

The new form of the problem can be described in terms of a game which we call the "imitation game." It is played with three people, a man (A), a woman (B), and an interrogator (C) who may be of either sex. The interrogator stays in a room apart front the other two. The object of the game for the interrogator is to determine which of the other two is the man and which is the woman. He knows them by labels X and Y, and at the end of the game he says either "X is A and Y is B" or "X is B and Y is A." The interrogator is allowed to put questions to A and B thus:

C: Will X please tell me the length of his or her hair?

Now suppose X is actually A, then A must answer. It is A's object in the game to try and cause C to make the wrong identification. His answer might therefore be:

"My hair is shingled, and the longest strands are about nine inches long."

In order that tones of voice may not help the interrogator the answers should be written, or better still, typewritten. The ideal arrangement is to have a teleprinter communicating between the two rooms. Alternatively the question and answers can be repeated by an intermediary. The object of the game for the third player (B) is to help the interrogator. The best strategy for her is probably to give truthful answers. She can add such things as "I am the woman, don't listen to him!" to her answers, but it will avail nothing as the man can make similar remarks.

We now ask the question, "What will happen when a machine takes the part of A in this game?" Will the interrogator decide wrongly as often when the game is played like this as he does when the game is played between a man and a woman? These questions replace our original, "Can machines think?"

2. CRITIQUE OF THE NEW PROBLEM

As well as asking, "What is the answer to this new form of the question," one may ask, "Is this new question a worthy one to investigate?" This latter question we investigate without further ado, thereby cutting short an infinite regress.

The new problem has the advantage of drawing a fairly sharp line between the physical and the intellectual capacities of a man. No engineer or chemist claims to be able to produce a material which is indistinguishable from the human skin. It is possible that at some time this might be done, but even supposing this invention available we should feel there was little point in trying to make a "thinking machine" more human by dressing it up in such artificial flesh. The form in which we have set the problem reflects this fact in the condition which prevents the interrogator from seeing or touching the other competitors, or hearing their voices. Some other advantages of the proposed criterion may be shown up by specimen questions and answers. Thus:

Q: Please write me a sonnet on the subject of the Forth Bridge.

A: Count me out on this one. I never could write poetry.

Q: Add 34957 to 70764.

A: (Pause about 30 seconds and then give as answer) 105621.

Q: Do you play chess?

A: Yes.

Q: I have K at my K1, and no other pieces. You have only K at K6 and R at R1. It is your move. What do you play?

A: (After a pause of 15 seconds) R-R8 mate.

The question and answer method seems to be suitable for introducing almost any one of the fields of human endeavor that we wish to include. We do not wish to penalize the machine for its inability to shine in beauty competitions, nor to penalize a man for losing in a race against an airplane. The conditions of our game make these disabilities irrelevant. The "witnesses" can brag, if they consider it advisable, as much as they please about their charms, strength or heroism, but the interrogator cannot demand practical demonstrations.

The game may perhaps be criticized on the ground that the odds are weighted too heavily against the machine. If the man were to try and pretend to be the machine he would clearly make a very poor showing. He would be given away at once by slowness and inaccuracy in arithmetic. May not machines carry out something which ought to be described as thinking but which is very different from what a man does? This objection is a very strong one, but at least we can say that if, nevertheless, a machine can be constructed to play the imitation game satisfactorily, we need not be troubled by this objection.

It might be urged that when playing the "imitation game" the best strategy for the machine may possibly be something other than imitation of the behavior of a man. This may be, but I think it is unlikely that there is any great effect of this kind. In any case there is no intention to investigate here the theory of the game, and it will be assumed that the best strategy is to try to provide answers that would naturally be given by a man.

3. THE MACHINES CONCERNED IN THE GAME

The question which we put in 1 will not be quite definite until we have specified what we mean by the word "machine." It is natural that we should wish to permit every kind of engineering technique to be used in our machines. We also wish to allow the possibility that an engineer or team of engineers may construct a machine which works, but whose manner of operation cannot be satisfactorily described by its constructors because they have applied a method which is largely experimental. Finally, we wish to exclude from the machines men born in the usual manner. It is difficult to frame the definitions so as to satisfy these three conditions. One might for instance insist that the team of engineers should be all of one sex, but this would not really be satisfactory, for it is probably possible to rear a complete individual from a single cell of the skin (say) of a man. To do so would be a feat of biological technique deserving of the very highest praise, but we would not be inclined to regard it as a case of "constructing a thinking machine." This prompts us to abandon the requirement that every kind of technique should be permitted. We are the more ready to do so in view of the fact that the present interest in "thinking machines" has been aroused by a particular kind of machine, usually called an "electronic computer" or "digital computer." Following this suggestion we only permit digital computers to take part in our game.

This restriction appears at first sight to be a very drastic one. I shall attempt to show that it is not so in reality. To do this necessitates a short account of the nature and properties of these computers.

It may also be said that this identification of machines with digital computers, like our criterion for "thinking," will only be unsatisfactory if (contrary to my belief), it turns out that digital computers are unable to give a good showing in the game.

There are already a number of digital computers in working order, and it may be asked, "Why not try the experiment straight away? It would be easy to satisfy the conditions of the game. A number of interrogators could be used, and statistics compiled to show how often the right identification was given." The short answer is that we are not asking whether all digital computers would do well in the game nor whether the computers at present available would do well, but whether there are imaginable computers which would do well. But this is only the short answer. We shall see this question in a different light later.

4. DIGITAL COMPUTERS

The idea behind digital computers may be explained by saying that these machines are intended to carry out any operations which could be done by a human computer. The human computer is supposed to be following fixed rules; he has no authority to deviate from them in any detail. We may suppose that these rules are supplied in a book, which is altered whenever he is put on to a new job. He has also an unlimited supply of paper on which he does his calculations. He may also do his multiplications and additions on a "desk machine," but this is not important.

If we use the above explanation as a definition we shall be in danger of circularity of argument. We avoid this by giving an outline of the means by which the desired effect is achieved. A digital computer can usually be regarded as consisting of three parts:

1. Store.
2. Executive unit.
3. Control.

The store is a store of information, and corresponds to the human computer's paper, whether this is the paper on which he does his calculations or that on which his book of rules is printed. In so far as the human computer does calculations in his head a part of the store will correspond to his memory.

The executive unit is the part which carries out the various individual operations involved in a calculation. What these individual operations are will vary from machine to machine. Usually fairly lengthy operations can be done such as "Multiply 3540675445 by 7076345687" but in some machines only very simple ones such as "Write down 0" are possible.

We have mentioned that the "book of rules" supplied to the computer is replaced in the machine by a part of the store. It is then called the "table of instructions." It is the duty of the control to see that these instructions are obeyed correctly and in the right order. The control is so constructed that this necessarily happens.

The information in the store is usually broken up into packets of moderately small size. In one machine, for instance, a packet might consist of ten decimal digits. Numbers are assigned to the parts of the store in which the various packets of information are stored, in some systematic manner. A typical instruction might say—

"Add the number stored in position 6809 to that in 4302 and put the result back into the latter storage position."

Needless to say it would not occur in the machine expressed in English. It would more likely be coded in a form such as 6809430217. Here 17 says which of various possible operations is to be performed on the two numbers. In this case the operation is that described above, viz., "Add the number. . . ." It will be noticed that the instruction takes up 10 digits and so forms one packet of information, very conveniently. The control will normally take the instructions to be obeyed in the order of the positions in which they are stored, but occasionally an instruction such as

"Now obey the instruction stored in position 5606, and continue from there" may be encountered, or again

"If position 4505 contains 0 obey next the instruction stored in 6707, otherwise continue straight on."

Instructions of these latter types are very important because they make it possible for a sequence of operations to be replaced over and over again until some condition is fulfilled, but in doing so to obey, not fresh instructions on each repetition, but the same ones over and over again. To take a domestic analogy. Suppose Mother wants Tommy to call at the cobbler's every morning on his way to school to see if her shoes are done, she can ask him afresh every morning. Alternatively she can stick up a notice once and for all in the hall which he will see when he leaves for school and which tells him to call for the shoes, and also to destroy the notice when he comes back if he has the shoes with him.

The reader must accept it as a fact that digital computers can be constructed, and indeed have been constructed, according to the principles we have described, and that they can in fact mimic the actions of a human computer very closely.

The book of rules which we have described our human computer as using is of course a convenient fiction. Actual human computers really remember what they have got to do. If one wants to make a machine mimic the behavior of the human computer in some complex operation one has to ask him how it is done, and then translate the answer into the form of an instruction table. Constructing instruction tables is usually described as "programming." To "program a machine to carry out the operation A" means to put the appropriate instruction table into the machine so that it will do A.

An interesting variant on the idea of a digital computer is a "digital computer with a random element." These have instructions involving the throwing of a die or some equivalent electronic process; one such instruction might for instance be, "Throw the die and put the resulting number into store 1000." Sometimes such a machine is described as having free will (though I would not use this phrase myself). It is not normally possible to determine from observing a machine whether it has a random element, for a similar effect can be produced by such devices as making the choices depend on the digits of the decimal for.

Most actual digital computers have only a finite store. There is no theoretical difficulty in the idea of a computer with an unlimited store. Of course only a finite part can have been used at any one time. Likewise only a finite amount can have been constructed, but we can imagine more and more being added as required. Such computers have special theoretical interest and will be called infinitive capacity computers.

The idea of a digital computer is an old one. Charles Babbage, Lucasian Professor of Mathematics at Cambridge from 1828 to 1839, planned such a machine, called the Analytical Engine, but it was never completed. Although Babbage had all the essential ideas, his machine was not at that time such a very attractive prospect. The speed which would have been available would be definitely faster than a human computer but something like 100 times slower than the Manchester machine, itself one of the slower of the modern machines. The storage was to be purely mechanical, using wheels and cards.

The fact that Babbage's Analytical Engine was to be entirely mechanical will help us to rid ourselves of a superstition. Importance is often attached to the fact that modern digital computers are electrical, and that the nervous system also is electrical. Since Babbage's machine was not electrical, and since all digital computers are in a sense equivalent, we see that this use of electricity cannot be of theoretical importance. Of course electricity usually comes in where fast signaling is concerned, so that it is not surprising that we find it in both these connections. In the nervous system chemical phenomena are at least as important as electrical. In certain computers the storage system is mainly acoustic. The feature of using electricity is thus seen to be only a very superficial similarity. If we wish to find such similarities we should look rather for mathematical analogies of function.

5. UNIVERSALITY OF DIGITAL COMPUTERS

The digital computers considered in the last section may be classified amongst the "discrete-state machines." These are the machines which move by sudden jumps or clicks from one quite definite state to another. These states are sufficiently different for the possibility of confusion between them to be ignored. Strictly speaking there are no such machines. Everything really moves continuously. But there are many kinds of machine which can profitably be thought of as being discrete-state machines. For instance in considering the switches for a lighting system it is a convenient fiction that each switch must be definitely on or definitely off. There must be intermediate positions, but for most purposes we can forget about them. As an example of a discrete-state machine we might consider a wheel which clicks round through 120 once a second, but may be stopped by a lever which can be operated from outside; in addition a lamp is to light in one of the positions of the wheel. This machine could be described abstractly as follows. The internal state of the machine (which is described by the position of the wheel) may be q_1, q_2 or q_3. There is an input signal i_0 or i_1 (position of lever). The internal state at any moment is determined by the last state and input signal according to the table.

		Last State		
		q_1	q_2	q_3
	i_0	q_2	q_3	q_1
Input				
	i_1	q_1	q_2	q_3

The output signals, the only externally visible indication of the internal state (the light) are described by the table:

State	q_1	q_2	q_3
Output	o_0	o_0	o_1

This example is typical of discrete-state machines. They can be described by such tables provided they have only a finite number of possible states.

It will seem that given the initial state of the machine and the input signals it is always possible to predict all future states. This is reminiscent of Laplace's view that from the complete state of the universe at one moment of time, as described by the positions and velocities of all particles, it should be possible to predict all future states. The prediction which we are considering is, however, rather nearer to practicability than that considered by Laplace. The system of the "universe as a whole" is such that quite small errors in the initial conditions can have an overwhelming effect at a later time. The displacement of a single electron by a billionth of a centimeter at one moment might make the difference between a man being killed by an avalanche a year later, or escaping. It is an essential property of the mechanical systems which we have called "discrete-state machines" that this phenomenon does not occur. Even when we consider the actual physical machines instead of the idealized machines, reasonably accurate knowledge of the state at one moment yields reasonably accurate knowledge any number of steps later.

As we have mentioned, digital computers fall within the class of discrete-state machines. But the number of states of which such a machine is capable is usually enormously large. For instance, the number for the machine now working at Manchester is about $2^{165,000}$, i.e., about $10^{50,000}$. Compare this with our example of the clicking wheel described above, which had three states. It is not difficult to see why the number of states should be so immense. The computer includes a store corresponding to the paper used by a human computer. It must be possible to write into the store any one of the combinations of symbols which might have been written on the paper. For simplicity suppose that only digits from 0 to 9 are used as symbols. Variations in handwriting are ignored. Suppose the computer is allowed 100 sheets of paper each containing 50 lines each with room for 30 digits. Then the number of states is 10 100 $\times$ 50 $\times$ 30 i.e., $10^{150,000}$. This is about the number of states of three Manchester machines put together. The logarithm to the base two of the number of states is usually called the "storage capacity" of the machine. Thus the Manchester machine has a storage capacity of about 165,000 and the wheel machine of our example about 1.6. If two machines are put together their capacities must be added to obtain the capacity of the resultant machine. This leads to the possibility of statements such as "The Manchester machine contains 64 magnetic tracks each with a capacity of 2560, eight electronic tubes with a capacity of 1280. Miscellaneous storage amounts to about 300 making a total of 174,380."

Given the table corresponding to a discrete-state machine it is possible to predict what it will do. There is no reason why this calculation should not be carried out by means of a digital computer. Provided it could be carried out sufficiently quickly the digital computer could mimic the behavior of any discrete-state machine. The imitation game could then be played with the machine in question (as B) and the mimicking digital computer (as A) and the interrogator would be unable to distinguish them. Of course the digital computer must have an adequate storage capacity as well as working sufficiently fast. Moreover, it must be programmed afresh for each new machine which it is desired to mimic.

This special property of digital computers, that they can mimic any discrete-state machine, is described by saying that they are *universal* machines. The existence of machines with this property has the important consequence that, considerations of speed apart, it is unnecessary to design various new machines to do various computing processes. They can all be done with one digital computer, suitably programmed for each case. It will be seen that as a consequence of this all digital computers are in a sense equivalent.

We may now consider again the point raised at the end of §3. It was suggested tentatively that the question, "Can machines think?" should be replaced by "Are there imaginable digital computers which would do well in the imitation game?" If we wish we can make this superficially more general and ask "Are there discrete-state machines which would do well?" But in view of the universality property we see that either of these questions is equivalent to this, "Let us fix our attention on one particular digital computer C. Is it true that by modifying this computer to have an adequate storage, suitably increasing its speed of action, and providing it with an appropriate program, C can be made to play satisfactorily the part of A in the imitation game, the part of B being taken by a man?"

6. CONTRARY VIEWS ON THE MAIN QUESTION

We may now consider the ground to have been cleared and we are ready to proceed to the debate on our question, "Can machines think?" and the variant of it quoted at the end of the last section. We cannot altogether abandon the original form of the problem, for opinions will differ as to the appropriateness of the substitution and we must at least listen to what has to be said in this connection.

It will simplify matters for the reader if I explain first my own beliefs in the matter. Consider first the more accurate form of the question. I believe that in about fifty years' time it will be possible, to program computers, with a storage capacity of about 10^9, to make them play the imitation game so well that an average interrogator will not have more than 70 per cent chance of making the right identification after five minutes of questioning. The original question, "Can machines think?" I believe to be too meaningless to deserve discussion. Nevertheless I believe that at the end of the century the use of words and general educated opinion will have altered so much that one will be able to speak of machines thinking without expecting to be contradicted. I believe further that no useful purpose is served by concealing these beliefs. The popular view that scientists proceed inexorably from well-established fact to well-established fact, never being influenced by any improved conjecture, is quite mistaken. Provided it is made clear which are proved facts and which are conjectures, no harm can result. Conjectures are of great importance since they suggest useful lines of research.

I now proceed to consider opinions opposed to my own.

(1) The Theological Objection

Thinking is a function of man's immortal soul. God has given an immortal soul to every man and woman, but not to any other animal or to machines. Hence no animal or machine can think.

I am unable to accept any part of this, but will attempt to reply in theological terms. I should find the argument more convincing if animals were classed with men, for there is a greater difference, to my mind, between the typical animate and the inanimate than there is between man and the other animals. The arbitrary character of the orthodox view becomes clearer if we consider how it might appear to a member of some other religious community. How do Christians regard the Moslem view that women have no souls? But let us leave this point aside and return to the main argument. It appears to me that the argument quoted above implies a serious restriction of the omnipotence of the Almighty. It is admitted that there are certain things that He cannot do such as making one equal to two, but should we not believe that He has freedom to confer a soul on an elephant if He sees fit? We might expect that He would only exercise this power in conjunction with a mutation which provided the elephant with an appropriately improved brain to minister to the needs of this sort. An argument of exactly similar form may be made for the case of machines. It may seem different because it is more difficult to "swallow." But this really only means that we think it would be less likely that He would consider the circumstances suitable for conferring a soul. The circumstances in question are discussed in the rest of this paper. In attempting to construct such machines we should not be irreverently usurping His power of creating souls, any more than we are in the procreation of children: rather we are, in either case, instruments of His will providing mansions for the souls that He creates.

However, this is mere speculation. I am not very impressed with theological arguments whatever they may be used to support. Such arguments have often been found unsatisfactory in the past. In the time of Galileo it was argued that the texts, "And the sun stood still . . . and hasted not to go down about a whole day" (Joshua x. 13) and "He laid the foundations of the earth, that it should not move at any time" (Psalm cv. 5) were an adequate refutation of the Copernican theory. With our present knowledge such an argument appears futile. When that knowledge was not available it made a quite different impression.

(2) The "Heads in the Sand" Objection

"The consequences of machines thinking would be too dreadful. Let us hope and believe that they cannot do so."

This argument is seldom expressed quite so openly as in the form above. But it affects most of us who think about it at all. We like to believe that Man is in some subtle way superior to the rest of creation. It is best if he can be shown to be necessarily superior, for then there is no danger of him losing his commanding position. The popularity of the theological argument is clearly connected with this feeling. It is likely to be quite strong in intellectual people, since they value the power of thinking more highly than others, and are more inclined to base their belief in the superiority of Man on this power.

I do not think that this argument is sufficiently substantial to require refutation. Consolation would be more appropriate: perhaps this should be sought in the transmigration of souls.

(3) The Mathematical Objection

There are a number of results of mathematical logic which can be used to show that there are limitations to the powers of discrete-state machines. The best known of these results is known as Godel's theorem (1931) and shows that in any sufficiently powerful logical system statements can be formulated which can neither be proved nor disproved within the system, unless possibly the system itself is inconsistent. There are other, in some respects similar, results due to Church (1936), Kleene (1935), Rosser, and Turing (1937). The latter result is the most convenient to consider, since it refers directly to machines, whereas the others can only be used in a comparatively indirect argument: for instance if Godel's theorem is to be used we need in addition to have some means of describing logical systems in terms of machines, and machines in terms of logical systems. The result in question refers to a type of machine which is essentially a digital computer with an infinite capacity. It states that there are certain things that such a machine cannot do. If it is rigged up to give answers to questions as in the imitation game, there will be some questions to which it will either give a wrong answer, or fail to give an answer at all however much time is allowed for a reply. There may, of course, be many such questions, and questions which cannot be answered by one machine may be satisfactorily answered by another. We are of course supposing for the present that the questions are of the kind to which an answer "Yes" or "No" is appropriate, rather than questions such as "What do you think of Picasso?" The questions that we know the machines must fail on are of this type, "Consider the machine specified as follows. . . . Will this machine ever answer 'Yes' to any question?" The dots are to be replaced by a description of some machine in a standard form, which could be something like that used in §5. When the machine described bears a certain comparatively simple relation to the machine which is under interrogation, it can be shown that the answer is either wrong or not forthcoming. This is the mathematical result: it is argued that it proves a disability of machines to which the human intellect is not subject.

The short answer to this argument is that although it is established that there are limitations to the powers of any particular machine, it has only been stated, without any sort of proof, that no such limitations apply to the human intellect. But I do not think this view can be dismissed quite so lightly. Whenever one of these machines is asked the appropriate critical question, and gives a definite answer, we know that this answer must be wrong, and this gives us a certain feeling of superiority. Is this feeling illusory? It is no doubt quite genuine, but I do not think too much importance should be attached to it. We too often give wrong answers to questions ourselves to be justified in being very pleased at such evidence of fallibility on the part of the machines. Further, our superiority can only be felt on such an occasion in relation to the one machine over which we have scored our petty triumph. There would be no question of triumphing simultaneously over all machines. In short, then, there might be men cleverer than any given machine, but then again there might be other machines cleverer again, and so on.

Those who hold to the mathematical argument would, I think, mostly be willing to accept the imitation game as a basis for discussion. Those who believe in the two previous objections would probably not be interested in any criteria.

(4) The Argument from Consciousness

This argument is very well expressed in Professor Jefferson's Lister Oration for 1949, from which I quote. "Not until a machine can write a sonnet or compose a concerto because of thoughts and emotions felt, and not by the chance fall of symbols, could we agree that machine equals brain—that is, not only write it but know that it had written it. No mechanism could feel (and not merely artificially signal, an easy contrivance) pleasure at its successes, grief when its valves fuse, be warmed by flattery, be made miserable by its mistakes, be charmed by sex, be angry or depressed when it cannot get what it wants."

This argument appears to be a denial of the validity of our test. According to the most extreme form of this view the only way by which one could be sure that machine thinks is to be the machine and to feel oneself thinking. One could then describe these feelings to the world, but of course no one would be justified in taking any notice. Likewise according to this view the only way to know that a man thinks is to be that particular man. It is in fact the solipsist point of view. It may be the most logical view to hold but it makes communication of ideas difficult. A is liable to believe "A thinks but B does not" whilst B believes "B thinks but A does not." Instead of arguing continually over this point it is usual to have the polite convention that everyone thinks.

I am sure that Professor Jefferson does not wish to adopt the extreme and solipsist point of view. Probably he would be quite willing to accept the imitation game as a test. The game (with the player B omitted) is frequently used in practice under the name of viva voce to discover whether some one really understands something or has "learnt it parrot fashion." Let us listen in to a part of such a viva voce:

> Interrogator: In the first line of your sonnet which reads "Shall I compare thee to a summer's day," would not "a spring day" do as well or better?
> Witness: It wouldn't scan.
> Interrogator: How about "a winter's day." That would scan all right.
> Witness: Yes, but nobody wants to be compared to a winter's day.
> Interrogator: Would you say Mr. Pickwick reminded you of Christmas?
> Witness: In a way.
> Interrogator: Yet Christmas is a winter's day, and I do not think Mr. Pickwick would mind the comparison.
> Witness: I don't think you're serious. By a winter's day one means a typical winter's day, rather than a special one like Christmas.

And so on. What would Professor Jefferson say if the sonnet-writing machine was able to answer like this in the viva voce? I do not know whether he would regard the machine as "merely artificially signaling" these answers, but if the answers were as satisfactory and sustained as in the above passage I do not think he would describe it as "an easy contrivance." This phrase is, I think, intended to cover such devices as the inclusion in the machine of a record of someone reading a sonnet, with appropriate switching to turn it on from time to time.

In short then, I think that most of those who support the argument from consciousness could be persuaded to abandon it rather than be forced into the solipsist position. They will then probably be willing to accept our test.

I do not wish to give the impression that I think there is no mystery about consciousness. There is, for instance, something of a paradox connected with any attempt to localize it. But I do not think these mysteries necessarily need to be solved before we can answer the question with which we are concerned in this paper.

(5) Arguments from Various Disabilities

These arguments take the form, "I grant you that you can make machines do all the things you have mentioned but you will never be able to make one to do X." Numerous features X are suggested in this connection. I offer a selection:

Be kind, resourceful, beautiful, friendly, have initiative, have a sense of humor, tell right from wrong, make mistakes, fall in love, enjoy strawberries and cream, make some one fall in love with it, learn from experience, use words properly, be the subject of its own thought, have as much diversity of behavior as a man, do something really new.

No support is usually offered for these statements. I believe they are mostly founded on the principle of scientific induction. A man has seen thousands of machines in his lifetime. From what he sees of them he draws a number of general conclusions. They are ugly, each is designed for a very limited purpose, when required for a minutely different purpose they are useless, the variety of behavior of any one of them is very small, etc., etc. Naturally he concludes that these are necessary properties of machines in general. Many of these limitations are associated with the very small storage capacity of most machines. (I am assuming that the idea of storage capacity is extended in some way to cover machines other than discrete-state machines. The exact definition does not matter as no mathematical accuracy is claimed in the present discussion.) A few years ago, when very little had been heard of digital computers, it was possible to elicit much incredulity concerning them, if one mentioned their properties without describing their construction. That was presumably due to a similar application of the principle of scientific induction. These applications of the principle are of course largely unconscious. When a burnt child fears the fire and shows that he fears it by avoiding it, I should say that he was applying scientific induction. (I could of course also describe his behavior in many other ways.) The works and customs of mankind do not seem to be very suitable material to which to apply scientific induction. A very large part of space-time must be investigated, if reliable results are to be obtained. Otherwise we may (as most English children do) decide that everybody speaks English, and that it is silly to learn French.

There are, however, special remarks to be made about many of the disabilities that have been mentioned. The inability to enjoy strawberries and cream may have struck the reader as frivolous. Possibly a machine might be made to enjoy this delicious dish, but any attempt to make one do so would be idiotic. What is important about this disability is that it contributes to some of the other disabilities, e.g., to the difficulty of the same kind of friendliness occurring between man and machine as between white man and white man, or between black man and black man.

The claim that "machines cannot make mistakes" seems a curious one. One is tempted to retort, "Are they any the worse for that?" But let us adopt a more sympathetic attitude, and try to see what is really meant. I think this criticism can be explained in terms of the imitation game. It is claimed that the interrogator could distinguish the machine from the man simply by setting them a number of problems in arithmetic. The machine would be unmasked because of its deadly accuracy. The reply to this is simple. The machine (programmed for playing the game) would not attempt to give the right answers to the arithmetic problems. It would deliberately introduce mistakes in a manner calculated to confuse the interrogator. A mechanical fault would probably show itself through an unsuitable decision as to what sort of a mistake to make in the arithmetic. Even this interpretation of the criticism is not sufficiently sympathetic. But we cannot afford the space to go into it much further. It seems to me that this criticism depends on a confusion between two kinds of mistake. We may call them "errors of functioning" and "errors of conclusion." Errors of functioning are due to some mechanical or electrical fault which causes the machine to behave otherwise than it was designed to do. In philosophical discussions one likes to ignore the possibility of such errors; one is therefore discussing "abstract machines." These abstract machines are mathematical fictions rather than physical objects. By definition they are incapable of errors of functioning. In this sense we can truly say that "machines can never make mistakes." Errors of conclusion can only arise when some meaning is attached to the output signals from the machine. The machine might, for instance, type out mathematical equations, or sentences in English. When a false proposition is typed we say that the machine has committed an error of conclusion. There is clearly no reason at all for saying that a machine cannot make this kind of mistake. It might do nothing but type out repeatedly "O = I." To take a less perverse example, it might have some method for drawing conclusions by scientific induction. We must expect such a method to lead occasionally to erroneous results.

The claim that a machine cannot be the subject of its own thought can of course only be answered if it can be shown that the machine has some thought with some subject matter. Nevertheless, "the subject matter of a machine's operations" does seem to mean something, at least to the people who deal with it. If, for instance, the machine was trying to find a solution of the equation $x2 - 40x - 11 = 0$ one would be tempted to describe this equation as part of the machine's subject matter at that moment. In this sort of sense a machine undoubtedly can be its own subject matter. It may be used to help in making up its own programs, or to predict the effect of alterations in its own structure. By observing the results of its own behavior it can modify its own programs so as to achieve some purpose more effectively. These are possibilities of the near future, rather than Utopian dreams.

The criticism that a machine cannot have much diversity of behavior is just a way of saying that it cannot have much storage capacity. Until fairly recently a storage capacity of even a thousand digits was very rare.

The criticisms that we are considering here are often disguised forms of the argument from consciousness, Usually if one maintains that a machine can do one of these things, and describes the kind of method that the machine could use, one will not make much of an impression. It is thought that tile method (whatever it may be, for it must be mechanical) is really rather base. Compare the parentheses in Jefferson's statement quoted above.

(6) Lady Lovelace's Objection

Our most detailed information of Babbage's Analytical Engine comes from a memoir by Lady Lovelace (1842). In it she states, "The Analytical Engine has no pretensions to *originate* anything. It can do *whatever we know how to order it to perform*" (her italics). This statement is quoted by Hartree (1949) who adds: "This does not imply that it may not be possible to construct electronic equipment which will 'think for itself,' or in which, in biological terms, one could set up a conditioned reflex, which would serve as a basis for 'learning.' Whether this is possible in principle or not is a stimulating and exciting question, suggested by some of these recent developments. But it did not seem that the machines constructed or projected at the time had this property."

I am in thorough agreement with Hartree over this. It will be noticed that he does not assert that the machines in question had not got the property, but rather that the evidence available to Lady Lovelace did not encourage her to believe that they had it. It is quite possible that the machines in question had in a sense got this property. For suppose that some discrete-state machine has the property. The Analytical Engine was a universal digital computer, so that, if its storage capacity and speed were adequate, it could by suitable programming be made to mimic the machine in question. Probably this argument did not occur to the Countess or to Babbage. In any case there was no obligation on them to claim all that could be claimed.

This whole question will be considered again under the heading of learning machines.

A variant of Lady Lovelace's objection states that a machine can "never do anything really new." This may be parried for a moment with the saw, "There is nothing new under the sun." Who can be certain that "original work" that he has done was not simply the growth of the seed planted in him by teaching, or the effect of following well-known general principles. A better variant of the objection says that a machine can never "take us by surprise." This statement is a more direct challenge and can be met directly. Machines take me by surprise with great frequency. This is largely because I do not do sufficient calculation to decide what to expect them to do, or rather because, although I do a calculation, I do it in a hurried, slipshod fashion, taking risks. Perhaps I say to myself, "I suppose the Voltage here ought to be the same as there: anyway let's assume it is." Naturally I am often wrong, and the result is a surprise for me for by the time the experiment is done these assumptions have been forgotten. These admissions lay me open to lectures on the subject of my vicious ways, but do not throw any doubt on my credibility when I testify to the surprises I experience.

I do not expect this reply to silence my critic. He will probably say that the surprises are due to some creative mental act on my part, and reflect no credit on the machine. This leads us back to the argument from consciousness, and far from the idea of surprise. It is a line of argument we must consider closed, but it is perhaps worth remarking that the appreciation of something as surprising requires as much of a "creative mental act" whether the surprising event originates from a man, a book, a machine or anything else.

The view that machines cannot give rise to surprises is due, I believe, to a fallacy to which philosophers and mathematicians are particularly subject. This is the assumption that as soon as a fact is presented to a mind all consequences of that fact spring into the mind simultaneously with it. It is a very useful assumption under many circumstances, but one too easily forgets that it is false. A natural consequence of doing so is that one then assumes that there is no virtue in the mere working out of consequences from data and general principles.

(7) Argument from Continuity in the Nervous System

The nervous system is certainly not a discrete-state machine. A small error in the information about the size of a nervous impulse impinging on a neuron, may make a large difference to the size of the outgoing impulse. It may be argued that, this being so, one cannot expect to be able to mimic the behavior of the nervous system with a discrete-state system.

It is true that a discrete-state machine must be different from a continuous machine. But if we adhere to the conditions of the imitation game, the interrogator will not be able to take any advantage of this difference. The situation can be made clearer if we consider some other simpler continuous machine. A differential analyzer will do very well. (A differential analyzer is a certain kind of machine not of the discrete-state type used for some kinds of calculation.) Some of these provide their answers in a typed form, and so are suitable for taking part in the game. It would not be possible for a digital computer to predict exactly what answers the differential analyzer would give to a problem, but it would be quite capable of giving the right sort of answer. For instance, if asked to give the value of pi (actually about 3.1416) it would be reasonable to choose at random between the values 3.12, 3.13, 3.14, 3.15, 3.16 with the probabilities of 0.05, 0.15, 0.55, 0.19, 0.06 (say). Under these circumstances it would be very difficult for the interrogator to distinguish the differential analyzer from the digital computer.

(8) The Argument from Informality of Behavior

It is not possible to produce a set of rules purporting to describe what a man should do in every conceivable set of circumstances. One might for instance have a rule that one is to stop when one sees a red traffic light, and to go if one sees a green one, but what if by some fault both appear together? One may perhaps decide that it is safest to stop. But some further difficulty may well arise from this decision later. To attempt to provide rules of conduct to cover every eventuality, even those arising from traffic lights, appears to be impossible. With all this I agree.

From this it is argued that we cannot be machines. I shall try to reproduce the argument, but I fear I shall hardly do it justice. It seems to run something like this: "If each man had a definite set of rules of conduct by which he regulated his life he would be no better than a machine. But there are no such rules, so men cannot be machines." The undistributed middle is glaring. I do not think the argument is ever put quite like this, but I believe this is the argument used nevertheless. There may however be a certain confusion between "rules of conduct" and "laws of behavior" to cloud the issue. By "rules of conduct" I mean precepts such as "Stop if you see red lights," on which one can act, and of which one can be conscious. By "laws of behavior" I mean laws of nature as applied to a man's body such as "if you pinch him he will squeak." If we substitute "laws of behavior which regulate his life" for "laws of conduct by which he regulates his life" in the argument quoted the undistributed middle is no longer insuperable. For we believe that it is not only true that being regulated by laws of behavior implies being some sort of machine (though not necessarily a discrete-state machine), but that conversely being such a machine implies being regulated by such laws. However, we cannot so easily convince ourselves of the absence of complete laws of behavior as of complete rules of conduct. The only way we know of for finding such laws is scientific observation, and we certainly know of no circumstances under which we could say, "We have searched enough. There are no such laws."

We can demonstrate more forcibly that any such statement would be unjustified. For suppose we could be sure of finding such laws if they existed. Then given a discrete-state machine it should certainly be possible to discover by observation sufficient about it to predict its future behavior, and this within a reasonable time, say a thousand years. But this does not seem to be the case. I have set up on the Manchester computer a small program using only 1,000 units of storage, whereby the machine supplied with one sixteen-figure number replies with another within two seconds. I would defy anyone to learn from these replies sufficient about the program to be able to predict any replies to untried values.

7. LEARNING MACHINES

The reader will have anticipated that I have no very convincing arguments of a positive nature to support my views. If I had I should not have taken such pains to point out the fallacies in contrary views. Such evidence as I have I shall now give.

Let us return for a moment to Lady Lovelace's objection, which stated that the machine can only do what we tell it to do. One could say that a man can "inject" an idea into the machine, and that it will respond to a certain extent and then drop into quiescence, like a piano string struck by a hammer. Another simile would be an atomic pile of less than critical size: an injected idea is to correspond to a neutron entering the pile from without. Each such neutron will cause a certain disturbance which eventually dies away. If, however, the size of the pile is sufficiently increased, the disturbance caused by such an incoming neutron will very likely go on and on increasing until the whole pile is destroyed. Is there a corresponding phenomenon for minds, and is there one for machines? There does seem to be one for the human mind. The majority of them seem to be "subcritical," i.e., to correspond in this analogy to piles of subcritical size. An idea presented to such a mind will on average give rise to less than one idea in reply. A smallish proportion are supercritical. An idea presented to such a mind then may give rise to a whole "theory" consisting of secondary, tertiary and more remote ideas. Animals' minds seem to be very definitely subcritical. Adhering to this analogy we ask, "Can a machine be made to be supercritical?"

The "skin-of-an-onion" analogy is also helpful. In considering the functions of the mind or the brain we find certain operations which we can explain in purely mechanical terms. This we say does not correspond to the real mind: it is a sort of skin which we must strip off if we are to find the real mind. But then in what remains we find a further skin to be stripped off, and so on. Proceeding in this way do we ever come to the "real" mind, or do we eventually come to the skin which has nothing in it? In the latter case the whole mind is mechanical. (It would not be a discrete-state machine however. We have discussed this.)

These last two paragraphs do not claim to be convincing arguments. They should rather be described as "recitations tending to produce belief."

The only really satisfactory support that can be given for the view expressed at the beginning of §6, will be that provided by waiting for the end of the century and then doing the experiment described. But what can we say in the meantime? What steps should be taken now if the experiment is to be successful?

As I have explained, the problem is mainly one of programming. Advances in engineering will have to be made too, but it seems unlikely that these will not be adequate for the requirements. Estimates of the storage capacity of the brain vary from 10^{10} to 10^{15} binary digits. I incline to the lower values and believe that only a very small fraction is used for the higher types of thinking. Most of it is probably used for the retention of visual impressions, I should be surprised if more than 10^9 was required for satisfactory playing of the imitation game, at any rate against a blind man. (Note: The capacity of the *Encyclopedia Britannica*, 11th edition, is 2 X 10^9.) A storage capacity of 10^7 would be a very practicable possibility even by present techniques. It is probably not necessary to increase the speed of operations of the machines at all. Parts of modern machines which can be regarded as analogs of nerve cells work about a thousand times faster than the latter. This should provide a "margin of safety" which could cover losses of speed arising in many ways. Our problem then is to find out how to program these machines to play the game. At my present rate of working I produce about a thousand digits of program a day, so that about sixty workers, working steadily through the fifty years, might accomplish the job, if nothing went into the wastepaper basket. Some more expeditious method seems desirable.

In the process of trying to imitate an adult human mind we are bound to think a good deal about the process which has brought it to the state that it is in. We may notice three components.

(a) The initial state of the mind, say at birth,
(b) The education to which it has been subjected,
(c) Other experience, not to be described as education, to which it has been subjected.

Instead of trying to produce a program to simulate the adult mind, why not rather try to produce one which simulates the child's? If this were then subjected to an appropriate course of education one would obtain the adult brain. Presumably the child brain is something like a notebook as one buys it from the stationer's. Rather little mechanism, and lots of blank sheets. (Mechanism and writing are from our point of view almost synonymous.) Our hope is that there is so little mechanism in the child brain that something like it can be easily programmed. The amount of work in the education we can assume, as a first approximation, to be much the same as for the human child.

We have thus divided our problem into two parts. The child program and the education process. These two remain very closely connected. We cannot expect to find a good child machine at the first attempt. One must experiment with teaching one such machine and see how well it learns. One can then try another and see if it is better or worse. There is an obvious connection between this process and evolution, by the identifications

Structure of the child machine = hereditary material,
Changes of the child machine = mutation,
Natural selection = judgment of the experimenter

One may hope, however, that this process will be more expeditious than evolution. The survival of the fittest is a slow method for measuring advantages. The experimenter, by the exercise of intelligence, should he able to speed it up. Equally important is the fact that he is not restricted to random mutations. If he can trace a cause for some weakness he can probably think of the kind of mutation which will improve it.

It will not be possible to apply exactly the same teaching process to the machine as to a normal child. It will not, for instance, be provided with legs, so that it could not be asked to go out and fill the coal scuttle. Possibly it might not have eyes. But however well these deficiencies might be overcome by clever engineering, one could not send the creature to school without the other children making excessive fun of it. It must be given some tuition. We need not be too concerned about the legs, eyes, etc. The example of Miss Helen Keller shows that education can take place provided that communication in both directions between teacher and pupil can take place by some means or other.

We normally associate punishments and rewards with the teaching process. Some simple child machines can be constructed or programmed on this sort of principle. The machine has to be so constructed that events which shortly preceded the occurrence of a punishment signal are unlikely to be repeated, whereas a reward signal increased the probability of repetition of the events which led up to it. These definitions do not presuppose any feelings on the part of the machine. I have done some experiments with one such child machine, and succeeded in teaching it a few things, but the teaching method was too unorthodox for the experiment to be considered really successful.

The use of punishments and rewards can at best be a part of the teaching process. Roughly speaking, if the teacher has no other means of communicating to the pupil, the amount of information which can reach him does not exceed the total number of rewards and punishments applied. By the time a child has learnt to repeat "Casabianca" he would probably feel very sore indeed, if the text could only be discovered by a "Twenty Questions" technique, every "NO" taking the form of a blow. It is necessary therefore to have some other "unemotional" channels of communication. If these are available it is possible to teach a machine by punishments and rewards to obey orders given in some language, e.g., a symbolic language. These orders are to be transmitted through the "unemotional" channels. The use of this language will diminish greatly the number of punishments and rewards required.

Opinions may vary as to the complexity which is suitable in the child machine. One might try to make it as simple as possible consistently with the general principles. Alternatively one might have a complete system of logical inference "built in." In the latter case the store would be largely occupied with definitions and propositions. The propositions would have various kinds of status, e.g., well-established facts, conjectures, mathematically proved theorems, statements given by an authority, expressions having the logical form of proposition but not belief-value. Certain propositions may be described as "imperatives." The machine should be so constructed that as soon as an imperative is classed as "well established" the appropriate action automatically takes place. To illustrate this, suppose the teacher says to the machine, "Do your homework now." This may cause "Teacher says 'Do your homework now'" to be included amongst the well-established facts. Another such fact might be, "Everything that teacher says is true." Combining these may eventually lead to the imperative, "Do your homework now," being included amongst the well-established facts, and this, by the construction of the machine, will mean that the homework actually gets started, but the effect is very satisfactory. The processes of inference used by the machine need not be such as would satisfy the most exacting logicians. There might for instance be no hierarchy of types. But this need not mean that type fallacies will occur, any more than we are bound to fall over unfenced cliffs. Suitable imperatives (expressed within the systems, not forming part of the rules of the system) such as "Do not use a class unless it is a subclass of one which has been mentioned by teacher" can have a similar effect to "Do not go too near the edge."

The imperatives that can be obeyed by a machine that has no limbs are bound to be of a rather intellectual character, as in the example (doing homework) given above. Important amongst such imperatives will be ones which regulate the order in which the rules of the logical system concerned are to be applied. For at each stage when one is using a logical system, there is a very large number of alternative steps, any of which one is permitted to apply, so far as obedience to the rules of the logical system is concerned. These choices make the difference between a brilliant and a footling reasoner, not the difference between a sound and a fallacious one. Propositions leading to imperatives of this kind might be "When Socrates is mentioned, use the syllogism in Barbara" or "If one method has been proved to be quicker than another, do not use the slower method." Some of these may be "given by authority," but others may be produced by the machine itself, e.g. by scientific induction.

The idea of a learning machine may appear paradoxical to some readers. How can the rules of operation of the machine change? They should describe completely how the machine will react whatever its history might be, whatever changes it might undergo. The rules are thus quite time-invariant. This is quite true. The explanation of the paradox is that the rules which get changed in the learning process are of a rather less pretentious kind, claiming only an ephemeral validity. The reader may draw a parallel with the Constitution of the United States.

An important feature of a learning machine is that its teacher will often be very largely ignorant of quite what is going on inside, although he may still be able to some extent to predict his pupil's behavior. This should apply most strongly to the later education of a machine arising from a child machine of well-tried design (or program). This is in clear contrast with normal procedure when using a machine to do computations. One's object is then to have a clear mental picture of the state of the machine at each moment in the computation. This object can only be achieved with a struggle. The view that "the machine can only do what we know how to order it to do," appears strange in face of this. Most of the programs which we can put into the machine will result in its doing something that we cannot make sense (of at all, or which we regard as completely random behavior. Intelligent behavior presumably consists in a departure from the completely disciplined behavior involved in computation, but a rather slight one, which does not give rise to random behavior, or to pointless repetitive loops. Another important result of preparing our machine for its part in the imitation game by a process of teaching and learning is that "human fallibility" is likely to be omitted in a rather natural way, i.e., without special "coaching." (The reader should reconcile this with the point of view on pages 64–66.) Processes that are learnt do not produce a hundred per cent certainty of result; if they did they could not be unlearnt.

It is probably wise to include a random element in a learning machine. A random element is rather useful when we are searching for a solution of some problem. Suppose for instance we wanted to find a number between 50 and 200 which was equal to the square of the sum of its digits, we might start at 51 then try 52 and go on until we got a number that worked. Alternatively we might choose numbers at random until we got a good one. This method has the advantage that it is unnecessary to keep track of the values that have been tried, but the disadvantage that one may try the same one twice, but this is not very important if there are several solutions. The systematic method has the disadvantage that there may be an enormous block without any solutions in the region which has to be investigated first, Now the learning process may be regarded as a search for a form of behavior which will satisfy the teacher (or some other criterion). Since there is probably a very large number of satisfactory solutions the random method seems to be better than the systematic. It should be noticed that it is used in the analogous process of evolution. But there the systematic method is not possible. How could one keep track of the different genetical combinations that had been tried, so as to avoid trying them again?

We may hope that machines will eventually compete with men in all purely intellectual fields. But which are the best ones to start with? Even this is a difficult decision. Many people think that a very abstract activity, like the playing of chess, would be best. It can also be maintained that it is best to provide the machine with the best sense organs that money can buy, and then teach it to understand and speak English. This process could follow the normal teaching of a child. Things would be pointed out and named, etc. Again I do not know what the right answer is, but I think both approaches should be tried.

We can only see a short distance ahead, but we can see plenty there that needs to be done.

NOTES

Alan Turing, "Computing Machinery and Intelligence," *Mind*, 1950, vol. LIX, no. 236, pp. 433–60, by permission of Oxford University Press.

Online resources:

Alan Turing
www.alanturing.net/
www.turing.org.uk/turing/

6

Psychophysical and Theoretical Identifications

David Lewis

Psychophysical identity theorists often say that the identifications they anticipate between mental and neural states are essentially like various uncontroversial theoretical identifications: the identification of water with H_2O, of light with electromagnetic radiation, and so on. Such theoretical identifications are usually described as pieces of voluntary theorizing, as follows. Theoretical advances make it possible to simplify total science by positing bridge laws identifying some of the entities discussed in one theory with entities discussed in another theory. In the name of parsimony, we posit those bridge laws forthwith. Identifications are made, not found.

In 'An Argument for the Identity Theory,'[1] I claimed that this was a bad picture of psychophysical identification, since a suitable physiological theory could *imply* psychophysical identities—not merely make it reasonable to posit them for the sake of parsimony. The implication was as follows:

Mental state M = the occupant of causal role R (by definition of M).
Neural state N = the occupant of causal role R (by the physiological theory).
Mental state M = neural state N (by transitivity of =).

If the meanings of the names of mental states were really such as to provide the first premise, and if the advance of physiology were such as to provide the second premise, then the conclusion would follow. Physiology and the meanings of words would leave us no choice but to make the psychophysical identification.

In this sequel, I shall uphold the view that psychophysical identifications thus described would be like theoretical identifications, though they would not fit the usual account thereof. For the usual account, I claim, is wrong; theoretical identifications *in general* are implied by the theories that make them possible—not posited independently. This follows from a general hypothesis about the meanings of theoretical terms: that they are definable functionally, by reference to causal roles.[2] Applied to common sense psychology—folk science rather than professional science, but a theory nonetheless—we get the hypothesis of my previous paper[3] that a mental state M (say, an experience) is definable as the occupant of a certain causal role R, that is, as the state, of whatever sort, that is causally connected in specified ways to sensory stimuli, motor responses, and other mental states.

First, I consider an example of theoretical identification chosen to be remote from past philosophizing; then I give my general account of the meanings of theoretical terms and the nature of theoretical identifications; finally I return to the case of psychophysical identity.

I

We are assembled in the drawing room of the country house; the detective reconstructs the crime. That is, he proposes a *theory* designed to be the best explanation of phenomena we have observed: the death of Mr. Body, the blood on the wallpaper, the silence of the dog in the night, the clock seventeen minutes fast, and so on. He launches into his story:

X, Y and Z conspired to murder Mr. Body. Seventeen years ago, in the gold fields of Uganda, X was Body's partner . . . Last week, Y and Z conferred in a bar in Reading . . . Tuesday night at 11:17, Y went to the attic and set a time bomb . . . Seventeen minutes later, X met Z in the billiard room and gave him the lead pipe . . . Just when the bomb went off in the attic, X fired three shots into the study through the French windows. . . .

And so it goes: a long story. Let us pretend that it is a single long conjunctive sentence.

The story contains the three names 'X', 'Y' and 'Z'. The detective uses these new terms without explanation, as though we knew what they meant. But we do not. We never used them before, at least not in the senses they bear in the present context. All we know about their meanings is what we gradually gather from the story itself. Call these *theoretical terms* (*T-terms* for short) because they are introduced by a theory. Call the rest of the terms in the story *O-terms*. These are all the *other* terms except the T-terms; they are all the *old, original* terms we understood before the theory was proposed. We could call them our 'pre-theoretical' terms. But 'O' does not stand for 'observational.' Not all the O-terms are observational terms, whatever those may be. They are just any old terms. If part of the story was mathematical—if it included a calculation of the trajectory that took the second bullet to the chandelier without breaking the vase—then some of the O-terms will be mathematical. If the story says that something happened because of something else, then the O-terms will include the intensional connective 'because,' or the operator 'it is a law that,' or something of the sort.

Nor do the theoretical terms name some sort of peculiar theoretical, unobservable, semi-fictitious entities. The story makes plain that they name *people*. Not theoretical people, different somehow from ordinary, observational people—just people!

On my account, the detective plunged right into his story, using '*X*', '*Y*' and '*Z*' as if they were names with understood denotation. It would have made little difference if he had started, instead, with initial existential quantifiers: 'There exist X, Y and Z such that . . .' and then told the story. In that case, the terms '*X*', '*Y*' and '*Z*' would have been bound variables rather than T-terms. But the story would have had the same explanatory power. The second version of the story, with the T-terms turned into variables bound by existential quantifiers, is the Ramsey sentence of the first. Bear in mind, as evidence for what is to come, how little difference the initial quantifiers seem to make to the detective's assertion.

Suppose that after we have heard the detective's story, we learn that it is true of a certain three people: Plum, Peacock and Mustard. If we put the name 'Plum' in place of '*X*', 'Peacock' in place of '*Y*', and 'Mustard' in place of '*Z*' throughout, we get a true story about the doings of those three people. We will say that Plum, Peacock and Mustard together *realize* (or are a *realization* of) the detective's theory.

We may also find out that the story is not true of any other triple.[4] Put in any three names that do not name Plum, Peacock and Mustard (in that order) and the story we get is false. We will say that Plum, Peacock and Mustard *uniquely realize* (are the *unique realization* of) the theory.

We might learn both of these facts. (The detective might have known them all along, but, held them back to spring his trap; or he, like us, might learn them only after his story had been told.) And if we did, we would surely conclude that X, Y and Z in the story were Plum, Peacock and Mustard. I maintain that we would be compelled so to conclude, given the senses borne by the terms '*X*', '*Y*' and '*Z*' in virtue of the way the detective introduced them in his theorizing, and given our information about Plum, Peacock and Mustard.

In telling his story, the detective set forth three roles and said that they were occupied by X, Y and Z. He must have specified the meanings of the three: T-terms '*X*', '*Y*' and '*Z*' thereby; for they had meanings afterwards, they had none before, and nothing else was done to give them meanings. They were introduced by an implicit functional definition, being reserved to name the occupants of the three roles. When we find out who are the occupants of the three roles, we find out who are X, Y and Z. Here is our theoretical identification.

In saying that the roles were occupied by X, Y and Z, the detective implied that they were occupied. That is, his theory implied its Ramsey sentence. That seems right; if we learnt that no triple realized the story, or even came close, we would have to conclude that the story was false. We would also have to deny that the names 'X', 'Y' and 'Z' named anything; for they were introduced as names for the occupants of roles that turned out to be unoccupied.

I also claim that the detective implied that the roles were uniquely occupied, when he reserved names for their occupants and proceeded as if those names had been given definite referents. Suppose we learnt that two different triples realized the theory: Plum, Peacock, Mustard; and Green, White, Scarlet. (Or the two different triples might overlap; Plum, Peacock, Mustard; and Green, Peacock, Scarlet.) I think we would be most inclined to say that the story was false, and that the names 'X', 'Y' and 'Z' did not name anything. They were introduced as names for the occupants of certain roles; but there is no such thing as *the* occupant of a doubly occupied role, so there is nothing suitable for them to name.

II

We now proceed to a general account of the functional definability of T-terms and the nature of theoretical identification. Suppose we have a new theory, T, introducing the new terms $t_1 \ldots t_n$. These are our T-terms. (Let them be names.) Every other term in our vocabulary, therefore, is an O-term. The theory T is presented in a sentence called the *postulate* of T. Assume this is a single sentence, perhaps a long conjunction. It says of the entities—states, magnitudes, species, or whatever—named by the T-terms that they occupy certain *causal roles*; that they stand in specified causal (and other) relations to entities named by O-terms, and to one another.

If I am right, T-terms are eliminable—we can always replace them by their definientia. Of course, this is not to say that theories are fictions, or that theories are uninterpreted formal abacuses, or that theoretical entities are unreal. Quite the opposite! Because we understand the O-terms, and we can define the T-terms from them, theories are fully meaningful; we have reason to think a good theory true; and if a theory is true, then whatever exists according to the theory really *does* exist.

III

And that is how, someday, we will infer that[5] the mental states M_1, M_2, . . . are the neural states N_1, N_2, . . . Think of common-sense psychology as a term-introducing scientific theory, though one invented long before there was any such institution as professional science. Collect all the platitudes you can think of regarding the causal relations of mental states, sensory stimuli, and motor responses. Perhaps we can think of them as having the form: When someone is in so-and-so combination of mental states and receives sensory stimuli of so-and-so kind, he tends with so-and-so probability to be caused thereby to go into so-and-so mental states and produce so-and-so motor responses. Add also all the platitudes to the effect that one mental state falls under another, "toothache is a kind of pain," and the like. Perhaps there are platitudes of other forms as well. Include only platitudes which are common knowledge among us—everyone knows them, everyone knows that everyone else knows them, and so on. For the meanings of our words are common knowledge, and I am going to claim that names of mental states derive their meaning from these platitudes. Form the conjunction of these platitudes; or better, form a cluster of them—a disjunction of all conjunctions of *most* of them. (That way it will not matter if a few are wrong.) This is the postulate of our term-introducing theory. The names of mental states are the T-terms. The O-terms used to introduce them must be sufficient for speaking of stimuli and responses, and for speaking of causal relations among these and states of unspecified nature. From the postulate, form the definition of the T-terms; it defines the mental states by reference to their causal relations to stimuli, responses, and each other. When we learn what sort of states occupy those causal roles definitive of the mental states, we will learn what states the mental states are—exactly as we found out who X was when we found out that Plum was the man who occupied a certain role, and exactly as we found out what light was when we found that electromagnetic radiation was the phenomenon that occupied a certain role.

NOTES

Originally printed in the *Australasian Journal of Philosophy*.
    1. *Journal of Philosophy*, 63 (1966): 17–25.
    2. See my 'How to Define Theoretical Terms': *Journal of Philosophy*, 67 (1970): 427–446.
    3. Since advocated also by D. M. Armstrong in a *Materialist Theory of Mind* (New York: Humanities Press, 1968). He expresses it thus: "The concept of a mental state is primarily the concept of a state of the person apt for bringing about a certain

sort of behaviour [and secondarily also, in some cases] apt for being brought about by a certain sort of stimulus.' p. 82.

4. The story itself might imply this. If, for instance, the story said 'X saw Y give Z the candlestick while the three of them were alone in the billiard room at 9:17; then the story could not possibly be true of more than one triple.

5. In general, or in the case of a given species, or in the case of a given person. It might turn out that the causal roles definitive of mental states are occupied by different neural (or other) states in different organisms. See my discussion of Hilary Putnam 'Psychological Predicates' in *Journal of Philosophy*, 66 (1969): 23–25.

Online resources:

David Lewis
David Lewis on the Internet
www.david-lewis.org/links.php
Obituary from Princeton University
www.princeton.edu/pr/news/01/q4/1019-lewis.htm

7

The Mind-Body Problem

Jerry A. Fodor

Modern philosophy of science has been devoted largely to the formal and systematic description of the successful practices of working scientists. The philosopher does not try to dictate how scientific inquiry and argument ought to be conducted. Instead he tries to enumerate the principles and practices that have contributed to good science. The philosopher has devoted the most attention to analyzing the methodological peculiarities of the physical sciences. The analysis has helped to clarify the nature of confirmation, the logical structure of scientific theories, the formal properties of statements that express laws and the question of whether theoretical entities actually exist.

It is only rather recently that philosophers have become seriously interested in the methodological tenets of psychology. Psychological explanations of behavior refer liberally to the mind and to states, operations and processes of the mind. The philosophical difficulty comes in stating in unambiguous language what such references imply.

Traditional philosophies of mind can be divided into two broad categories: dualist theories and materialist theories. In the dualist approach the mind is a nonphysical substance. In materialist theories the mental is not distinct from the physical; indeed all mental states, properties, processes and operations are in principle identical with physical states, properties, processes and operations. Some materialists, known as behaviorists, maintain that all talk of mental causes can be eliminated from the language of psychology in favor of talk of environmental stimuli and behavioral responses. Other materialists, the identity theorists, contend that there are mental causes and that they are identical with neurophysiological events in the brain.

In the past fifteen years a philosophy of mind called functionalism that is neither dualist nor materialist has emerged from philosophical reflection on developments in artificial intelligence, computational theory, linguistics, cybernetics and psychology. All these fields, which are collectively known as the cognitive sciences, have in common a certain level of abstraction and a concern with systems that process information. Functionalism, which seeks to provide a philosophical account of this level of abstraction, recognizes the possibility that systems as diverse as human beings, calculating machines and disembodied spirits could all have mental states. In the functionalist view the psychology of a system depends not on the stuff it is made of (living cells, metal or spiritual energy) but on how the stuff is put together. Functionalism is a difficult concept, and one way of coming to grips with it is to review the deficiencies of the dualist and materialist philosophies of mind it aims to displace.

The chief drawback of dualism is its failure to account adequately for mental causation. If the mind is nonphysical, it has no position in physical space. How, then, can a mental cause give rise to a behavioral effect that has a position in space? To put it another way, how can the nonphysical give rise to the physical without violating the laws of the conversation of mass, of energy and of momentum?

The dualist might respond that the problem of how an immaterial substance can cause physical events is not much obscurer than the problem of how one physical event can cause another. Yet there is an important difference: there are many clear cases of physical causation but not one clear case of nonphysical causation. Physical interaction is something philosophers, like all other people, have to live with. Nonphysical interaction, however, may be no more than an artifact of the immaterialist construal of the mental. Most philosophers now agree that no argument has successfully demonstrated why mind-body causation should not be regarded as a species of physical causation.

Dualism is also incompatible with the practices of working psychologists. The psychologist frequently applies the experimental methods of the physical sciences to the study of the mind. If mental processes were different in kind from physical processes, there would be no reason to expect these methods to work in the realm of the mental. In order to justify their experimental methods many psychologists urgently sought an alternative to dualism.

In the 1920s John B. Watson of Johns Hopkins University made the radical suggestion that behavior does not have mental causes. He regarded the behavior of an organism as its observable responses to stimuli, which he took to be the causes of its behavior. Over the next thirty years psychologists such as B. F. Skinner of Harvard University developed Watson's ideas into an elaborate world view in which the role of psychology was to catalogue the laws that determine causal relations between stimuli and responses. In this "radical behaviorist" view the problem of explaining the nature of the mind-body interaction vanishes; there is no such interaction.

Radical behaviorism has always worn an air of paradox. For better or worse, the idea of mental causation is deeply ingrained in our everyday language and in our ways of understanding our fellow men and ourselves. For example, people commonly attribute behavior to beliefs, to knowledge and to expectations. Brown puts gas in his tank because he believes the car will not run without it. Jones writes not "acheive" but "achieve" because he knows the rule about putting i before e. Even when a behavioral response is closely tied to an environmental stimulus, mental processes often intervene. Smith carries an umbrella because the sky is cloudy, but the weather is only part of the story. There are apparently also mental links in the causal chain: observation and expectation. The clouds affect Smith's behavior only because he observes them and because they induce in him an expectation of rain.

The radical behaviorist is unmoved by appeals to such cases. He is prepared to dismiss references to mental causes, however plausible they may seem, as the residue of outworn creeds. The radical behaviorist predicts that as psychologists come to understand more about the relations between stimuli and responses they will find it increasingly possible to explain behavior without postulating mental causes.

The strongest argument against behaviorism is that psychology has not turned out this way; the opposite has happened. As psychology has matured, the framework of mental states and processes that is apparently needed to account for experimental observations has grown all the more elaborate. Particularly in the case of human behavior psychological theories satisfying the methodological tenets of radical behaviorism have proved largely sterile, as would be expected if the postulated mental processes are real and causally effective.

Nevertheless, many philosophers were initially drawn to radical behaviorism because, paradoxes and all, it seemed better than dualism. Since a psychologist committed to immaterial substances was unacceptable, philosophers turned to radical behaviorism because it seemed to be the only alternative materialist philosophy of mind. The choice, as they saw it, was between radical behaviorism and ghosts.

By the early 1960s philosophers began to have doubts that dualism and radical behaviorism exhausted the possible approaches to the philosophy of mind. Since the two theories seemed unattractive, the right strategy might be to develop a materialist philosophy of mind that nonetheless allowed for mental causes. Two such philosophies emerged, one called logical behaviorism and the other called the central-state identity theory.

Logical behaviorism is a semantic theory about what mental terms mean.

The basic idea is that attributing a mental state (say thirst) to an organism is the same as saying that the organism is disposed to behave in a particular way (for example to drink if there is water available). On this view every mental ascription is equivalent in meaning to an if-then statement (called a behavioral hypothetical) that expresses a behavioral disposition. For example, "Smith is thirsty" might be taken to be equivalent to the dispositional statement "if there were water available, then Smith would drink some." By definition a behavioral hypothetical includes no mental terms. The if-clause of the hypothetical speaks only of stimuli and the then-clause speaks only of behavioral responses. Since stimuli and responses are physical events, logical behaviorism is a species of materialism.

The strength of logical behaviorism is that by translating mental language into the language of stimuli and responses it provides an interpretation of psychological explanations in which behavioral effects are attributed to mental causes. Mental causation is simply the manifestation of a behavioral disposition. More precisely, mental causation is what happens when an organism has a behavioral disposition and the if-clause of the behavioral hypothetical expressing the disposition happens to be true. For example, the causal statement "Smith drank some water because he was thirsty" might be taken to mean "if there were water available, then Smith would drink some, and there was water available."

I have somewhat oversimplified logical behaviorism by assuming that each mental ascription can be translated by a unique behavioral hypothetical. Actually the logical behaviorist often maintains that it takes an open-ended set (perhaps an infinite set) of behavioral hypotheticals to spell out the behavioral disposition expressed by a mental term. The mental ascription "Smith is thirsty" might also be satisfied by the hypothetical "If there were orange juice available, then Smith would drink some" and by a host of other hypotheticals. In any event the logical behaviorist does not usually maintain he can actually enumerate all the hypotheticals that correspond to a behavioral disposition expressing a given mental term. He only insists that in principle the meaning of any mental term can be conveyed by behavioral hypotheticals.

The way the logical behaviorist has interpreted a mental term such as thirsty is modeled after the way many philosophers have interpreted a physical disposition such as fragility. The physical disposition "The glass is fragile" is often taken to mean something like "If the glass were struck, then it would break." By the same token the logical behaviorist's analysis of mental causation is similar to the received analysis of one kind of physical causation. The causal statement "The glass broke because it was fragile" is taken to mean something like "If the glass were struck, then it would break, and the glass was struck."

By equating mental terms with behavioral dispositions the logical behaviorist has put mental terms on a par with the nonbehavioral dispositions of the physical sciences. That is a promising move, because the analysis of non-behavioral dispositions is on relatively solid philosophical ground. An explanation attributing the breaking of a glass to its fragility is surely something even the staunchest materialist can accept. By arguing that mental terms are synonymous with dispositional terms, the logical behaviorist has provided something the radical behaviorist could not: a materialist account of mental causation.

Nevertheless, the analogy between mental causation as construed by the logical behaviorist and physical causation goes only so far. The logical behaviorist treats the manifestation of a disposition as the sole form of mental causation, whereas the physical sciences recognize additional kinds of causation. There is the kind of causation where one physical event causes another, as when the breaking of a glass is attributed to its having been struck. In fact, explanations that involve event-event causation are presumably more basic than dispositional explanations, because the manifestation of a disposition (the breaking of a fragile glass) always involves event-event causation and not vice versa. In the realm of the mental many examples of event-event causation involve one mental state's causing another, and for this kind of causation logical behaviorism provides no analysis. As a result the logical behaviorist is committed to the tacit and implausible assumption that psychology requires a less robust notion of causation than the physical sciences require.

Event-event causation actually seems to be quite common in the realm of the mental. Mental causes typically give rise to behavioral effects by virtue of their interaction with other mental causes. For example, having a headache causes a disposition to take aspirin only if one also has the desire to get rid of the headache, the belief that aspirin exists, the belief that taking aspirin reduces headaches and so on. Since mental states interact in generating behavior, it will be necessary to find a construal of psychological explanations that posits mental processes: causal sequences of mental events. It is this construal that logical behaviorism fails to provide.

Such considerations bring out a fundamental way in which logical behaviorism is quite similar to radical behaviorism. It is true that the logical behaviorist, unlike the radical behaviorist, acknowledges the existence of mental states. Yet since the underlying tenet of logical behaviorism is that references to mental states can be translated out of psychological explanations by employing behavioral hypotheticals, all talk of mental states and processes is in a sense heuristic. The only facts to which the behaviorist is actually committed are facts about relations between stimuli and responses. In this respect logical behaviorism is just radical behaviorism in a semantic form. Although the former theory offers a construal of mental causation, the construal is Pickwickian. What does not really exist cannot cause anything, and the logical behaviorist, like the radical behaviorist, believes deep down that mental causes do not exist.

An alternative materialist theory of the mind to logical behaviorism is the central-state identity theory. According to this theory, mental events, states and processes are identical with neurophysiological events in the brain, and the property of being in a certain mental state (such as having a headache or believing it will rain) is identical with the property of being in a certain neurophysiological state. On this basis it is easy to make sense of the idea that a behavioral effect might sometimes have a chain of mental causes; that will be the case whenever a behavioral effect is contingent on the appropriate sequence of neurophysiological events.

The central-state identity theory acknowledges that it is possible for mental causes to interact causally without ever giving rise to any behavioral effect, as when a person thinks for a while about what he ought to do and then decides to do nothing. If mental processes are neurophysiological, they must have the causal properties of neurophysiological processes. Since neurophysiological processes are presumably physical processes, the central-state identity theory ensures that the concept of mental causation is as rich as the concept of physical causation.

The central-state identity theory provides a satisfactory account of what the mental terms in psychological explanations refer to, and so it is favored by psychologists who are dissatisfied with behaviorism. The behaviorist maintains that mental terms refer to nothing or that they refer to the parameters of stimulus-response relations. Either way the existence of mental entities is only illusory. The identity theorist, on the other hand, argues that mental terms refer to neurophysiological states. Thus he can take seriously the project of explaining behavior by appealing to its mental causes.

The chief advantage of the identity theory is that it takes the explanatory constructs of psychology at face value, which is surely something a philosophy of mind ought to do if it can. The identity theory shows how the mentalistic explanations of psychology could be not mere heuristics but literal accounts of the causal history of behavior. Moreover, since the identity theory is not a semantic thesis, it is immune to many arguments that cast in doubt logical behaviorism. A drawback of logical behaviorism is that the observation "John has a headache" does not seem to mean the same thing as a statement of the form "John is disposed to behave in such and such a way." The identity theorist, however, can live with the fact that "John has a headache" and "John is in such and such a brain state" are not synonymous. The assertion of the identity theorist is not that these sentences mean the same thing but only that they are rendered true (or false) by the same neurophysiological phenomena.

The identity theory can be held either as a doctrine about mental particulars (John's current pain or Bill's fear of animals) or as a doctrine about mental universals, or properties (having a pain or being afraid of animals). The two doctrines, called respectively token physicalism and type physicalism, differ in strength and plausibility. Token physicalism maintains only that all of the mental particulars that happen to exist are neurophysiological, whereas type physicalism makes the more sweeping assertion that all the mental particulars there could possibly be are neurophysiological. Token physicalism does not rule out the logical possibility of machines and disembodied spirits having mental properties. Type physicalism dismisses this possibility because neither machines nor disembodied spirits have neurons.

Type physicalism is not a plausible doctrine about mental properties even if token physicalism is right about mental particulars. The problem with type physicalism is that the psychological constitution of a system seems to depend not on its hardware, or physical composition, but on its software, or program. Why should the philosopher dismiss the possibility that silicon-based Martians have pains, assuming that the silicon is properly organized? And why should the philosopher rule out the possibility of machines having beliefs, assuming that the machines are correctly programmed? If it is logically possible that Martians and machines could have mental properties, then mental properties and neurophysiological processes cannot be identical, however much they may prove to be coextensive.

What it all comes down to is that there seems to be a level of abstraction at which the generalizations of psychology are most naturally pitched. This level of abstraction cuts across differences in the physical composition of the systems to which psychological generalizations apply. In the cognitive sciences, at least, the natural domain for psychological theorizing seems to be all systems that process information. The problem with type physicalism is that there are possible information-processing systems with the same psychological constitution as human beings but not the same physical organization. In principle all kinds of physically different things could have human software.

This situation calls for a relational account of mental properties that abstracts them from the physical structure of their bearers. In spite of the objections to logical behaviorism that I presented above, logical behaviorism was at least on the right track in offering a relational interpretation of mental properties: to have a headache is to be disposed to exhibit a certain pattern of relations between the stimuli one encounters and the responses one exhibits. If that is what having a headache is, however, there is no reason in principle why only heads that are physically similar to ours can ache. Indeed, according to logical behaviorism, it is a necessary truth that any system that has our stimulus-response contingencies also has our headaches.

All of this emerged ten or fifteen years ago as a nasty dilemma for the materialist program in the philosophy of mind. On the one hand the identity theorist (and not the logical behaviorist) had got right the causal character of the interactions of mind and body. On the other the logical behaviorist (and not the identity theorist) had got right the relational character of mental properties. Functionalism has apparently been able to resolve the dilemma. By stressing the distinction computer science draws between hardware and software the functionalist can make sense of both the causal and the relational character of the mental.

The intuition underlying functionalism is that what determines the psychological type to which a mental particular belongs is the causal role of the particular in the mental life of the organism. Functional individuation is differentiation with respect to causal role. A headache, for example, is identified with the type of mental state that among other things causes a disposition for taking aspirin in people who believe aspirin relieves a headache, causes a desire to rid oneself of the pain one is feeling, often causes someone who speaks English to say such things as "I have a headache" and is brought on by overwork, eyestrain and tension. This list is presumably not complete. More will be known about the nature of a headache as psychological and physiological research discovers more about its causal role.

The functionalism construes the concept of causal role in such a way that a mental state can be defined by its causal relations to other mental states. In this respect functionalism is completely different from logical behaviorism. Another major difference is that functionalism is not a reductionist thesis. It does not foresee, even in principle, the elimination of mentalistic concepts from the explanatory apparatus of psychological theories.

The difference between functionalism and logical behaviorism is brought out by the fact that functionalism is fully compatible with token physicalism. The functionalist would not be disturbed if brain events turn out to be the only things with the functional properties that define mental states. Indeed, most functionalists fully expect it will turn out that way.

Since functionalism recognizes that mental particulars may be physical, it is compatible with the idea that mental causation is a species of physical causation. In other words, functionalism tolerates the materialist solution to the mind-body problem provided by the central-state identity theory. It is possible for the functionalist to assert both that mental properties are typically defined in terms of their relations and that interactions of mind and body are typically causal in however robust a motion of causality is required by psychological explanations. The logical behaviorist can endorse only the first assertion and the type physicalist only the second. As a result functionalism seems to capture the best features of the materialist alternatives to dualism. It is no wonder that functionalism has become increasingly popular.

Machines provide good examples of two concepts that are central to functionalism: the concept that mental states are interdefined and the concept that they can be realized by many systems. The illustration contrasts a behavioristic Coke machine with a mentalistic one. Both machines dispense a Coke for 10 cents. (The price has not been affected by inflation.) The states of the machines are defined by reference to their causal roles, but only one machine would satisfy the behaviorist. Its single state (SO) is completely specified in terms of stimuli and responses. SO is the state a machine is in if, and only if, given a dime as the input, it dispenses a Coke as the output.

The machine in the illustration had interdefined states (S1 and S2), which are characteristic of functionalism. S1 is the state a machine is in if, and only if, (1) given a nickel, it dispenses nothing and proceeds to S2, and (2) given a dime, it dispenses a Coke and stays in S1. S2 is the state a machine is in if, and only if, (1) given a nickel, it dispenses a Coke and proceeds to S1, and (2) given a dime, it dispenses a Coke and a nickel and proceeds to S1. What S1 and S2 jointly amount to is the machine's dispensing a Coke if it is given a dime, dispensing a Coke and a nickel if it is given a dime and a nickel and waiting to be given a second nickel if it has been given a first one.

Since S1 and S2 are each defined by hypothetical statements, they can be viewed as dispositions. Nevertheless, they are not behavioral dispositions because the consequences an input has for a machine in S1 or S2 are not specified solely in terms of the output of the machine. Rather, the consequences also involve the machine's internal states.

Nothing about the way I have described the behavioristic and mentalistic Coke machines puts constraints on what they could be made of. Any system whose states bore the proper relations to inputs, outputs and other states could be one of these machines. No doubt it is reasonable to expect such a system to be constructed out of such things as wheels, levers and diodes (token physicalism for Coke machines). Similarly, it is reasonable to expect that our minds may prove to be neurophysiological (token physicalism for human beings).

Nevertheless, the software description of a Coke machine does not logically require wheels, levers and diodes for its concrete realization. By the same token, the software description of the mind does not logically require neurons. As far as functionalism is concerned a Coke machine with states S1 and S2 could be made of ectoplasm, if there is such stuff and if its states have the right causal properties. Functionalism allows for the possibility of disembodied Coke machines in exactly the same way and to the same extent that it allows for the possibility of disembodied minds.

To say that S1 and S2 are interdefined and realizable by different kinds of hardware is not, of course, to say that a Coke machine has a mind. Although interdefinition and functional specification are typical features of mental states, they are clearly not sufficient for mentality. What more is required is a question to which I shall return below.

Some philosophers are suspicious of functionalism because it seems too easy. Since functionalism licenses the individuation of states by reference to their causal role, it appears to allow a trivial explanation of any observed event E, that is, it appears to postulate an E-causer. For example, what makes the valves in a machine open? Why, the operation of a valve opener. And what is a valve opener? Why, anything that has the functionally defined property of causing valves to open.

In psychology this kind of question-begging often takes the form of theories that in effect postulate homunculi with the selfsame intellectual capacities the theorist set out to explain. Such is the case when visual perception is explained by simply postulating psychological mechanisms that process visual information. The behaviorist has often charged the mentalist, sometimes justifiably of mongering this kind of question-begging pseudo explanation. The charge will have to be met if functionally defined mental states are to have a serious role in psychological theories.

The burden of the accusation is not untruth but triviality. There can be no doubt that it is a valve opener that opens valves, and it is likely that visual perception is mediated by the processing of visual information. The charge is that such putative functional explanations are mere platitudes. The functionalist can meet this objection by allowing functionally defined theoretical constructs only where mechanisms exist that can carry out the function and only where he has some notion of what such mechanisms might be like. One way of imposing this requirement is to identify the mental processes that psychology postulates with the operations of the restricted class of possible computers called Turing machines.

A Turing machine can be informally characterized as a mechanism with a finite number of program states. The inputs and outputs of the machine are written on a tape that is divided into squares each of which includes a symbol from a finite alphabet. The machine scans the tape one square at a time. It can erase the symbol on a scanned square and print a new one in its place. The machine can execute only the elementary mechanical operations of scanning, erasing, printing, moving the tape and changing state.

The program states of the Turing machine are defined solely in terms of the input symbols on the tape, the output symbols on the tape, the elementary operations and the other states of the program. Each program state is therefore functionally defined by the part it plays in the overall operation of the machine. Since the functional role of a state depends on the relation of the state to other states as well as to inputs and outputs, the relational character of the mental is captured by the Turing-machine version of functionalism. Since the definition of a program state never refers to the physical structure of the system running the program, the Turing-machine version of functionalism also captures the idea that the character of a mental state is independent of its physical realization. A human being, a roomful of people, a computer and a disembodied spirit would be a Turing machine if they operated according to a Turing machine program.

The proposal is to restrict the functional definition of psychological states to those that can be expressed in terms of the program states of Turing machines. If this restriction can be enforced, it provides a guarantee that psychological theories will be compatible with the demands of mechanisms. Since Turing machines are very simple devices, they are in principle quite easy to build. Consequently by formulating a psychological explanation as a Turing-machine program the psychologist ensures that the explanation is mechanistic, even though the hardware realizing the mechanism is left open.

There are many kinds of computational mechanisms other than Turing machines, and so the formulation of a functionalist psychological theory in Turing-machine notation provides only a sufficient condition for the theory's being mechanically realizable. What makes the condition interesting, however, is that the simple Turing machine can perform many complex tasks. Although the elementary operations of the Turing machine are restricted, iterations of the operations enable the machine to carry out any well-defined computation on discrete symbols.

An important tendency in the cognitive sciences is to treat the mind chiefly as a device that manipulates symbols. If a mental process can be functionally defined as an operation on symbols, there is a Turing machine capable of carrying out the computation and a variety of mechanisms for realizing the Turing machine. Where the manipulation of symbols is important the Turing machine provides a connection between functional explanation and mechanistic explanation.

The reduction of a psychological theory to a program for a Turing machine is a way of exorcising the homunculi. The reduction ensures that no operations have been postulated except those that could be performed by a familiar mechanism. Of course, the working psychologist usually cannot specify the reduction for each functionally individuated process in every theory he is prepared to take seriously. In practice the argument usually goes in the opposite direction; if the postulation of a mental operation is essential to some cherished psychological explanation, the theorist tends to assume that there must be a program for a Turing machine that will carry out that operation.

The "black boxes" that are common in flow charts drawn by psychologists often serve to indicate postulated mental processes for which Turing reductions are wanting. Even so, the possibility in principle of such reductions serves as a methodological constraint on psychological theorizing by determining what functional definitions are to be allowed and what it would be like to know that everything has been explained that could possibly need explanation.

Such is the origin, the provenance and the promise of contemporary functionalism. How much has it actually paid off? This question is not easy to answer because much of what is now happening in the philosophy of mind and the cognitive sciences is directed at exploring the scope and limits of the functionalist explanations of behavior. I shall, however, give a brief overview.

An obvious objection to functionalism as a theory of the mind is that the functionalist definition is not limited to mental states and processes. Catalysts, Coke machines, valve openers, pencil sharpeners, mousetraps and ministers of finance are all in one way or another concepts that are functionally defined, but none is a mental concept such as pain, belief and desire. What, then, characterizes the mental? And can it be captured in a functionalist framework?

The traditional view in the philosophy of mind has it that mental states are distinguished by their having what are called either qualitative content or intentional content. I shall discuss qualitative content first.

It is not easy to say what qualitative content is; indeed, according to some theories, it is not even possible to say what it is because it can be known not by description but only by direct experience. I shall nonetheless attempt to describe it. Try to imagine looking at a blank wall through a red filter. Now change the filter to a green one and leave everything else exactly the way it was. Something about the character of your experience changes when the filter does, and it is this kind of thing that philosophers call qualitative content. I am not entirely comfortable about introducing qualitative content in this way, but it is a subject with which many philosophers are not comfortable.

The reason qualitative content is a problem for functionalism is straightforward. Functionalism is committed to defining mental states in terms of their causes and effects. It seems, however, as if two mental states could have all the same causal relations and yet could differ in their qualitative content. Let me illustrate this with the classic puzzle of the inverted spectrum.

It seems possible to imagine two observers who are alike in all relevant psychological respects except that experiences having the qualitative content of red for one observer would have the qualitative content of green for the other. Nothing about their behavior need reveal the difference because both of them see ripe tomatoes and flaming sunsets as being similar in color and both of them call that color "red." Moreover, the causal connection between their (qualitatively distinct) experiences and their other mental states could also be identical. Perhaps they both think of Little Red Riding Hood when they see ripe tomatoes, feel depressed when they see the color green and so on. It seems as if anything that could be packed into the notion of the causal role of their experiences could be shared by them, and yet the qualitative content of the experiences could be as different as you like. If this is possible, then the functionalist account does not work for mental states that have qualitative content. If one person is having a green experience while another person is having a red one, then surely they must be in different mental states.

The example of the inverted spectrum is more than a verbal puzzle. Having qualitative content is supposed to be a chief factor in what makes a mental state conscious. Many psychologists who are inclined to accept the functionalist framework are nonetheless worried about the failure of functionalism to reveal much about the nature of consciousness. Functionalists have made a few ingenious attempts to talk themselves and their colleagues out of this worry, but they have not, in my view, done so with much success. (For example, perhaps one is wrong in thinking one can imagine what an inverted spectrum would be like.) As matters stand, the problem of qualitative content poses a serious threat to the assertion that functionalism can provide a general theory of the mental.

Functionalism has fared much better with the intentional content of mental states. Indeed, it is here that the major achievements of recent cognitive science are found. To say that a mental state has intentional content is to say that is has certain semantic properties. For example, for Enrico to believe Galileo was Italian apparently involves a three-way relation between Enrico, a belief and a proposition that is the content of the belief (namely the proposition that Galileo was Italian). In particular it is an essential property of Enrico's belief that it is about Galileo (and not about, say, Newton) and that it is true if, and only if, Galileo was indeed Italian. Philosophers are divided on how these considerations fit together, but it is widely agreed that beliefs involve semantic properties such as expressing a proposition, being true or false and being about one thing rather than another.

It is important to understand the semantic properties of beliefs because theories in the cognitive sciences are largely about the beliefs organisms have. Theories of learning and perception, for example, are chiefly accounts of how the host of beliefs an organism has are determined by the character of its experiences and its genetic endowment. The functionalist account of mental states does not by itself provide the required insights. Mousetraps are functionally defined, yet mousetraps do not express propositions and they are not true or false.

There is at least one kind of thing other than a mental state that has intentional content: a symbol. Like thoughts, symbols seem to be about things. If someone says "Galileo was Italian," his utterance, like Enrico's belief, expresses a proposition about Galileo that is true or false depending on Galileo's homeland. This parallel between the symbolic and the mental underlies the traditional quest for a unified treatment of language and mind. Cognitive science is now trying to provide such a treatment.

The basic concept is simple but striking. Assume that there are such things as mental symbols (mental representations) and that mental symbols have semantic properties. On this view having a belief involves being related to a mental symbol, and the belief inherits its semantic properties from the mental symbol that figures in the relation. Mental processes (thinking, perceiving, learning and so on) involve causal interactions among relational states such as having a belief. The semantic properties of the words and sentences we utter are in turn inherited from the semantic properties of the mental states that language expresses.

Associating the semantic properties of mental states with those of mental symbols is fully compatible with the computer metaphor, because it is natural to think of the computer as a mechanism that manipulates symbols. A computation is a causal chain of computer states and the links in the chain are operations on semantically interpreted formulas in a machine code. To think of a system (such as the nervous system) as a computer is to raise questions about the nature of the code in which it computes and the semantic properties of the symbols in the code. In fact, the analogy between minds and computers actually implies the postulation of mental symbols. There is no computation without representation.

The representational account of the mind, however, predates considerably the invention of the computing machine. It is a throwback to classical epistemology, which is a tradition that includes philosophers as diverse as John Locke, David Hume, George Berkeley, Rene Descartes, Immanuel Kant, John Stuart Mill and William James.

Hume, for one, developed a representational theory of the mind that included five points. First, there exist "Ideas," which are a species of mental symbol. Second, having a belief involves entertaining an Idea. Third, mental processes are causal associations of Ideas. Fourth, Ideas are like pictures. And fifth, Ideas have their semantic properties by virtue of what they resemble: the Idea of John is about John because it looks like him.

Contemporary cognitive psychologists do not accept the details of Hume's theory, although they endorse much of its spirit. Theories of computation provide a far richer account of mental processes than the mere association of Ideas. And only a few psychologists still think that imagery is the chief vehicle of mental representation. Nevertheless, the most significant break with Hume's theory lies in the abandoning of resemblance as an explanation of the semantic properties of mental representations.

Many philosophers, starting with Berkeley, have argued that there is something seriously wrong with the suggestion that the semantic relation between a thought and what the thought is about could be one of resemblance. Consider the thought that John is tall. Clearly the thought is true only of the state of affairs consisting of John's being tall. A theory of the semantic properties of a thought should therefore explain how this particular thought is related to this particular state of affairs. According to the resemblance theory, entertaining the thought involves having a mental image that shows John to be tall. To put it another way, the relation between the thought that John is tall and his being tall is like the relation between a tall man and his portrait.

The difficulty with the resemblance theory is that any portrait showing

John to be tall must also show him to be many other things: clothed or naked, lying, standing or sitting, having a head or not having one, and so on. A portrait of a tall man who is sitting down resembles a man's being seated as much as it resembles a man's being tall. On the resemblance theory it is not clear what distinguishes thoughts about John's height from thoughts about his posture.

The resemblance theory turns out to encounter paradoxes at every turn. The possibility of construing beliefs as involving relations to semantically interpreted mental representations clearly depends on having an acceptable account of what the semantic properties of the mental representations come from. If resemblance will not provide this account, what will?

The current idea is that the semantic properties of a mental representation are determined by aspects of its functional role. In other words, a significant condition for having semantic properties can be specified in causal terms. This is the connection between functionalism and the representational theory of the mind. Modern cognitive psychology rests largely on the hope that these two doctrines can be made to support each other.

No philosopher is now prepared to say exactly how the functional role of a mental representation determines its semantic properties. Nevertheless, the functionalist recognizes three types of causal relation among psychological states involving mental representations, and they might serve to fix the semantic properties of mental representations. The three types are causal relations among mental states and stimuli, mental states and responses and some mental states and other ones.

Consider the belief that John is tall. Presumably the following facts, which correspond respectively to the three types of causal relation, are relevant to determining the semantic properties of the mental representation involved in the belief. First, the belief is a normal effect of certain stimulations, such as seeing John in circumstances that reveal his height. Second, the belief is the normal cause of certain behavioral effects, such as uttering "John is tall." Third, the belief is a normal cause of certain other beliefs and a normal effect of certain other beliefs. For example, anyone who believes John is tall is very likely also to believe someone is tall. Having the first belief is normally causally sufficient for having the second belief. And anyone who believes everyone in the room is tall and also believes John is in the room will very likely believe John is tall. The third belief is a normal effect of the first two. In short, the functionalist maintains that the proposition expressed by a given mental representation depends on the causal properties of the mental states in which that mental representation figures.

The concept that the semantic properties of mental representations are determined by aspects of their functional role is at the center of current work in the cognitive sciences. Nevertheless, the concept may not be true. Many philosophers who are unsympathetic to the cognitive turn in modern psychology doubt its truth, and many psychologists would probably reject it in the bald and unelaborated way that I have sketched it. Yet even in its skeletal form, there is this much to be said in its favor: It legitimizes the notion of mental representation, which has become increasingly important to theorizing in every branch of the cognitive sciences. Recent advances in formulating and testing hypotheses about the character of mental representations in fields ranging from phonetics to computer vision suggest that the concept of mental representation is fundamental to empirical theories of the mind.

The behaviorist has rejected the appeal to mental representation because it runs counter to his view of the explanatory mechanisms that can figure in psychological theories. Nevertheless, the science of mental representation is now flourishing. The history of science reveals that when a successful theory comes into conflict with a methodological scruple, it is generally the scruple that gives way. Accordingly the functionalist has relaxed the behaviorist constraints on psychological explanations. There is probably no better way to decide what is methodologically permissible in science than by investigating what successful science requires.

NOTES

Reprinted with permission. Copyright © 1981 by Scientific American, Inc. All rights reserved.

8

Troubles with Functionalism

Ned Block

1.2. HOMUNCULI-HEADED ROBOTS

In this section I shall describe a class of devices that embarrass all versions of functionalism in that they indicate functionalism is guilty of liberalism—classifying systems that lack mentality as having mentality.

Consider the simple version of machine functionalism already described. It says that each system having mental states is described by at least one Turing-machine table of a certain kind, and each mental state of the system is identical to one of the machine-table states specified by the machine table. I shall consider inputs and outputs to be specified by descriptions of neural impulses in sense organs and motor-output neurons. This assumption should not be regarded as restricting what will be said to Psychofunctionalism rather than Functionalism. As already mentioned, every version of functionalism assumes *some* specification of inputs and outputs. A Functionalist specification would do as well for the purposes of what follows.

Imagine a body externally like a human body, say yours, but internally quite different. The neurons from sensory organs are connected to a bank of lights in a hollow cavity in the head. A set of buttons connects to the motor-output neurons. Inside the cavity resides a group of little men. Each has a very simple task: to implement a "square" of a reasonably adequate machine table that describes you. On one wall is a bulletin board on which is posted a state card, i.e., a card that bears a symbol designating one of the states specified in the machine table. Here is what the little men do: Suppose the posted card has a 'G' on it. This alerts the little men who implement G squares—'G-men' they call themselves. Suppose the light representing input I goes on.

97

One of the G-men has the following as his sole task: when the card reads 'G' and the I light goes on, he presses output button O and changes the state card to 'M'. This G-man is called upon to exercise his task only rarely. In spite of the low level of intelligence required of each little man, the system as a whole manages to simulate you because the functional organization they have been trained to realize is yours. A Turing machine can be represented as a finite set of quadruples (or quintuples, if the output is divided into two parts)—current state, current input; next state, next output. Each little man has the task corresponding to a single quadruple. Through the efforts of the little men, the system realizes the same (reasonably adequate) machine table as you do and is thus functionally equivalent to you.

I shall describe a version of the homunculi-headed simulation, which is more clearly nomologically possible. How many homunculi are required? Perhaps a billion are enough; after all, there are only about a billion neurons in the brain.

Suppose we convert the government of China to functionalism, and we convince its officials that it would enormously enhance their international prestige to realize a human mind for an hour. We provide each of the billion people in China (I chose China because it has a billion inhabitants) with a specially designed two-way radio that connects them in the appropriate way to other persons and to the artificial body mentioned in the previous example. We replace the little men with a radio transmitter and receiver connected to the input and output neurons. Instead of a bulletin board, we arrange to have letters displayed on a series of satellites placed so that they can be seen from anywhere in China. Surely such a system is not physically impossible. It could be functionally equivalent to you for a short time, say an hour.

"But," you may object, "how could something be functionally equivalent to me for *an hour*? Doesn't my functional organization determine, say, how I would react to doing nothing for a week but reading *Reader's Digest*?" Remember that a machine table specifies a set of conditionals of the form: if the machine is in S and receives input I, it emits output O and goes into S. Any system that has a set of inputs, outputs, and states related in the way described realizes that machine table, even if it exists for only an instant. For the hour the Chinese system is "on," it *does* have a set of inputs, outputs, and states of which such conditionals are true. Whatever the initial state, the system will respond in whatever way the machine table directs. This is how *any* computer realizes the machine table it realizes.

Of course, there are signals the system would respond to that you would not respond to, e.g., massive radio interference or a flood of the Yangtze River. Such events might cause a malfunction, scotching the simulation, just as a bomb in a computer can make it fail to realize the machine table it was built to realize. But just as the computer *without* the bomb *can* realize the machine table, the system consisting of the people and artificial body can realize the machine table so long as there are no catastrophic interferences, e.g., floods, etc.

"But," someone may object, "there is a difference between a bomb in a computer and a bomb in the Chinese system, for in the case of the latter (unlike the former), inputs as specified in the machine table can be the cause of the malfunction. Unusual neural activity in the sense organs of residents of Chungking Province caused by a bomb or by a flood of the Yangtze can cause the system to go haywire."

Reply: the person who says what system he or she is talking about gets to say what counts as inputs and outputs. I count as inputs and outputs only neural activity in the artificial body connected by radio to the people of China. Neural signals in the people of Chungking count no more as inputs to this system than input tape jammed by a saboteur between the relay contacts in the innards of a computer count as an input to the computer.

Of course, the object consisting of the people of China + the artificial body has *other* Turing machine descriptions under which neural signals in the inhabitants of Chungking *would* count as inputs. Such a new system (i.e., the object under such a new Turing-machine description) would not be functionally equivalent to you. Likewise, any commercial computer can be redescribed in a way that allows tape jammed into its innards to count as inputs. In describing an object as a Turing machine, one draws a line between the inside and the outside. (If we count only neural impulses as inputs and outputs, we draw that line inside the body. If *we* count only peripheral stimulations as inputs and only bodily movements as outputs, we draw that line at the skin.) In describing the Chinese system as a Turing machine, I have drawn the line in such a way that it satisfies a certain type of functional description—one that you *also* satisfy, and one that, according to functionalism, justifies attributions of mentality. Functionalism does not claim that every mental system has a machine table of a sort that justifies attributions of mentality with respect to *every* specification of inputs and outputs, but rather, only with respect to *some* specification.

Objection: The Chinese system would work too slowly. The kind of events and processes with which we normally have contact would pass by far too quickly for the system to detect them. Thus, we would be unable to converse with it, play bridge with it, etc.[1]

Reply: It is hard to see why the system's time scale should matter. What reason is there to believe that *your* mental operations could not be very much slowed down, yet remain mental operations? Is it really contradictory or nonsensical to suppose we could meet a race of intelligent beings with whom we could communicate only by devices such as time-lapse photography? When we observe these creatures, they seem almost inanimate. But when we view the time-lapse movies, we see them conversing with one another. Indeed, we find they are saying that the only way they can make any sense of us is by viewing movies greatly slowed down. To take time scale as all important seems crudely behavioristic. Further, even if the time-scale objection is right, I can elude it by retreating to the point that a homunculus-head that works in normal time is *metaphysically* possible, even if not nomologically possible. Metaphysical possibility is all my argument requires (see Section 1.3).[2]

'What makes the homunculi-headed system (count the two systems as variants of a single system) just described a prima facie counterexample to (machine) functionalism is that there is prima facie doubt whether it has any mental states at all—especially whether it has what philosophers have variously called "qualitative states," "raw feels," or "immediate phenomenological qualities.' (You ask: What is it that philosophers have called qualitative states? I answer, only half in jest: As Louis Armstrong said when asked what jazz is, "If you got to ask, you ain't never gonna get to know.') In Nagel's terms (1974), there is a prima facie doubt whether there is anything which it is like to be the homunculi-headed system.

The force of the prima facie counterexample can be made clearer as follows: Machine functionalism says that each mental state is identical to a machine-table state. For example, a particular qualitative state, Q, is identical to a machine table state, S. But if there is nothing it is like to be the homunculi-headed system, it cannot be in Q even when it is in S. Thus, if there is prima facie doubt about the homunculi-headed system's mentality, there is prima facie doubt that Q = S, i.e., doubt that the kind of functionalism under consideration is true.[3] Call this argument the Absent Qualia Argument.

NOTES

Ned Block, "Troubles with Functionalism," in *Perception and Cognition: Issues in the Foundations of Psychology, Minnesota Studies in the Philosophy of Science*, vol. IX, edited by C. W. Savage. Copyright © 1978. Reprinted by permission of the University of Minnesota Press.

1. This point has been raised with me by persons too numerous to mention.

2. One potential difficulty for Functionalism is provided by the possibility that one person may have two radically different Functional descriptions of the sort that justify attribution of mentality. In such a case, Functionalists might have to ascribe two radically different systems of belief, desire, etc., to the same person, or suppose that there is no fact of the matter about what the person's propositional attitudes are. Undoubtedly, Functionalists differ greatly on what they make of this possibility, and the differences reflect positions on such issues as indeterminacy of translation.

3. Shoemaker, 1975, argues (in reply to Block & Fodor, 1972) that absent qualia are logically impossible, that is, that it is logically impossible that two systems be in the same functional state yet one's state have and the other's state lack qualitative

content. If Shoemaker is right, it is wrong to doubt whether the homunculi-headed system has qualia. I attempt to show Shoemaker's argument to be fallacious in Block, 1980.

REFERENCES

Block, N. Are absent qualia impossible? *Philosophical Review*, 1980, 89, 257–74.

Block, N. & Fodor J. What psychological states are not. *Philosophical Review*, 1972, 81, 159–81.

Chisholm, Roderick, *Perceiving*. Ithaca: Cornell University Press, 1957.

Fodor, J. Explanations in psychology. In M. Black (Ed.), *Philosophy in America*, London: Routledge & Kegan Paul, 1965.

Gendron, B. On the relation of neurological and psychological theories: A critique of the hardware thesis. In R. C. Buck and R. S. Cohen (Eds.), *Boston studies in the philosophy of Science VIII*. Dordrecht: Reidel, 1971.

Hempel, C. Reduction: Ontological and linguistic facets. In S. Morgenbesser, P. Suppes & M. White (Eds.), *Essays in honor of Ernest Nagel*. New York: St. Martin's Press, 1970.

Kalke, W. What is wrong with Fodor and Putnam's functionalism? *Nous*, 1969, 3, 83–93.

Kim, J. Phenomenal properties, psychophysical laws, and the identity theory. *The Monist*, 1972, 56(2), 177–92.

Mucciolo, L. F. The identity thesis and neuropsychology. *Nous*, 1974, 8, 327–42.

Nagel, T. What is it like to be a bat? *Philosophical Review*, 1974, 83, 435–50.

Putnam, H. Brains and behavior. 1963. Reprinted as are all Putnam's articles referred to here (except "On properties") in *Mind, language and reality; philosophical papers*, Vol. 2. London: Cambridge University Press, 1975.

———. The mental life of some machines. 1966.

———. On properties. In *Mathematics, matter and method; philosophical papers*, Vol. 1. London: Cambridge University Press, 1970.

Shoemaker, S. Functionalism and qualia. *Philosophical studies*, 1975. 27, 291–315.

Online resources:

Ned Block
www.nyu.edu/gsas/dept/philo/faculty/block/

9

Epiphenomenal Qualia

Frank Jackson

It is undeniable that the physical, chemical and biological sciences have provided a great deal of information about the world we live in and about ourselves. I will use the label 'physical information' for this kind of information, and also for information that automatically comes along with it. For example, if a medical scientist tells me enough about the processes that go on in my nervous system, and about how they relate to happenings in the world around me, to what has happened in the past and is likely to happen in the future, to what happens to other similar and dissimilar organisms, and the like, he or she tells me—if I am clever enough to fit it together appropriately—about what is often called the functional role of those states in me (and in organisms in general in similar cases). This information, and its kin, I also label 'physical'.

I do not mean these sketchy remarks to constitute a definition of 'physical information', and of the correlative notions of physical property, process, and so on, but to indicate what I have in mind here. It is well known that there are problems with giving a precise definition of these notions, and so of the thesis of Physicalism that all (correct) information is physical information.[1] But—unlike some—I take the question of definition to cut across the central problems I want to discuss in this paper.

I am what is sometimes known as a "qualia freak." I think that there are certain features of the bodily sensations especially, but also of certain perceptual experiences, which no amount of purely physical information includes. Tell me everything physical there is to tell about what is going on in a living brain, the kind of states, their functional role, their relation to what goes on at other times and in other brains, and so on and so forth, and be I as clever as can be in fitting it all together, you won't have told me about the hurtfulness of pains, the itchiness of itches, pangs of jealousy, or about the characteristic experience of tasting a lemon, smelling a rose, hearing a loud noise or seeing the sky.

There are many qualia freaks, and some of them say that their rejection of Physicalism is an unargued intuition.[2] I think that they are being unfair to themselves. They have the following argument. Nothing you could tell of a physical sort captures the smell of a rose, for instance. Therefore, Physicalism is false. By our lights this is a perfectly good argument. It is obviously not to the point to question its validity, and the premise is intuitively obviously true both to them and to me.

I must, however, admit that it is weak from a polemical point of view. There are, unfortunately for us, many who do not find the premise intuitively obvious. The task then is to present an argument whose premises are obvious to all, or at least to as many as possible. This I try to do in section I with what I will call "the Knowledge argument." In section II I contrast the Knowledge argument with the modal argument and in section III with the "What is it like to be" argument. In section IV I tackle the question of the causal role of qualia. The major factor in stopping people from admitting qualia is the belief that they would have to be given a causal role with respect to the physical world and especially the brain;[3] and it is hard to do this without sounding like someone who believes in fairies. I seek in section IV to turn this objection by arguing that the view that qualia are epiphenomenal is a perfectly possible one.

I: THE KNOWLEDGE ARGUMENT FOR QUALIA

People vary considerably in their ability to discriminate colors. Suppose that in an experiment to catalog this variation Fred is discovered. Fred has better color vision than anyone else on record; he makes every discrimination that anyone has ever made, and moreover he makes one that we cannot even begin to make. Show him a batch of ripe tomatoes and he sorts them into two roughly equal groups and does so with complete consistency. That is, if you blindfold him, shuffle the tomatoes up, and then remove the blindfold and ask him to sort them out again, he sorts them into exactly the same two groups.

We ask Fred how he does it. He explains that all ripe tomatoes do not look the same color to him, and in fact that this is true of a great many objects that we classify together as red. He sees two colors where we see one, and he has in consequence developed for his own use two words 'red1' and 'red2' to mark the difference. Perhaps he tells us that he has often tried to teach the difference between red1 and red2 to his friends but has got nowhere and has concluded that the rest of the world is red1-red2 color-blind—or perhaps he has had partial success with his children; it doesn't matter. In any case he explains to us that it would be quite wrong to think that because 'red' appears in both 'red1' and 'red2' that the two colors are shades of the one color. He only uses the common term 'red' to fit more easily into our restricted usage. To him red1 and red2 are as different from each other and all the other colors as yellow is from blue. And his discriminatory behavior bears this out: he sorts red1 from red2 tomatoes with the greatest of ease in a wide variety of viewing circumstances. Moreover, an investigation of the physiological basis of Fred's exceptional ability reveals that Fred's optical system is able to separate out two groups of wavelengths in the red spectrum as sharply as we are able to sort out yellow from blue.[4]

I think that we should admit that Fred can see, really see, at least one more color than we can; red1 is a different color from red2. We are to Fred as a totally red-green color-blind person is to us. H. G. Wells' story "The country of the blind" is about a sighted person in a totally blind community.[5] This person never manages to convince them that he can see, that he has an extra sense. They ridicule this sense as quite inconceivable, and treat his capacity to avoid falling into ditches, to win fights and so on as precisely that capacity and nothing more. We would be making their mistake if we refused to allow that Fred can see one more color than we can.

What kind of experience does Fred have when he sees red1 and red2? What is the new color or colors like? We would dearly like to know but do not; and it seems that no amount of physical information about Fred's brain and optical system tells us. We find out perhaps that Fred's cones respond differentially to certain light waves in the red section of the spectrum that make no difference to ours (or perhaps he has an extra cone) and that this leads in Fred to a wider range of those brain states responsible for visual discriminatory behavior. But none of this tells us what we really want to know about his color experience. There is something about it we don't know. But we know, we may suppose, everything about Fred's body, his behavior and dispositions to behavior and about his internal physiology, and everything about his history and relation to others that can be given in physical accounts of persons. We have all the physical information. Therefore, knowing all this is not knowing everything about Fred. It follows that Physicalism leaves something out.

To reinforce this conclusion, imagine that as a result of our investigations into the internal workings of Fred we find out how to make everyone's physiology like Fred's in the relevant respects; or perhaps Fred donates his body to science and on his death we are able to transplant his optical system into someone else—again the fine detail doesn't matter. The important point is that such a happening would create enormous interest. People would say "At last we will know what it is like to see the extra color, at last we will know how Fred has differed from us in the way he has struggled to tell us about for so long." Then it cannot be that we knew all along all about Fred. But ex hypothesi we did know all along everything about Fred that features in the physicalist scheme; hence the physicalist scheme leaves something out.

Put it this way. After the operation, we will know more about Fred and especially about his color experiences. But beforehand we had all the physical information we could desire about his body and brain, and indeed everything that has ever featured in physicalist accounts of mind and consciousness. Hence there is more to know than all that. Hence Physicalism is incomplete.

Fred and the new color(s) are of course essentially rhetorical devices. The same point can be made with normal people and familiar colors. Mary is a brilliant scientist who is, for whatever reason, forced to investigate the world from a black and white room via a black and white television monitor. She specializes in the neurophysiology of vision and acquires, let us suppose, all the physical information there is to obtain about what goes on when we see ripe tomatoes, or the sky, and use terms like 'red', 'blue', and so on. She discovers, for example, just which wavelength combinations from the sky stimulate the retina, and exactly how this produces via the central nervous system the contraction of the vocal chords and expulsion of air from the lungs that results in the uttering of the sentence 'The sky is blue'. (It can hardly be denied that it is in principle possible to obtain all this physical information from black and white television, otherwise the Open University would of necessity need to use color television.)

What will happen when Mary is released from her black and white room or is given a color television monitor? Will she learn anything or not? It seems just obvious that she will learn something about the world and our visual experience of it. But then it is inescapable that her previous knowledge was incomplete. But she had all the physical information. Ergo there is more to have than that, and Physicalism is false.

Clearly the same style of Knowledge argument could be deployed for taste, hearing, the bodily sensations and generally speaking for the various mental states which are said to have (as it is variously put) raw feels, phenomenal features or qualia. The conclusion in each case is that the qualia are left out of the physicalist story. And the polemical strength of the Knowledge argument is that it is so hard to deny the central claim that one can have all the physical information without having all the information there is to have.

II: THE MODAL ARGUMENT

By the Modal argument I mean an argument of the following style.[6] Skeptics about other minds are not making a mistake in deductive logic, whatever else may be wrong with their position. No amount of physical information about another logically entails that he or she is conscious or feels anything at all. Consequently there is a possible world with organisms exactly like us in every physical respect (and remember that includes functional states, physical history et al.) but which differ from us profoundly in that they have no conscious mental life at all. But then what is it that we have and they lack? Not anything physical ex hypothesis. In all physical regards we and they are exactly alike. Consequently there is more to us than the purely physical. Thus Physicalism is false.[7]

It is sometimes objected that the Modal argument misconceives Physicalism on the ground that that doctrine is advanced as a contingent truth.[8] But to say this is only to say that physicalists restrict their claim to some possible worlds, including especially ours; and the Modal argument is only directed against this lesser claim. If we in our world, let alone beings in any others, have features additional to those of our physical replicas in other possible worlds, then we have non-physical features or qualia.

The trouble rather with the modal argument is that it rests on a disputable modal intuition. Disputable because it is disputed. Some sincerely deny that there can be physical replicas of us in other possible worlds which nevertheless lack consciousness. Moreover, at least one person who once had the intuition now has doubts.[9]

Head-counting may seem a poor approach to a discussion of the modal argument. But frequently we can do no better when modal intuitions are in question, and remember our initial goal was to find the argument with the greatest polemical utility.

Of course, qua protagonists of the Knowledge argument we may well accept the modal intuition in question; but this will be a consequence of our already having an argument to the conclusion that qualia are left out of the physicalist story, not our ground for that conclusion. Moreover, the matter is complicated by the possibility that the connection between matters physical and qualia is like that sometimes held to obtain between esthetic qualities and natural ones. Two possible worlds which agree in all "natural" respects (including the experiences of sentient creatures) must agree in all esthetic qualities also, but it is plausibly held that the esthetic qualities cannot be reduced to the natural.

III: THE "WHAT IS IT LIKE TO BE" ARGUMENT

In "What is it like to be a bat?" Thomas Nagel argues that "no amount of physical information can tell us what it is like to be a bat, and indeed that we, human beings, cannot imagine what it is like to be a bat."[10] His reason is that what this is like can only be understood from a bat's point of view, which is not our point of view and is not something capturable in physical terms which are essentially terms understandable equally from many points of view.

It is important to distinguish this argument from the Knowledge argument. When I complained that all the physical knowledge about Fred was not enough to tell us what his special color experience was like, I was not complaining that we weren't finding out what it is like to be Fred. I was complaining that there is something about his experience, a property of it, of which we were left ignorant. And if and when we come to know what this property is we still will not know what it is like to be Fred, but we will know more about him. No amount of knowledge about Fred, be it physical or not, amounts to knowledge "from the inside" considering Fred. We are not Fred. There is thus a whole set of items of knowledge expressed by forms of words like 'that is I myself who is . . .' which Fred has and we simply cannot have because we are not him.[11]

When Fred sees the color he alone can see, one thing he knows is the way his experience of it differs from his experience of seeing red and so on; another is that he himself is seeing it. Physicalist and qualia freaks alike should acknowledge that no amount of information of whatever kind that others have about Fred amounts to knowledge of the second. My complaint though concerned the first and was that the special quality of his experience is certainly a fact about it and one which Physicalism leaves out because no amount of physical information told us what it is.

Nagel speaks as if the problem he is raising is one of extrapolating from knowledge of one experience to another, of imagining what an unfamiliar experience would be like on the basis of familiar ones. In terms of Hume's example, from knowledge of some shades of blue we can work out what it would be like to see other shades of blue. Nagel argues that the trouble with bats et al. is that they are too unlike us. It is hard to see an objection to Physicalism here. Physicalism makes no special claims about the imaginative or extrapolative powers of human beings, and it is hard to see why it need do so.[12]

Anyway, our Knowledge argument makes no assumptions on this point. If Physicalism were true, enough physical information about Fred would obviate any need to extrapolate or to perform special feats of imagination or understanding in order to know all about his special color experience. The information would already be in our possession. But it clearly isn't. That was the nub of the argument.

IV: THE BOGEY OF EPIPHENOMENALISM

Is there any really good reason for refusing to countenance the idea that qualia are causally impotent with respect to the physical world? I will argue for the answer no, but in doing this I will say nothing about two views associated with the classical epiphenomenalist position. The first is that mental states are inefficacious with respect to the physical world. All I will be concerned to defend is that it is possible to hold that certain properties of certain mental states, namely those I've called qualia, are such that their possession or absence makes no difference to the physical world. The second is that the mental is totally causally inefficacious. For all I will say it may be that you have to hold that the instantiation of qualia makes a difference to other mental states though not to anything physical. Indeed general considerations to do with how you could come to be aware of the instantiation of qualia suggest such a position.[13]

Three reasons are standardly given for holding that a quale like the hurtfulness of a pain must be causally efficacious in the physical world, and so, for instance, that its instantiation must sometimes make a difference to what happens in the brain. None, I will argue, has any real force. (I am much indebted to Alec Hyslop and John Lucas for convincing me of this.)

(i) It is supposed to be just obvious that the hurtfulness of pain is partly responsible for the subject seeking to avoid pain, saying 'It hurts' and so on. But, to reverse Hume, anything can fail to cause anything. No matter how often B follows A, and no matter how initially obvious the causality of the connection seems, the hypothesis that A causes B can be overturned by an over-arching theory which shows the two as distinct effects of a common underlying causal process.

To the untutored the image on the screen of Lee Marvin's fist moving from left to right immediately followed by the image of John Wayne's head moving in the same general direction looks as causal as anything.[14] And of course throughout countless Westerns images similar to the first are followed by images similar to the second. All this counts for precisely nothing when we know the over-arching theory concerning how the relevant images are both effects of an underlying causal process involving the projector and the film. The epiphenomenalist can say exactly the same about the connection between, for example, hurtfulness and behavior. It is simply a consequence of the fact that certain happenings in the brain cause both.

(ii) The second objection relates to Darwin's Theory of Evolution. According to natural selection the traits that evolve over time are those conducive to physical survival. We may assume that qualia evolved over time—we have them, the earliest forms of life do not—and so we should expect qualia to be conducive to survival. The objection is that they could hardly help us to survive if they do nothing to the physical world.

The appeal of this argument is undeniable, but there is a good reply to it. Polar bears have particularly thick, warm coats. The Theory of Evolution explains this (we suppose) by pointing out that having a thick warm coat is conducive to survival in the Arctic. But having a thick coat goes along with having a heavy coat, and having a heavy coat is not conducive to survival. It slows the animal down.

Does this mean that we have refuted Darwin because we have found an evolved trait—having a heavy coat—which is not conducive to survival? Clearly not. Having a heavy coat is an unavoidable concomitant of having a warm coat (in the context, modern insulation was not available), and the advantages for survival of having a warm coat outweighed the disadvantages of having a heavy one. The point is that all we can extract from Darwin's theory is that we should expect any evolved characteristic to be either conducive to survival or a by-product of one that is so conducive. The epiphenomenalist holds that qualia fall into the latter category. They are a by-product of certain brain processes that are highly conducive to survival.

(iii) The third objection is based on a point about how we come to know about other minds. We know about other minds by knowing about other behavior, at least in part. The nature of the inference is a matter of some controversy, but it is not a matter of controversy that it proceeds from behavior. That is why we think that stones do not feel and dogs do feel. But, runs the objection, how can a person's behavior provide any reason for believing he has qualia like mine, or indeed any qualia at all, unless this behavior can be regarded as the outcome of the qualia. Man Friday's footprint was evidence of Man Friday because footprints are causal outcomes of feet attached to people. And an epiphenomenalist cannot regard behavior, or indeed anything physical, as an outcome of qualia.

But consider my reading in *The Times* that Spurs won. This provides excellent evidence that the *Telegraph* has also reported that Spurs won, despite the fact that (I trust) the *Telegraph* does not get the results from *The Times*. They each send their own reporters to the game. The *Telegraph*'s report is in no sense an outcome of *The Times*', but the latter provides good evidence for the former nevertheless.

The reasoning involved can be reconstructed thus. I read in *The Times* that Spurs won. This gives me reason to think that Spurs won because I know that Spurs' winning is the most likely candidate to be what caused the report in *The Times*. But I also know that Spurs' winning would have had many effects, including almost certain a report in the *Telegraph*.

I am arguing from one effect back to its cause and out again to another effect. The fact that neither effect causes the other is irrelevant. Now the epiphenomenalist allows that qualia are effects of what goes on in the brain. Qualia cause nothing physical but are caused by something physical. Hence the epiphenomenalist can argue from the behavior of others to the qualia of others by arguing from the behavior of others back to its causes in the brains of others and out again to their qualia.

You may well feel for one reason or another that this is a more dubious chain of reasoning than its model in the case of newspaper reports. You are right. The problem of other minds is a major philosophical problem, the problem of other newspaper reports is not. But there is no special problem for Epiphenomenalism as opposed to, say, Interactionism here.

There is a very understandable response to the three replies I have just made. "All right, there is no knockdown refutation of the existence of epiphenomenal qualia. But the fact remains that they are an excrescence. They do nothing, they explain nothing, they serve merely to soothe the intuitions of dualists, and it is left a total mystery how they fit into the world view of science. In short we do not and cannot understand the how and why of them."

This is perfectly true; but it is no objection to qualia, for it rests on an overly optimistic view of the human animal, and its powers. We are the products of Evolution. We understand and sense what we need to understand and sense in order to survive. Epiphenomenal qualia are totally irrelevant to survival. At no stage of our evolution did natural selection favor those who could make sense of how they are caused and the laws governing them, or in fact why they exist at all. And that is why we can't.

It is not sufficiently appreciated that Physicalism is an extremely optimistic view of our powers. If it is true, we have, in very broad outline admittedly, a grasp of our place in the scheme of things. Certain matters of sheer complexity defeat us—there are an awful lot of neurons—but in principle we have it all. But consider the antecedent probability that everything in the Universe be of a kind that is relevant in some way or other to the survival of Homo sapiens. It is very low surely. But then one must admit that it is very likely that there is a part of the whole scheme of things, maybe a big part, which no amount of evolution will ever bring us near to knowledge about or understanding of. For the simple reason that such knowledge and understanding is irrelevant to survival.

Physicalists typically emphasize that we are a part of nature on their view, which is fair enough. But if we are a part of nature, we are as nature has left us after however many years of evolution it is, and each step in that evolutionary progression has been a matter of chance constrained just by the need to preserve or increase survival value. The wonder is that we understand as much as we do, and there is no wonder that there should be matters which fall quite outside our comprehension. Perhaps exactly how epiphenomenal qualia fit into the scheme of things is one such.

This may seem an unduly pessimistic view of our capacity to articulate a truly comprehensive picture of our world and our place in it. But suppose we discovered living on the bottom of the deepest oceans a sort of sea slug which manifested intelligence. Perhaps survival in the conditions required rational powers. Despite their intelligence, these sea slugs have only a very restricted conception of the world by comparison with ours, the explanation for this being the nature of their immediate environment. Nevertheless they have developed sciences which work surprisingly well in these restricted terms. They also have philosophers, called slugists. Some call themselves tough-minded slugists, others confess to being soft-minded slugists.

The tough-minded slugists hold that the restricted terms (or ones pretty like them which may be introduced as their sciences progress) suffice in principle to describe everything without remainder. These tough-minded slugists admit in moments of weakness to a feeling that their theory leaves something out. They resist this feeling and their opponents, the soft-minded slugists, by pointing out—absolutely correctly—that no slugist has ever succeeded in spelling out how this mysterious residue fits into the highly successful view that their sciences have and are developing of how their world works.

Our sea slugs don't exist, but they might. And there might also exist super beings which stand to us as we stand to these slugs. We cannot adopt the perspective of these super beings, because we are not them, but the possibility of such a perspective is, I think, an antidote to excessive optimism.[15]

NOTES

1. See, e.g., D. H. Mellor, "Materialism and phenomenal qualities," *Aristotelian Society Supp.* Vol. 47 (1973), 107–19; and J. W. Cornman, *Materialism and Sensations*, New Haven and London, 1971.

2. Particularly in discussion, but see, e.g., Keith Campbell, *Metaphysics*, Belmont, 1976, p. 67.

3. See, e.g., D. C. Dennett, "Current issues in the philosophy of mind," *American Philosophical Quarterly* 15 (1978), 249–61.

4. Put this, and similar specifications below, in terms of Land's theory if you prefer. See, e.g., Edwin H. Land, "Experiments in color vision," *Scientific American* 200 (5 May 1959), 84–99.

5. H. G. Wells, The Country of the Blind and Other Stories, London, n.d.

6. See, e.g., Keith Campbell, *Body and Mind*, New York, 1970; and Robert Kirk, "Sentience and behavior," *Mind* 83 (1974), 43–60.

7. I have presented the argument in an inter-world rather than the more usual intra-world fashion to avoid inessential complications to do with supervenience, causal anomalies and the like.

8. See, e.g., W. G. Lycan, "A new Lilliputian argument against machine functionalism," *Philosophical Studies* 35 (1979), 279–87, p. 280; and Don Locke, "Zombies, schizophrenics and purely physical objects," *Mind* 85 (1976), 97–9.

9. See R. Kirk, "From physical explicability to full-blooded materialism," *Philosophical Quarterly* 29 (1979), 229–37. See also the arguments against the modal intuition in, e.g., Sydney Shoemaker, "Functionalism and qualia," *Philosophical Studies* 27 (1975), 291–315.

10. *Philosophical Review* 83 (1974), 435-50. Two things need to be said about this article. One is that, despite my dissociations to come, I am much indebted to it. The

other is that the emphasis changes through the article, and by the end Nagel is objecting not so much to Physicalism as to all extant theories of mind for ignoring points of view, including those that admit (irreducible) qualia.

11. Knowledge de se in the terms of David Lewis, "Attitudes de dicto and de se," *Philosophical Review* 88 (1979), 513–43.

12. See Laurence Nemirow's comments on "What it is . . ." in his review of T. Nagel *Mortal Questions* in *Philosophical Review* 89 (1980), 473–7. I am indebted here in particular to a discussion with David Lewis.

13. See my review of K. Campbell, *Body and Mind*, in *Australasian Journal of Philosophy* 50 (1972), 77–80.

14. Cf. Jean Piaget, "The child's conception of physical causality," reprinted in *The Essential Piaget*, London, 1977.

15. I am indebted to Robert Pargetter for a number of comments and, despite his dissent, to section IV of Paul E. Meehl's "The complete autocerebroscopist," in Paul Feyerabend and Grover Maxwell (eds.), *Mind, Matter and Method*, Minneapolis, 1966.

Online resources:

Frank Jackson
http://rsss.anu.edu.au/director.htm

Eliminativist Materialism

The readings in this section address a theory of the mind known as "**eliminativism**" or "**eliminativist materialism**." This is a materialist view of the mind that holds that our ordinary, everyday understanding of the mind and the language we use to express this understanding is incorrect. This commonsense view of the mind and terms signifying mental states will be replaced—eliminated—by neuro-scientific theory and its terminology that correctly explain the brain. Mental states, like pains, desires, and beliefs, are terms belonging to a pre-scientific theory of the human mind that explains and predicts human behavior and the mental states relating to it. This theory of mind is called "**folk-psychology**." It provides us with a way of understanding what mental states people have, given a certain set of circumstances that cause mental states and the reactions that are caused by mental states. For example, the term 'pain' denotes a state of mind that is caused by damage to the body. This state of mind, posited by folk-psychology, causes the person in pain to yell and scream, attempt to get aid and so on. Thus, when you see someone bleeding and wounded, screaming and begging for help, you understand that this person is in a state of pain. You don't actually see this mental state—you infer that the person is in this mental state due to your understanding of what is known as "folk-psychology." According to the eliminativist, this pre-scientific theory of the mind will no longer be a useful way to explain and predict human behavior once our scientific understanding of the mind improves. The eliminativist's most controversial claim is that our folk-psychology, including our ordinary way of speaking about the mind, will not match up with neuro-scientific discoveries about the brain. Eventually, we will not speak of our mental states as pains or beliefs at all (since this theory will turn out to be false) but will speak of particular states of the brain and its chemistry.

Our first reading, "Eliminative Materialism," is by Paul M. Churchland and is a chapter from his book, *Matter and Consciousness*. Churchland reviews the eliminativist position, explaining the thesis itself and its radical implications for our ordinary conception of the mind. He presents three arguments supporting eliminativism and three arguments against it, attempting to show that eliminativism is more plausible than one might initially suspect and that the arguments against the position are weak, at best. The second reading is a selection from Daniel C. Dennett, "True Believers: The Intentional Strategy and Why it Works." Dennett does not defend radical eliminativism in precisely the same way that Paul Churchland does. For Dennett, human behavior must be explained through what he terms "the **intentional stance**." We must, in other words, interpret people's behavior through attributing beliefs—intentions—to them using our folk-psychology and its concepts of mental states like beliefs. The other interpretive **stances**, the physical stance and design stance, will not reveal, explain, or predict the patterns present in human behavior. Folk-psychology, for Dennett, does real explanatory work as a theory of mind. However, the intentional stance is nevertheless an *interpretive* strategy, and it should not be confused with a scientific theory of the brain. The third reading, "I am John's Brain" by Andy Clark, is an account of the relationship between John's brain and John, written from the perspective of John's brain. John hardly knows anything about his brain and its workings, according to his brain, and the beliefs he does have about it are largely false. Clark creatively illustrates the difficulty involved in matching our commonsense understanding of our minds with what the sciences uncover about the brain. Our expectation that the ways we presently understand our minds and ourselves will be borne out by further scientific investigation may be disappointed, according to eliminativism.

10

Eliminative Materialism [Selection from *Matter and Consciousness*]

Paul M. Churchland

The identity theory was called into doubt not because the prospects for a materialist account of our mental capacities were thought to be poor, but because it seemed unlikely that the arrival of an adequate materialist theory would bring with it the nice one-to-one match-ups, between the concepts of folk psychology and the concepts of theoretical neuroscience, that intertheoretic reduction requires. The reason for that doubt was the great variety of quite different physical systems that could instantiate the required functional organization. *Eliminative materialism* also doubts that the correct neuroscientific account of human capacities will produce a neat reduction of our common-sense framework, but here the doubts arise from a quite different source.

As the eliminative materialists see it, the one-to-one match-ups will not be found, and our common-sense psychological framework will not enjoy an intertheoretic reduction, *because our common-sense psychological framework is a false and radically misleading conception of the causes of human behavior and the nature of cognitive activity.* On this view, folk psychology is not just an incomplete representation of our inner natures; it is an outright *mis*representation of our internal states and activities. Consequently, we cannot expect a truly adequate neuroscientific account of our inner lives to provide theoretical categories that match up nicely with the categories of our common-sense framework. Accordingly, we must expect that the older framework will simply be eliminated, rather than be reduced, by a matured neuroscience.

HISTORICAL PARALLELS

As the identity theorist can point to historical cases of successful intertheoretic reduction, so the eliminative materialist can point to historical cases
of the outright elimination of the ontology of an older theory in favor of
the ontology of a new and superior theory. For most of the eighteenth and
nineteenth centuries, learned people believed that heat was a subtle *fluid* held
in bodies, much in the way water is held in a sponge. A fair body of moderately successful theory described the way this fluid substance—called "caloric"—flowed within a body, or from one body to another, and how it
produced thermal expansion, melting, boiling, and so forth. But by the end
of the last century it had become abundantly clear that heat was not a substance at all, but just the energy of motion of the trillions of jostling molecules that make up the heated body itself. The new theory—the
"corpuscular/kinetic theory of matter and heat"—was much more successful than the old in explaining and predicting the thermal behavior of bodies.
And since we were unable to *identify* caloric fluid with kinetic energy
(according to the old theory, caloric is a material *substance;* according to the
new theory, kinetic energy is a form of *motion),* it was finally agreed that
there is *no such thing* as caloric. Caloric was simply eliminated from our
accepted ontology.

A second example. It used to be thought that when a piece of wood burns,
or a piece of metal rusts, a spirit-like substance called "phlogiston" was
being released: briskly, in the former case, slowly in the latter. Once gone,
that 'noble' substance left only a base pile of ash or rust. It later came to be
appreciated that both processes involve, not the loss of something, but the
gaining of a substance taken from the atmosphere: oxygen. Phlogiston
emerged, not as an incomplete description of what was going on, but as a
radical misdescription. Phlogiston was therefore not suitable for reduction
to or identification with some notion from within the new oxygen chemistry, and it was simply eliminated from science.

Admittedly, both of these examples concern the elimination of something
nonobservable, but our history also includes the elimination of certain
widely accepted 'observables'. Before Copernicus' views became available,
almost any human who ventured out at night could look up at *the starry
sphere of the heavens,* and if he stayed for more than a few minutes he could
also see that it *turned,* around an axis through Polaris. What the sphere was
made of (crystal?) and what made it turn (the gods?) were theoretical questions that exercised us for over two millennia. But hardly anyone doubted
the existence of what everyone could observe with their own eyes. In the
end, however, we learned to reinterpret our visual experience of the night
sky within a very different conceptual framework, and the turning sphere
evaporated.

Witches provide another example. Psychosis is a fairly common affliction among humans, and in earlier centuries its victims were standardly seen as cases of demonic possession, as instances of Satan's spirit itself, glaring malevolently out at us from behind the victims' eyes. That witches exist was not a matter of any controversy. One would occasionally see them, in any city or hamlet, engaged in incoherent, paranoid, or even murderous behavior. But observable or not, we eventually decided that witches simply do not exist. We concluded that the concept of a witch is an element in a conceptual framework that misrepresents so badly the phenomena to which it was standardly applied that literal application of the notion should be permanently withdrawn. Modern theories of mental dysfunction led to the elimination of witches from our serious ontology.

The concepts of folk psychology—belief, desire, fear, sensation, pain, joy, and so on—await a similar fate, according to the view at issue. And when neuroscience has matured to the point where the poverty of our current conceptions is apparent to everyone, and the superiority of the new framework is established, we shall then be able to set about *reconceiving* our internal states and activities, within a truly adequate conceptual framework at last. Our explanations of one another's behavior will appeal to such things as our neuropharmacological states, the neural activity in specialized anatomical areas, and whatever other states are deemed relevant by the new theory. Our private introspection will also be transformed, and may be profoundly enhanced by reason of the more accurate and penetrating framework it will have to work with—just as the astronomer's perception of the night sky is much enhanced by the detailed knowledge of modern astronomical theory that he or she possesses.

The magnitude of the conceptual revolution here suggested should not be minimized: it would be enormous. And the benefits to humanity might be equally great. If each of us possessed an accurate neuroscientific understanding of (what we now conceive dimly as) the varieties and causes of mental illness, the factors involved in learning, the neural basis of emotions, intelligence, and socialization, then the sum total of human misery might be much reduced. The simple increase in mutual understanding that the new framework made possible could contribute substantially toward a more peaceful and humane society. Of course, there would be dangers as well: increased knowledge means increased power, and power can always be misused.

ARGUMENTS FOR ELIMINATIVE MATERIALISM

The arguments for eliminative materialism are diffuse and less than decisive, but they are stronger than is widely supposed. The distinguishing feature of this position is its denial that a smooth intertheoretic reduction is to be expected—even a species-specific reduction—of the framework of folk psychology to the framework of a matured neuroscience. The reason for this denial is the eliminative materialist's conviction that folk psychology is a hopelessly primitive and deeply confused conception of our internal activities. But why this low opinion of our common-sense conceptions?

There are at least three reasons. First, the eliminative materialist will point to the widespread explanatory, predictive, and manipulative failures of folk psychology. So much of what is central and familiar to us remains a complete mystery from within folk psychology. We do not know what *sleep* is, or why we have to have it, despite spending a full third of our lives in that condition. (The answer, "For rest," is mistaken. Even if people are allowed to rest continuously, their need for sleep is undiminished. Apparently, sleep serves some deeper functions, but we do not yet know what they are.) We do not understand how *learning* transforms each of us from a gaping infant to a cunning adult, or how differences in *intelligence* are grounded. We have not the slightest idea how *memory* works, or how we manage to retrieve relevant bits of information instantly from the awesome mass we have stored. We do not know what *mental illness* is, nor how to cure it.

In sum, the most central things about us remain almost entirely mysterious from within folk psychology. And the defects noted cannot be blamed on inadequate time allowed for their correction, for folk psychology has enjoyed no significant changes or advances in well over 2,000 years, despite its manifest failures. Truly successful theories may be expected to reduce, but significantly unsuccessful theories merit no such expectation.

This argument from explanatory poverty has a further aspect. So long as one sticks to normal brains, the poverty of folk psychology is perhaps not strikingly evident. But as soon as one examines the many perplexing behavioral and cognitive deficits suffered by people with *damaged* brains, one's descriptive and explanatory resources start to claw the air. As with other humble theories asked to operate successfully in unexplored extensions of their old domain (for example, Newtonian mechanics in the domain of velocities close to the velocity of light, and the classical gas law in the domain of high pressures or temperatures), the descriptive and explanatory inadequacies of folk psychology become starkly evident.

The second argument tries to draw an inductive lesson from our conceptual history. Our early folk theories of motion were profoundly confused, and were eventually displaced entirely by more sophisticated theories. Our early folk theories of the structure and activity of the heavens were wildly off the mark, and survive only as historical lessons in how wrong we can be. Our folk theories of the nature of fire, and the nature of life, were similarly cockeyed. And one could go on, since the vast majority of our past folk conceptions have been similarly exploded. All except folk psychology, which survives to this day and has only recently begun to feel pressure. But the phenomenon of conscious intelligence is surely a more complex and difficult phenomenon than any of those just listed. So far as accurate understanding is concerned, it would be a *miracle* if we had got *that* one right the very first time, when we fell down so badly on all the others. Folk psychology has survived for so very long, presumably, not because it is basically correct in its representations, but because the phenomena addressed are so surpassingly difficult that any useful handle on them, no matter how feeble, is unlikely to be displaced in a hurry.

A third argument attempts to find an a priori advantage for eliminative materialism over the identity theory and functionalism. It attempts to counter the common intuition that eliminative materialism is distantly possible, perhaps, but is much less probable than either the identity theory or functionalism. The focus again is on whether the concepts of folk psychology will find vindicating match-ups in a matured neuroscience. The eliminativist bets no; the other two bet yes. (Even the functionalist bets yes, but expects the match-ups to be only species-specific, or only person-specific. Functionalism denies the existence only of *universal* type/type identities.)

The eliminativist will point out that the requirements on a reduction are rather demanding. The new theory must entail a set of principles and embedded concepts that mirrors very closely the specific conceptual structure to be reduced. And the fact is, there are vastly many more ways of being an explanatorily successful neuroscience while *not* mirroring the structure of folk psychology, than there are ways of being an explanatorily successful neuroscience while also *mirroring* the very specific structure of folk psychology. Accordingly, the a priori probability of eliminative materialism is not lower, but substantially *higher* than that of either of its competitors. One's initial intuitions here are simply mistaken.

Granted, this initial a priori advantage could be reduced if there were a very strong presumption in favor of the truth of folk psychology—true theories are better bets to win reduction. But according to the first two arguments, the presumptions on this point should run in precisely the opposite direction.

ARGUMENTS AGAINST
ELIMINATIVE MATERIALISM

The initial plausibility of this rather radical view is low for almost everyone, since it denies deeply entrenched assumptions. That is at best a question-begging complaint, of course, since those assumptions are precisely what is at issue. But the following line of thought does attempt to mount a real argument.

Eliminative materialism is false, runs the argument, because one's introspection reveals directly the existence of pains, beliefs, desires, fears, and so forth. Their existence is as obvious as anything could be.

The eliminative materialist will reply that this argument makes the same mistake that an ancient or medieval person would be making if he insisted that he could just see with his own eyes that the heavens form a turning sphere, or that witches exist. The fact is, all observation occurs within some system of concepts, and our observation judgments are only as good as the conceptual framework in which they are expressed. In all three cases—the starry sphere, witches, and the familiar mental states—precisely what is challenged is the integrity of the background conceptual frameworks in which the observation judgments are expressed. To insist on the validity of one's experiences, *traditionally interpreted,* is therefore to beg the very question at issue. For in all three cases, the question is whether we should *reconceive* the nature of some familiar observational domain.

A second criticism attempts to find an incoherence in the eliminative materialist's position. The bald statement of eliminative materialism is that the familiar mental states do not really exist. But that statement is meaningful, runs the argument, only if it is the expression of a certain *belief,* and an *intention* to communicate, and a *knowledge* of the language, and so forth. But if the statement is true, then no such mental states exist, and the statement is therefore a meaningless string of marks or noises, and cannot be true. Evidently, the assumption that eliminative materialism is true entails that it cannot be true.

The hole in this argument is the premise concerning the conditions necessary for a statement to be meaningful. It begs the question. If eliminative materialism is true, then meaningfulness must have some different source. To insist on the 'old' source is to insist on the validity of the very framework at issue. Again, an historical parallel may be helpful here. Consider the medieval theory that being biologically *alive* is a matter of being ensouled by an immaterial *vital spirit.* And consider the following response to someone who has expressed disbelief in that theory.

> My learned friend has stated that there is no such thing as vital spirit. But this statement is incoherent. For if it is true, then my friend does not have vital spirit, and must therefore be *dead.* But if he is dead, then his statement is just a string of noises, devoid of meaning or truth. Evidently, the assumption that antivitalism is true entails that it cannot be true! Q.E.D.

This second argument is now a joke, but the first argument begs the question in exactly the same way.

> A final criticism draws a much weaker conclusion, but makes a rather stronger case. Eliminative materialism, it has been said, is making mountains out of mole-

hills. It exaggerates the defects in folk psychology, and underplays its real successes. Perhaps the arrival of a matured neuroscience will require the elimination of the occasional folk-psychological concept, continues the criticism, and a minor adjustment in certain folk-psychological principles may have to be endured. But the large-scale elimination forecast by the eliminative materialist is just an alarmist worry or a romantic enthusiasm.

Perhaps this complaint is correct. And perhaps it is merely complacent. Whichever, it does bring out the important point that we do not confront two simple and mutually exclusive possibilities here: pure reduction versus pure elimination. Rather, these are the end points of a smooth spectrum of possible outcomes, between which there are mixed cases of partial elimination and partial reduction. Only empirical research can tell us where on that spectrum our own case will fall. Perhaps we should speak here, more liberally, of "revisionary materialism," instead of concentrating on the more radical possibility of an across-the-board elimination. Perhaps we should. But it has been my aim in this section to make it at least intelligible to you that our collective conceptual destiny lies substantially toward the revolutionary end of the spectrum.

NOTES

Paul Churchland, Matter and Consciousness (Revised Edition), revised material, new edition © 1988 Massachusetts Institute of Technology. Reprinted by permission of The MIT Press.

Online resources:

Paul Churchland
http://philosophy.ucsd.edu/Faculty/pmc.html

11

True Believers: The Intentional Strategy and Why it Works [Selection from *Scientific Explanation*]

Daniel C. Dennett

DEATH SPEAKS

There was a merchant in Baghdad who sent his servant to market to buy provisions and in a little while the servant came back, white and trembling, and said, Master, just now when I was in the market-place I was jostled by a woman in the crowd and when I turned I saw it was Death that jostled me. She looked at me and made a threatening gesture; now, lend me your horse, and I will ride away from this city and avoid my fate. I will go to Samarra and there Death will not find me. The merchant lent him his horse, and the servant mounted it, and he dug his spurs in its flanks and as fast as the horse could gallop he went. Then the merchant went down to the market-place and he saw me standing in the crowd, and he came to me and said, why did you make a threatening gesture to my servant when you saw him this morning? That was not a threatening gesture, I said, it was only a start of surprise. I was astonished to see him in Baghdad, for I had an appointment with him tonight in Samarra.

—W. Somerset Maugham

In the social sciences, talk about *belief* is ubiquitous. Since social scientists are typically self-conscious about their methods, there is also a lot of talk

about *talk about belief*. And since belief is a genuinely curious and perplexing phenomenon, showing many different faces to the world, there is abun-
dant controversy. Sometimes belief attribution appears to be a dark, risky,
and imponderable business—especially when exotic, and more particularly
religious or superstitious, beliefs are in the limelight. These are not the only
troublesome cases; we also court argument and skepticism when we attribute
beliefs to non-human animals, or to infants, or to computers or robots. Or
when the beliefs we feel constrained to attribute to an apparently healthy,
adult member of our own society are contradictory, or even just wildly false.
A biologist colleague of mine was once called on the telephone by a man in
a bar who wanted him to settle a bet. The man asked: 'Are rabbits birds?'
'No' said the biologist. 'Damn!' said the man as he hung up. Now could he
really have believed that rabbits were birds? Could anyone really and truly
be attributed that belief? Perhaps, but it would take a bit of a story to bring
us to accept it.

In all of these cases belief attribution appears beset with subjectivity,
infected with cultural relativism, prone to 'indeterminacy of radical translation'—clearly an enterprise demanding special talents: the art of phenomenological analysis, hermeneutics, empathy, *Verstehen*, and all that. On other
occasions, normal occasions, when familiar beliefs are the topic, belief attribution looks as easy as speaking prose, and as objective and reliable as counting beans in a dish. Particularly when these straightforward cases are before
us, it is quite plausible to suppose that *in principle* (if not yet in practice) it
would be possible to confirm these simple, objective belief attributions by
finding something inside the believer's head—by finding the beliefs themselves, in effect. 'Look', someone might say, 'You either believe there's milk
in the fridge or you don't believe there's milk in the fridge' (you might have
no opinion, in the latter case). But if you do believe this, that's a perfectly
objective fact about you, and it must come down in the end to your brain's
being in some particular physical state. If we knew more about physiological
psychology we could in principle determine the facts about your brain state,
and thereby determine whether or not you believe there is milk in the fridge,
even if you were determined to be silent, or disingenuous on the topic. In
principle, on this view physiological psychology could trump the results—or
non-results—of any 'black box' method in the social sciences that divines
beliefs (and other mental features) by behavioral, cultural, social, historical,
external criteria.

These differing reflections congeal into two opposing views on the nature
of belief attribution, and hence on the nature of belief. The latter, a variety
of *realism*, likens the question of whether a person has a particular belief to
the question of whether a person is infected with a particular virus—a perfectly objective internal matter of fact about which an observer can often
make educated guesses of great reliability. The former, which we could call

interpretationism if we absolutely had to give it a name, likens the question of whether a person has a particular belief to the question of whether a person is immoral, or has style, or talent, or would make a good wife. Faced with such questions, we preface our answers with 'Well, it all depends on what you're interested in', or make some similar acknowledgment of the relativity of the issue. 'It's a matter of interpretation', we say. These two opposing views, so baldly stated, do not fairly represent any serious theorists' positions, but they do express views that are typically seen as mutually exclusive and exhaustive; the theorist must be friendly with one and only one of these themes.

I think this is a mistake. My thesis will be that while belief is a perfectly objective phenomenon (that apparently makes me a realist), it can be discerned only from the point of view of one who adopts a certain *predictive strategy*, and its existence can be confirmed only by an assessment of the success of that strategy (that apparently makes me an interpretationist).

First I will describe the strategy, which I call the intentional strategy, or adopting the intentional stance. To a first approximation, the intentional strategy consists of treating the object whose behavior you want to predict as a rational agent with beliefs and desires and other mental states exhibiting what Brentano and others call *intentionality*. The strategy has often been described before, but I shall try to put this very familiar material in a new light, by showing *how* it works, and by showing *how well* it works.

Then I will argue that any object—or as I shall say, any *system*—whose behavior is well predicted by this strategy is in the fullest sense of the word a believer. *What it is* to be a true believer is to be an *intentional system*, a system whose behavior is reliably and voluminously predictable via the intentional strategy. I have argued for this position before,[1] and my arguments have so far garnered few converts and many presumed counterexamples. I shall try again here, harder, and shall also deal with several compelling objections.

THE INTENTIONAL STRATEGY
AND HOW IT WORKS

There are many strategies, some good, some bad. Here is a strategy, for instance, for predicting the future behavior of a person: determine the date and hour of the person's birth, and then feed this modest datum into one or another astrological algorithm for generating predictions of the person's prospects. This strategy is deplorably popular. Its popularity is deplorable only because we have such good reasons for believing that *it does not work*.[2] When astrological predictions come true, this is sheer luck, or the result of such vagueness or ambiguity in the prophecy that almost any eventuality can be construed to confirm it. But suppose the astrological strategy did in fact work well on some people. We could call those people *astrological systems*—systems whose behavior was, as a matter of fact, predictable by the astrological strategy. If there were such people, such astrological systems, we would be more interested than most of us in fact are in *how the astrological strategy works*—that is, we would be interested in the rules, principles, or methods of astrology. We could find out how the strategy works by asking astrologers, reading their books, and observing them in action. But we would also be curious about *why* it worked. We might find that astrologers had no useful opinions about this latter question—they either had no theory of why it worked, or their theories were pure hokum. Having a good strategy is one thing; knowing why it works is another.

So far as we know, however, the class of astrological systems is empty, so the astrological strategy is of interest only as a social curiosity. Other strategies have better credentials. Consider the physical strategy, or physical stance: if you want to predict the behavior of a system, determine its physical constitution (perhaps all the way down to the micro-physical level) and the physical nature of the impingements upon it, and use your knowledge of the laws of physics to predict the outcome for any input. This is the grand and impractical strategy of Laplace for predicting the entire future of everything in the universe, but it has more modest, local, actually usable versions. The chemist or physicist in the laboratory can use this strategy to predict the behavior of exotic materials, but equally the cook in the kitchen can predict the effect of leaving the pot on the burner too long. The strategy is not always practically available, but that it will always work *in principle* is a dogma of the physical sciences. (I ignore the minor complications raised by the sub-atomic indeterminancies of quantum physics.)

Sometimes, in any event, it is more effective to switch from the physical stance to what I call the design stance, where one ignores the actual (possibly messy) details of the physical constitution of an object, and, on the assumption that it has a certain design, predicts that it will behave *as it is designed to behave* under various circumstances. For instance, most users of computers have not the foggiest idea what physical principles are responsible for the computer's highly reliable, and hence predictable, behavior. But if they have a good idea of what the computer is designed to do (a description of its operation at any one of the many possible levels of abstraction), they can predict its behavior with great accuracy and reliability, subject to disconfirmation only in cases of physical malfunction. Less dramatically, almost anyone can predict when an alarm clock will sound on the basis of the most casual inspection of its exterior. One does not know or care to know whether it is spring wound, battery driven, sunlight powered, made of brass wheels and jewel bearings or silicon chips—one just assumes that it is designed so that the alarm will sound when it is set to sound, and it is set to sound where it appears to be set to sound, and the clock will keep on running until that time and beyond, and is designed to run more or less accurately, and so forth. For more accurate and detailed design stance predictions of the alarm clock, one must descend to a less abstract level of description of its design; for instance, to the level at which gears are described, but their material is not specified.

Only the designed behavior of a system is predictable from the design stance, of course. If you want to predict the behavior of an alarm clock when it is pumped full of liquid helium, revert to the physical stance. Not just artifacts, but also many biological objects (plants and animals, kidneys and hearts, stamens and pistils) behave in ways that can be predicted from the design stance. They are not just physical systems but designed systems.

Sometimes even the design stance is practically inaccessible, and then there is yet another stance or strategy one can adopt: the intentional stance. Here is how it works: first you decide to treat the object whose behavior is to be predicted as a rational agent; then you figure out what beliefs that agent ought to have, given its place in the world and its purpose. Then you figure out what desires it ought to have, on the same considerations, and finally you predict that this rational agent will act to further its goals in the light of its beliefs. A little practical reasoning from the chosen set of beliefs and desires will in many—but not all—instances yield a decision about what the agent ought to do; that is what you predict the agent *will* do.

The strategy becomes clearer with a little elaboration. Consider first how we go about populating each other's heads with beliefs. A few truisms: sheltered people tend to be ignorant; if you expose someone to something he comes to know all about it. In general, it seems, we come to believe all the truths about the parts of the world around us we are put in a position to learn about. *Exposure* to x, that is, sensory confrontation with x over some suitable period of time, is the *normally sufficient* condition for knowing (or having true beliefs) about x. As we say, we come to *know all about* the things around us. Such exposure is only *normally* sufficient for knowledge, but this is not the large escape hatch it might appear; our threshold for accepting abnormal ignorance in the face of exposure is quite high. 'I didn't know the gun was loaded', said by one who was observed to be present, sighted, and awake during the loading, meets with a variety of utter skepticism that only the most outlandish supporting tale could overwhelm.

Of course we do not come to learn or remember all the truths our sensory histories avail us. In spite of the phrase 'know all about', what we come to know, normally, are only all the *relevant* truths our sensory histories avail us. I do not typically come to know the ratio of spectacle-wearing people to trousered people in a room I inhabit, though if this interested me, it would be readily learnable. It is not just that some facts about my environment are below my thresholds of discrimination or beyond the integration and holding-power of my memory (such as the height in inches of all the people present), but that many perfectly detectable, graspable, memorable facts are of no interest to me, and hence do not come to be believed by me. So one rule for attributing beliefs in the intentional strategy is this: attribute as beliefs all the truths relevant to the system's interests (or desires) that the system's experience to date has made available. This rule leads to attributing somewhat too much—since we all are somewhat forgetful, even of important things. It also fails to capture the false beliefs we are all known to have. But the attribution of false belief, *any* false belief, requires a special genealogy, which will be seen to consist in the main in true beliefs. Two paradigm cases: S believes (falsely) that *p*, because S believes (truly) that Jones told him that *p*, that Jones is pretty clever, that Jones did not intend to deceive him, . . . etc. Second case: S believes (falsely) that there is a snake on the barstool, because S believes (truly) that he seems to see a snake on the barstool, is himself sitting in a bar not a yard from the barstool he sees, and so forth. The falsehood has to start somewhere; the seed may be sown in hallucination, illusion, a normal variety of simple misperception, memory deterioration, or deliberate fraud, for instance, but the false beliefs that are reaped grow in a culture medium of true beliefs.

An implication of the intentional strategy, then, is that true believers mainly believe truths. If anyone could devise an agreed-upon method of individuating and counting beliefs (which I doubt very much), we would see that all but the smallest portion (say, less than 10%) of a person's beliefs were attributable under our first rule.[3]

Note that this rule is a derived rule, an elaboration and further specification of the fundamental rule: attribute those beliefs the system *ought to have*. Note also that the rule interacts with the attribution of desires. How do we attribute the desires (preferences, goals, interests) on whose basis we will shape the list of beliefs? We attribute the desires the system *ought to have*. That is the fundamental rule. It dictates, on a first pass, that we attribute the familiar list of highest, or most basic, desires to people: survival, absence of pain, food, comfort, procreation, entertainment. Citing any one of these desires typically terminates the 'Why" game of reason giving. One is not supposed to need an ulterior motive for desiring comfort or pleasure or the prolongation of one's existence. Derived rules of desire attribution interact with belief attribution. Trivially, we have the rule: attribute desires for those things a system believes to be good for it. Somewhat more informatively, attribute desires for those things a system believes to be the best means to other ends it desires. The attribution of bizarre and detrimental desires thus requires, like the attribution of false beliefs, special stories.

I want to turn from the description of the strategy to the question of its use. Do people actually use this strategy? Yes, all the time. There may someday be other strategies for attributing belief and desire and for predicting behavior, but this is the only one we all know now. And when does it work?

It works with people almost all the time. Why would it not be a good idea to allow individual Oxford colleges to create and grant academic degrees whenever they saw fit? The answer is a long story, but very easy to generate. And there would be widespread agreement about the major points. We have no difficulty thinking of the reasons people would then have for acting in such ways as to give others reasons for acting in such ways as to give others reasons for . . . creating a circumstance we would not want. Our use of the intentional strategy is so habitual and effortless that the role it plays in shaping our expectations about people is easily overlooked. The strategy also works on most other mammals most of the time. For instance, you can use it to design better traps to catch those mammals, by reasoning about what the creature knows or believes about various things, what it prefers, what it wants to avoid. The strategy works on birds, and on fish, and on reptiles, and on insects and spiders, and even on such lowly and unenterprising creatures as clams (once a clam believes there is danger about, it will not relax its grip on its closed shell until it is convinced that the danger has passed). It also works on some artifacts: the chess-playing computer will not take your knight because it knows that there is a line of ensuing play that would lead to losing its rook, and it does not want that to happen. More modestly, the thermostat will turn off the boiler as soon as it comes to believe the room has reached the desired temperature.

The strategy even works for plants. In a locale with late spring storms you should plant apple varieties that are particularly cautious about concluding that it is spring—which is when they want to blossom, of course. It even works for such inanimate and apparently undesigned phenomena as lightning. An electrician once explained to me how he worked out how to protect my underground water pump from lightning damage: lightning, he said, always wants to find the best way to ground—or earth, as you say in England—but sometimes it gets tricked into taking second-best paths. You can protect the pump by making another, better path more obvious to the lightning.

TRUE BELIEVERS AS INTENTIONAL SYSTEMS

Now clearly this is a motley assortment of 'serious' belief attributions, dubious belief attributions, pedagogically useful metaphors, facons de parler, and perhaps worse: outright frauds. The next task would seem to be distinguishing those intentional systems that really have beliefs and desires from those we may find it handy to treat as if they had beliefs and desires. But that would be a Sisyphean labor, or else would be terminated by fiat. A better understanding of the phenomenon of belief begins with the observation that even in the worst of these cases, even when we are surest that the strategy works for the wrong reasons, it is nevertheless true that it does work, at least a little bit. This is an interesting fact, which distinguishes this class of objects, the class of intentional systems, from the class of objects for which the strategy never works. But is this so? Does our definition of an intentional system exclude any objects at all? For instance, it seems the lectern in this lecture room can be construed as an intentional system, fully rational, and believing that it is currently located at the centre of the civilized world (as some of you may also think); and desiring above all else to remain at that centre. What should such a rational agent so equipped with belief and desire do? Stay put, clearly, which is just what the lectern does. I predict the lectern's behavior, accurately, from the intentional stance, so is it an intentional system? If it is, anything at all is.

What should disqualify the lectern? For one thing, the strategy does not recommend itself in this case, for we get no predictive power from it that we did not antecedently have. We already knew what the lectern was going to do—namely nothing—and tailored the beliefs and desires to fit in a quite unprincipled way. In the case of people, or animals, or computers, however, the situation is different. In these cases often the only strategy that is at all practical is the intentional strategy; it gives us predictive power we can get by no other method. But, it will be urged, this is no difference in nature, but merely a difference that reflects upon our limited capacities as scientists. The Laplacean omniscient physicist could predict the behavior of a computer—or of a live human body, assuming it to be ultimately governed by the laws of physics—without any need for the risky, shortcut methods of either the design or intentional strategies. For people of limited mechanical aptitude, the intentional interpretation of a simple thermostat is a handy and largely innocuous crutch, but the engineers among us can quite fully grasp its internal operation without the aid of this anthropomorphizing. It may be true that the cleverest engineers find it practically impossible to maintain a clear conception of more complex systems, such as a time-sharing computer system or remote-controlled space probe, without lapsing into an intentional stance (and viewing these devices as asking and telling, trying and avoiding, wanting and believing), but this is just a more advanced case of human epistemic frailty. We would not want to classify these artifacts with the true believers—ourselves—on such variable and parochial grounds, would we? Would it not be intolerable to hold that some artifact, or creature, or person was a believer from the point of view of one observer, but not a believer at all from the point of view of another, cleverer observer? That would be a particularly radical version of interpretationism, and some have thought I espoused it in urging that belief be viewed in terms of the success of the intentional strategy. I must confess that my presentation of the view has sometimes invited that reading, but I now want to discourage it. The decision to adopt the intentional stance is free, but the facts about the success or failure of the stance, were one to adopt it, are perfectly objective.

Until now I have been stressing our kinship to clams and thermostats, in order to emphasize a view of the logical status of belief attributions, but the time has come to acknowledge the obvious differences, and say what can be made of them. The perverse claim remains; all there is to being a true believer is being a system whose behavior is reliably predictable via the intentional strategy, and hence all there is to really and truly believing that p (for any proposition p) is being an intentional system for which p occurs as a belief in the best (most predictive) interpretation. But once we turn our attention to the truly interesting and versatile intentional systems, we see that this apparently shallow and instrumentalistic criterion of belief puts a severe constraint on the internal constitution of a genuine believer, and thus yields a robust version of the belief after all.

Consider the lowly thermostat, as degenerate a case of an intentional system as could conceivably hold our attention for more than a moment. Going along with the gag we might agree to grant it the capacity for about half a dozen different beliefs and fewer desires—it can believe the room is too cold or too hot, that the boiler is on or off, and that if it wants the room warmer it should turn on the boiler, and so forth. But surely this is imputing too much to the thermostat; it has no concept of heat or of a boiler, for instance. So suppose we de-interpret its beliefs and desires; it can believe that A is too F or G, and if it wants the A to be more F it should do K, and so forth. After all, by attaching the thermostatic control mechanism to different input and output devices, it could be made to regulate the amount of water in a tank, or the speed of a train, for instance. Its attachment to a heat-sensitive 'transducer' and a boiler is too impoverished a link to the world to grant any rich semantics to its belief-like states.

But suppose we then enrich these modes of attachment. Suppose we give it more than one way of learning about the temperature, for instance. We give it an eye of sorts that can distinguish huddled, shivering occupants of the room, and an ear so that it can be told how cold it is. We give it some facts about geography so that it can conclude that it is probably in a cold place if it learns that its spatio-temporal location is Winnipeg in December. Of course giving it a visual system that is multi-purpose and general—not a mere shivering-object detector—will require vast complications of its inner structure. Suppose we also give our system more behavioral versatility: it chooses the boiler fuel, purchases it from the cheapest and most reliable dealer, checks the weather stripping and so forth. This adds another dimension of internal complexity; it gives individual belief-like states *more to do*, in effect, by providing more and different occasions for their derivation or deduction from other states, and by providing more and different occasions for them to serve as premises for further reasoning. The cumulative effect of enriching these connections between the device and the world in which it resides is to enrich the semantics of its dummy predicates, *F* and *G* and the rest. The more of this we add, the less amenable our device becomes to serving as the control structure of anything other than a room temperature maintenance system. A more formal way of saying this is that the class of indistinguishably satisfactory models of the formal system embodied in its internal states gets smaller and smaller as we add such complexities; the more we add, the richer or more demanding or specific the semantics of the system, until eventually we reach systems for which a *unique* semantic interpretation is *practically* (but never in *principle*) dictated.[4] At that point we say this device (or animal, or person) has beliefs *about heat,* and *about this very room,* and so forth, not only because of the system's *actual* location in, and operations on, the world, but because we cannot imagine another niche in which it could be placed *where it would work.*

Our original simple thermostat had a state we called a belief about a particular boiler, to the effect that it was on or off. Why about *that* boiler? Well, what *other* boiler would you want to say it was about? The belief is about the boiler because it is *fastened* to the boiler.[5] Given the actual, if minimal, causal link to the world that happened to be in effect, we could endow a state of the device with *meaning* (of a sort) and *truth conditions*, but it was altogether too easy to substitute a different minimal link and completely change the meaning (in this impoverished sense) of that internal state. But as systems become perceptually richer and behaviorally more versatile, it becomes harder and harder to make substitutions in the actual links of the system to the world without changing the organization of the system itself. If you change its environment, it will *notice*, in effect, and make a change in its internal state in response. There comes to be a two-way constraint of growing specificity between the device and the environment. Fix the device in any one state and it demands a very specific environment in which to operate properly (you can no longer switch it easily from regulating temperature to regulating speed or any thing else); but at the same time, if you do not *fix* the state it is in, but just plonk it down in a changed environment, its sensory attachments will be sensitive and discriminative enough to respond appropriately to the change, driving the system into a new state, in which it will operate effectively in the new environment. There is a familiar way to alluding to this tight relationship that can exist between the organization of a system and its environment; you say that the organism continuously *mirrors* the environment, or that there is a *representation* of the environment in—or implicit in—the organization of the system.

It is not that we attribute (or should attribute) beliefs and desires only to things in which we find internal representations, but rather that when we discover some object for which the intentional strategy works, we endeavor to interpret some of its internal states or processes as internal representations.

What makes some internal feature of a thing a representation could only be its role in regulating the behavior of an intentional system.

Now the reason for stressing our kinship with the thermostat should be clear. There is no magic moment in the transition from a single thermostat to a system that *really* has an internal representation of the world around it. The thermostat has a minimally demanding representation of the world, fancier thermostats have more demanding representations of the world, fancier robots for helping around the house would have still more demanding representations of the world. Finally you reach us. We are so multifariously and intricately connected to the world that almost no substitution is possible—though it is clearly imaginable in a thought experiment . . .

NOTES

"True Believer: The Intentional Strategy and Why It Works," by Daniel C. Dennett from *Scientific Explanation: Papers Based on Herbert Spencer Lectures* (1981), edited by A. F. Heath. By permission of Oxford University Press.

1. Intentional systems. *Journal of Philosophy* (1971). Conditions of personhood. In *The Identities of Persons* (ed. A. Rorty). University of California Press (1975). Both reprinted in *Brainstorms*. Montgomery, Vt.: Bradford (1978). Three kinds of intentional psychology. In *Mind, Psychology and Reductionism* (ed. R. A. Healey). Cambridge University Press (1981).

2. Paul Feyerabend, whose latest book, *Science in a Free Society*, New Left Books, London (1978), is heroically open-minded about astrology.

3. The idea that most of anyone's beliefs *must* be true seems obvious to some people. Support for the idea can be found in works by Quine, Putnam, Shoemaker, Davidson, and myself. Other people find the idea equally incredible—so probably each side is calling a different phenomenon belief. Once one makes the distinction between belief and opinion (in my technical sense—see How to change your mind. In *Brainstorms* Chapter 16), according to which opinions are linguistically infected, relatively sophisticated cognitive states—*roughly*, states of betting on the truth of a particular, formulated sentence, one can see the near triviality of the claim that most beliefs are true. A few reflections on peripheral matters should bring it out. Consider Democritus, who had a systematic, all-embracing, but (let us say, for the sake of argument) entirely false physics. He had things *all wrong*, though his views held together and had a sort of systematic utility. But even if every *claim* that scholarship permits us to attribute to Democritus (either explicit or implicit in his writing) is false, these represent a vanishingly small fraction of his *beliefs*, which include both the vast numbers of humdrum standing beliefs he must have had (about which house he lived in, what to look for in a good pair of sandals, and so forth), and also those occasional beliefs that came and went by the millions as his perceptual experience changed.

But, it may be urged, this isolation of his humdrum beliefs from his science relies on an insupportable distinction between truths of observation and truths of theory;

all Democritus' beliefs are theory-laden, and since his theory is false, they are false. The reply is as follows: Granted that all observation beliefs are theory laden, why should we choose Democritus' *explicit*, sophisticated theory (couched in his *opinions*) as the theory with which to burden his quotidian observations? Note that the least theoretical compatriot of Democritus also had myriad of theory-laden observation beliefs—and was, in one sense, none the wiser for it. Why should we not suppose their observations are laden with the same theory? If Democritus forgot his theory, or changed his mind, his observational beliefs would be *largely* untouched. To the extent that his sophisticated theory played a discernible role in his routine behaviour and expectations and so forth, it would be quite appropriate to couch his humdrum beliefs in terms of the sophisticated theory, but this will not yield a *mainly false* catalogue of beliefs, since so few of his beliefs will be affected. (The effect of theory on observation is nevertheless often underrated. See Paul Churchland, *Scientific Realism and the Plasticity of Mind*, Cambridge University Press [1979], for dramatic and convincing examples of the tight relationship that can sometimes exist between theory and experience.) (The discussion in this note was distilled from a useful conversation with Paul and Patricia Churchland and Michael Stack.)

4. Patrick Hayes explores this application of Tarskian model theory to the semantics of mental representation in *The Naïve Physics Manifesto* (forthcoming).

5. This idea is the ancestor in effect of the species of different ideas lumped together under the rubric of de re belief. If one builds from this idea towards its scions one can see better the difficulties with them, and how to repair them.

Online resources:

Daniel Dennett
http://ase.tufts.edu/cogstud/~ddennett.htm

Publications Online:

http://ase.tufts.edu/cogstud/incpages/publctns.shtml

12

I am John's Brain[1]

Andy Clark[2]

I am John's[3] brain. In the flesh, I am just a rather undistinguished looking grey/white mass of cells. My surface is heavily convoluted and I am possessed of a fairly differentiated internal structure. John and I are on rather close and intimate terms; indeed, sometimes it is hard to tell us apart. But at times, John takes this intimacy a little too far. When that happens, he gets very confused about my role and functioning. He imagines that I organize and process information in ways which echo his own perspective on the world. In short, he thinks that his thoughts are, in a rather direct sense, my thoughts. There is some truth to this of course. But things are really rather more complicated than John suspects, as I shall try to show.

In the first place, John is congenitally blind to the bulk of my daily activities. At best, he catches occasional glimpses and distorted shadows of my real work. Generally speaking, these fleeting glimpses portray only the products of my vast subterranean activity, rather than the processes which give rise to them. Such products include the play of mental images or the steps in a logical train of thought or flow of ideas.

John's access to these products is, moreover, itself a pretty rough and ready affair. What filters into his conscious awareness is somewhat akin to what gets on to the screen display of a personal computer. In both cases, what is displayed is just a specially tailored summary of the results of certain episodes of internal activity: results for which the user has some particular use. Evolution, after all, would not waste time and money (search & energy) to display to John a faithful record of inner goings-on unless they could help John to hunt, survive and reproduce. John, as a result, is appraised of the bare minimum of knowledge about my inner activities. All he needs to know is the overall significance of the upshot of a select few of these activities: that part of me is in a state which is associated with the presence of a dangerous predator and that flight is therefore indicated, and other things of that sort. What John gets from me is thus rather like what a driver gets from an electronic dashboard display: information pertaining to those few inner and outer parameters to which the gross activity of the agent can make a useful difference.

John, however, begs to differ. He thinks this is a crazy parallel since in his case there is no further agent to be informed by any 'dashboard display'. There is no 'driver' apart from me, his brain. But despite this undoubted fact, I insist that there is a dashboard display of sorts. The display consists of those select products of my activities which are able to play a role in those projects and decisions which the world at large ascribes to John-the-person (as opposed to those, like the maintenance of blood flow, ascribed not to John's decisions, but to John-the-biological-organism). The dashboard display thus consists of those products of my activity which are able to figure in what other humans would identify as John's plans, his choices and projects. Thus if one of my many sub-systems is appraised of some item of information, that item may or may not become available to support John's conscious planning and deliberate action. Information which is made available for such purposes can, of course, figure in John's on-going reflections on his own life and goals, while the rest, though often vital for John's continued success, remains invisible to John-the-agent. The fact that John has only limited access to my operations means, of course, that John can sometimes be unaware of the true causes of his own actions. In such cases, John is driven to create complex stories or narratives which try to make sense of his self-observed behaviors. This is a hard task, since the roots of much of that behavior lie, I am proud to report, in those other activities of mine to which John has no conscious access. As a result, his stories are often wildly imaginative (that is to say, false) attempts to make sense of his own activities on the restricted basis of the 'dashboard display' types of information.

And it gets worse. For John's reports, even of the favored 'dashboard display' products of my activity, are themselves filtered through the distorting lens of John's biased and limited vocabulary for reporting these facts to others. Thus John thinks (falsely) that introspection reveals the presence of entities he calls 'beliefs', others he calls 'desires', still others he calls 'hopes' and so on and so on. John is even inclined (in more philosophical moments) to picture these putative inner entities as sharing the basic structure of the very sentences he would use to report such facts to others. He thinks he finds in himself the belief that Rome is pretty, and the hope that St. Louis is pretty. And just as these sentences share a word 'pretty', so John believes the internal states which 'carry' the thoughts must share a component too. I do not know why John thinks this, although at times he has such a loose idea of a 'component' that what he says cannot help but be true. I assure you, however, that on any non-trivial reading, what he says is false. John should beware of confusing the structure of the language he uses to report his beliefs with the structure of my own encodings. I like to store information in ways which make my unseen labors easier and which come naturally given my evolutionary history—a proud and long one for most of which the recent fad of language-use had not even been invented. My modes of information storage and retrieval, I can safely say, bear no deep resemblance whatever to these new-fangled linguistic vehicles with which John is so misleadingly familiar.

A further complex of misapprehensions centers on the question of the provenance of thoughts. John thinks of me as the point source of the intellectual products he identifies as his thoughts. But, to put it crudely, I do not have John's thoughts. John has John's thoughts and I am just one item in the array of physical events and processes which enable that thinking to occur. John is an agent whose nature is fixed by a complex interplay between a mass of internal goings-on (including my activity) and a particular kind of physical embodiment and a certain embedding in the world. The combination of embodiment and embedding provides for persistent informational and physical couplings between John and his world; couplings which leave much of John's 'knowledge' out in the world and available for retrieval, transformation and use as and when required.

Take a simple example. A few days ago, John sat at his desk and worked rather hard for a sustained period of time. Eventually he got up and left his office, satisfied with his day's work. 'My brain', he reflected (for he prides himself on his physicalism), 'has done very well. It has come up with some neat ideas.' John's image of the events of the day depicted me as the point source of those ideas; ideas which he thinks he captured on paper as a mere convenience and a hedge against forgetting. I am, of course, grateful that John gives me so much credit. He attributes the finished intellectual products directly to me. But in this case, at least, the credit should be extended a little further. My role in the origination of these intellectual products is certainly a vital one: destroy me and the intellectual productivity will surely cease! But my role is more delicately constituted then John's simple image suggests. Those ideas of which he is so proud did not spring fully formed out of my activity. If truth be told, I acted rather as a mediating factor in some rather complex feedback loops encompassing John and selected chunks of his local environment. Bluntly, I spent the day in a variety of close and complex interactions with a number of external props. Without these, the finished intellectual products would never have taken shape. My role, as best I can recall, was to support John's re-reading of a bunch of old materials and notes, and to react to those materials by producing a few fragmentary ideas and criticisms. These small responses were stored as further marks on paper and in margins. Later on, I played a role in the re-organization of these marks on clean sheets of paper, adding new on-line reactions to the fragmentary ideas. The cycle of reading, responding and external re-organization was repeated again and again. At the end of the day, the 'good ideas' (with which John was so quick to credit me) emerged as the fruits of these repeated little interactions between me and the various external media. Credit thus belongs not so much to me as to the spatially and temporally extended process in which I played a role.

On reflection, John would probably agree to this description of my role on that day. But I would caution him that even this can be misleading. For so far I have allowed myself to speak as if I were a unified inner resource contributing to these interactive episodes. This is an illusion which the present literary device encourages and one which John seems to share. But once again, if truth be told, I am not one inner voice but many. I am so many inner voices, in fact, that the metaphor of the inner voice must itself mislead. For it surely suggests inner sub-agencies of some sophistication and perhaps possessed of a rudimentary kind of self-consciousness. In reality, I consist only of multiple mindless streams of highly parallel and often relatively independent computational processes. I am not a mass of little agents so much as a mass of non-agents, tuned and responsive to proprietary inputs and cleverly orchestrated by evolution so as to yield successful purposive behavior in most daily settings. My single voice, then, is no more than a literary conceit.

At root, John's mistakes are all variations on a single theme. He thinks that I see the world as he does, that I parcel things up as he would, that I think the way he would report his thoughts. None of this is the case. I am not the inner echo of John's conceptualizations. Rather, I am their somewhat alien source. To see just how alien I can be, John need only reflect on some of the rather extraordinary and unexpected ways that damage to brains like me can affect the cognitive profiles of beings like John. Damage to me could, for example, result in the selective impairment of John's capacity to recall the names of small manipulable objects, yet leave unscathed his capacity to name larger-scale ones. The reason for this has to do with my storing and retrieving heavily visually-oriented information in ways distinct from those I deploy for heavily functionally-oriented information; the former mode helps pick out the large-scale items and the latter the small-scale ones. The point, at any rate, is that this facet of my internal organization is altogether alien to John—it respects needs, principles and opportunities of which John is blissfully unaware. Unfortunately, instead of trying to comprehend my modes of information storage in their own terms, John prefers simply to imagine that I organize my knowledge the way he, heavily influenced by the particular words in his language, organizes his. Thus he supposes that I store information in clusters which respect what he calls 'concepts'—generally, names which figure in his linguistic classifications of worldly events, states and processes. Here, as usual, John is far too quick to identify my organization with his own perspective. Certainly I store and access bodies of information;

bodies which together, if I am functioning normally, support a wide range of successful uses of words and a variety of interactions with the physical and social worlds. But the 'concepts' which so occupy John's imagination correspond only to public names for grab-bags of knowledge and abilities whose neural underpinnings are in fact many and various. John's 'concepts' do not correspond to anything especially unified as far as I am concerned. And why should they? The situation is rather like that of a person who can build a boat. To speak of the ability to build a boat is to use a simple phrase to ascribe a whole panoply of skills whose cognitive and physical underpinnings are highly various. The unity exists only insofar as that particular grab-bag of cognitive and physical skills has special significance for a community of sea-faring agents. John's 'concepts', it seems to me, are just like that: names for complexes of skills whose unity rests not on facts about me, but on facts about John's way of life.

John's tendency to hallucinate his own perspective on to me extends to his conception of my knowledge of the external world. John walks around and feels as if he commands a stable, 3D image of his immediate surroundings. John's feelings notwithstanding, I command no such thing. I register small regions of detail in rapid succession as I fixate first on this, and then on that aspect of the visual scene. And I do not trouble myself to store all that detail in some internal model in need of constant maintenance and updating. Instead, I am adept at re-visiting parts of the scene so as to re-create detailed knowledge as and when required. As a result of this trick, and others, John has such a fluent capacity to negotiate his local environment that he thinks he commands a constant inner vision of the detail of his surroundings. In truth, what John sees has more to do with the abilities I confer on him to interact constantly, in real time, with rich external sources of information than with the kind of passive and enduring registration of information in terms of which he conceives his own seeings.

The sad fact, then, is that almost nothing about me is the way John imagines it to be. We remain strangers despite our intimacy (or perhaps because of it). John's language, introspections, and over-simplistic physicalism incline him to identify my organization too closely with his own limited perspective. He is thus blind to my fragmentary, opportunistic and generally alien nature. He forgets that I am in large part a survival-oriented device which greatly pre-dates the emergence of linguistic abilities, and that my role in promoting conscious and linguaform cognition is just a recent sideline. This sideline is, of course, a major root of his misconceptions. Possessed as John is of such a magnificent vehicle for the compact and communicable expression of knowledge, he often mistakes the forms and conventions of that vehicle for the structure of thought itself.

But hope springs eternal (more or less). I am of late heartened by the emergence of new investigative techniques such as non-invasive brain imaging, the study of artificial neural networks, and the use of real-world robotics. Such techniques bode well for a better understanding of the very complex relations between my activity, the local environment, and the patch-work construction of the sense of self. In the meantime, just bear in mind that despite our intimacy, John really knows very little about me. Think of me as the Martian in John's head.

NOTES

1. The ideas and themes pursued in this little fantasy owe much to the visions of P. M. and P. S. Churchland, Daniel Dennett, Marvin Minsky, Gilbert Ryle, John Haugeland and Rodney Brooks. In bringing these themes together I have tried for maximum divergence between agent- and brain-level facts. I do not mean to claim dogmatically that current neuroscience unequivocally posits quite such a radical divergence. Several of the issues on which I allow the brain to take a stand remain the subject of open neuroscientific debate. For a taste of the debate, see P. S. Churchland and T. J. Sejnowski, *The Computational Brain* (Cambridge, MA: MIT Press, 1992) and P. S. Churchland, V. S. Ramachandran and T. J. Sejnowski, "A critique of pure vision", in *Large-scale Neuronal Theories of the Brain*, ed. C. Koch and J. Davis (Cambridge, MA: MIT Press, 1994).

Explicit supporting references seemed out of place given the literary conceit adopted, but they would include especially: D. Dennett, *Brainstorms* (Cambridge, MA: MIT Press, 1980), D. Dennett, *Consciousness Explained* (Boston, MA: Little Brown, 1991), M. Minsky, *The Society of Mind* (New York: Simon & Schuster, 1985), P. M. Churchland, *A Neurocomputational Perspective* (Cambridge, MA: MIT Press, 1989), J. Haugeland, "Mind embodied and embedded", in *Mind and Cognition: Proceedings of the First International Conference on Mind and Cognition,* ed. Yu-Houng Houng (Taipei, Taiwan: Academia Sinica, to appear), R. Brooks, "Intelligence without representation", *Artificial Intelligence*, 41 (1991), pp. 139–59, G. Ryle, *The Concept of Mind* (London: Hutchinson, 1949) and C. Warrington and R. McCarthy, 'Categories of knowledge; further fractionations and an attempted integration', *Brain*, 110 (1987), pp. 1273–96.

For my own pursuit of some of these themes, see: A. Clark, *Associative Engines*: *Connectionism, Concepts and Representational Change* (Cambridge, MA: MIT Press, 1993) and A. Clark, 'Moving minds: situating content in the service of real-time success', in *Philosophical Perspectives*, 10, ed. J. Tomberlin (Atascadero, CA: Ridgeway, forthcoming).

2. Thanks to Daniel Dennett, Joseph Goguen, Keith Sutherland, David Chalmers and an anonymous referee for support, advice and suggestions.

3. Or Mary's, or Mariano's, or Pepa's. The choice of the classic male English name is intended only as a gentle reference to those old *Readers Digest* articles with titles like, "I am John's Liver," "I am John's Kidney," etc.

Online resources:

Andy Clark
www.cogs.indiana.edu/people/homepages/clark.html

III

ARTIFICIAL INTELLIGENCE

Research in **Artificial Intelligence** (AI) relies on a **functionalist** view of the mind, such as that presented by Alan Turing, and utilizes computer programs to *model* human cognitive processes. The interesting question arising as we look at debate about this research is the very significance of this aforementioned "modeling" in AI research. The answer might seem obvious: A model is distinct from whatever it is a model *of* in some manner. Yet, this is precisely where philosophical debate regarding AI begins. The functionalist account of the mind, as we have seen in Turing's paper, claims that all there is to cognitive process is the "program." Different kinds of matter, suitably organized, can implement a mind program. For a functionalist, an artificially intelligent computer is intelligent—if it can pass the **Turing Test**, performing functions indistinguishable from its human counterparts. It is "artificial" insofar as it is man-made, yet for the functionalist, at least in principle, a mind program is run on the material human brain just as it would be run on a computer. The first two papers in the section present a classic debate on AI in which philosophers assess whether or not a machine can truly think as humans do.

John Searle challenges the view he describes as "Strong AI," the thesis that a machine can be said to think by virtue of its implementing the right program, through a **thought experiment**, "the Chinese room argument." He asks us to consider a man with virtually no knowledge of Chinese who is placed in a room with a basket of Chinese symbols and a rule book telling him which Chinese symbols to match with others solely on the basis of their shape. The man uses the rule book to exchange symbols with people outside the room, and the rule book is written so that his answers to their questions are indistinguishable from those a native Chinese speaker would give on the basis of understanding the language. He, thus, performs just like an appropriately programmed computer, formally manipulating symbols in such a way as to pass the **Turing Test** with respect to the task. Yet, Searle inquires, "Does this man understand Chinese?" It seems to Searle (and others) that the answer is clearly no. Searle contends that if this is the case, his thought experiment shows us that formal symbol manipulation, the very heart of computer programming (whether in serial or parallel architecture), is insufficient for understanding a language—for "**semantics**," grasping the meanings of words. Just as the man in the Chinese room can manipulate symbols (perform **syntactical operations** with them) but does not understand their meaning, an artificially intelligent computer does the same. It cannot be said to think. Searle finds that the human mind is in a distinctive position when it comes to understanding, as the human brain (biologically) causes the mind. The specificity of this causal relationship makes it much more difficult for any other kind of system made of any other sort of material to possess the capacities our minds have, such as understanding language. Other beings' "hardware" would need to have the same sort of causal powers that the human brain has to be said to think. Strong AI, in other words, sets the standards much too low for "intelligence."

Paul and Patricia Churchland respond to Searle's Chinese room argument. They find it to be **question-begging**—assuming what he is seeking to prove. The question as to whether formal symbol manipulation (syntactical operations) is constitutive and sufficient for understanding is the very point at issue. (This is Searle's third axiom.) It is wrong to think that Searle's point in the Chinese room argument settles this question. The Churchlands illustrate their criticism with a thought experiment of their own taken from the history of science, the "luminous room argument," which reframes the Chinese room argument in terms of the 1864 discovery by James Maxwell that light and electromagnetic waves are identical, yet prior to further research that discovered the systematic parallels between the properties of light and those of electromagnetic waves. In the luminous room argument, the manipulation of electromagnetic forces does not intuitively appear to be constitutive of luminescence, just as Searle finds that the manipulation of symbols in the Chinese room as not comprising understanding. Yet, the **skeptic** running the luminous room argument against James Maxwell would turn out to be wrong. Scientific research settled the matter concerning what constituted light, and the Churchlands believe that, likewise, ongoing research will have to settle the question of whether symbol manipulation is constitutive of thought. The Churchlands agree with Searle that the **Turing Test** is inadequate to determine intelligence. The input-output relations must be the right ones, and not just any material can achieve this; yet the Churchlands also reject the Turing Test for different reasons than Searle's. They find that experimentally it fails to distinguish adequately between different computational strategies and architectures, some of which are better than others—the Turing Test does not capture these differences.

The final selection for this section is "The Practical Requirements for Making a Conscious Robot" by Daniel Dennett. In this article, Dennett explores AI and the possibility of building a conscious robot with both **skepticism** and optimism. His optimism comes from the fact that he finds fault with the classic philosophical objections to AI and outlines why he thinks none of these objections need dissuade us from this path of research. His skepticism is a scientist's skepticism. A **scientific hypothesis** must be confirmed or falsified through experimental observation. A scientist cannot know for sure at the start of an experiment what the outcome will be. Dennett supposes, however, that actual research will help us determine the real from the apparent difficulties in this line of research and settle our **intuitions** as to what counts as a conscious being.

Toward this goal, Dennett explains the Cog with which he is involved. Cog is a robot built by a team of MIT researchers, that/who is unusual in that it/he is not simply a computer simulation of human cognitive processes but also has been designed to interact with its/his environment—to perceive, establish relationships with human beings, and learn on its/his own. In this way the MIT researchers have taken into account many of the objections raised against AI research. For Dennett, Cog is an experiment through which we may be able to evaluate philosophical thought experiments of the past. If Cog turns out to be capable of acquiring a language through which it/he communicates effectively, things matter to it/him, and it/he becomes, like humans, a reliable and best source of information about itself/himself, we may find it/him a great aid to answering philosophical questions about human consciousness.

13

Is the Brain's Mind a Computer?

John Searle

Can a machine think? Can a machine have conscious thoughts in exactly the same sense that you and I have? If by "machine" one means a physical system capable of performing certain functions (and what else can one mean?), then humans are machines of a special biological kind, and humans can think, and so of course machines can think. And, for all we know, it might be possible to produce a thinking machine out of different materials altogether—say, out of silicon chips or vacuum tubes. Maybe it will turn out to be impossible, but we certainly do not know that yet.

In recent decades, however, the question of whether a machine can think has been given a different interpretation entirely. The question that has been posed in its place is, could a machine think just by virtue of implementing a computer program? Is the program by itself constitutive of thinking? This is a completely different question because it is not about the physical, causal properties of actual or possible physical systems but rather about the abstract, computational properties of formal computer programs that can be implemented in any sort of substance at all, provided only that the substance is able to carry the program.

A fair number of researchers in artificial intelligence (AI) believe the answer to the second question is yes; that is, they believe that by designing the right programs with the right inputs and outputs, they are literally creating minds. They believe furthermore that they have a scientific test for determining success or failure: the Turing test devised by Alan M. Turing, the founding father of artificial intelligence. The Turing test, as currently understood, is simply this: if a computer can perform in such a way that an expert cannot distinguish its performance from that of a human who has a certain cognitive ability—say, the ability to do addition or to understand Chinese—then the computer also has the ability. So the goal is to design programs that will simulate human cognition in such a way as to pass the Turing test. What is more, such a program would not merely be a model of the mind; it would literally be a mind, in the same sense that a human mind is a mind.

By no means does every worker in artificial intelligence accept so extreme a view. A more cautious approach is to think of computer models as being useful in studying the mind in the same way that they are useful in studying the weather, economics or molecular biology. To distinguish these two approaches, I call the first strong AI and second weak AI. It is important to see just how bold an approach strong AI is. Strong AI claims that thinking is merely the manipulation of formal symbols, and that is exactly what the computer does: manipulate formal symbols. This view is often summarized by saying, "The mind is to the brain as the program is to the hardware."

Strong AI is unusual among theories of the mind in at least two respects: it can be stated clearly, and it admits of a simple and decisive refutation. The refutation is one that any person can try for himself or herself. Here is how it goes. Consider a language you don't understand. In my case, I do not understand Chinese. To me Chinese writing looks like so many meaningless squiggles.

Now suppose I am placed in a room containing baskets full of Chinese symbols. Suppose also that I am given a rule book in English for matching Chinese symbols with other Chinese symbols. The rules identify the symbols entirely by their shapes and do not require that I understand any of them. The rules might say such things as, "Take a squiggle-squiggle sign from basket number one and put it next to a squoggle-squoggle sign from basket number two". Imagine that people outside the room who understand Chinese hand in small bunches of symbols and that in response I manipulate the symbols according to the rule book and hand back more small bunches of symbols. Now, the rule book is the "computer program". The people who wrote it are "programmers," and I am the "computer". The baskets full of symbols are the "data base", the small bunches that are handed in to me are "questions" and the bunches I then hand out are "answers".

Now suppose that the rule book is written in such a way that my "answers" to the "questions" are indistinguishable from those of a native Chinese speaker. For example, the people outside might hand me some symbols that unknown to me mean, "What's your favorite color?" and I might after going through the rules give back symbols that, also unknown to me, mean, "My favorite is blue, but I also like green a lot." I satisfy the Turing test for understanding Chinese. All the same, I am totally ignorant of Chinese. And there is no way I could come to understand Chinese in the system as described, since there is no way that I can learn the meanings of any of the symbols. Like a computer, I manipulate symbols, but I attach no meaning to the symbols.

The point of the thought experiment is this: if I do not understand Chinese solely on the basis of running a computer program for understanding Chinese, then neither does any other digital computer solely on that basis. Digital computers merely manipulate formal symbols according to rules in the program.

What goes for Chinese goes for other forms of cognition as well. Just manipulating the symbols is not by itself enough to guarantee cognition, perception, understanding, thinking and so forth. And since computers, qua computers, are symbol-manipulating devices, merely running the computer program is not enough to guarantee cognition.

This simple argument is decisive against the claims of strong AI. The first premise of the argument simply states the formal character of a computer program. Programs are defined in terms of symbol manipulations, and the symbols are purely formal, or "syntactic". The formal character of the program, by the way, is what makes computers so powerful. The same program can be run on an indefinite variety of hardwares, and one hardware system can run an indefinite range of computer programs. Let me abbreviate this "axiom" as

AXIOM 1. COMPUTER PROGRAMS ARE FORMAL (SYNTACTIC).

This point is so crucial that it is worth explaining in more detail. A digital computer processes information by first encoding it in the symbolism that the computer uses and then manipulating the symbols through a set of precisely stated rules. These rules constitute the program. For example, in Turing's early theory of computers, the symbols were simply 0's and 1's, and the rules of the program said such things as, "print a 0 on the tape, move one square to the left and erase a 1." The astonishing thing about computers is that any information that can be stated in a language can be encoded in such a system, and any information-processing task that can be solved by explicit rules can be programmed.

Two further points are important. First, symbols and programs are purely abstract notions: they have no essential physical properties to define them and can be implemented in any physical medium whatsoever. The 0's and 1's, qua symbols, have no essential physical properties and a fortiori have no physical, causal properties. I emphasize this point because it is tempting to identify computers with some specific technology—say, silicon chips and to think that the issues are about the physics of silicon chips or to think that syntax identifies some physical phenomenon that might have as yet unknown causal powers, in the way that actual physical phenomena such as electromagnetic radiation or hydrogen atoms have physical, causal properties. The second point is that symbols are manipulated without reference to any meanings. The symbols of the program can stand for anything the programmer or user wants. In this sense the program has syntax but no semantics.

The next axiom is just a reminder of the obvious fact that thoughts, perceptions, understandings and so forth have a mental content. By virtue of their content they can be about objects and states of affairs in the world. If the content involves language, there will be syntax in addition to semantics, but linguistic understanding requires at least a semantic framework. If, for example, I am thinking about the last presidential election, certain words will go through my mind, but the words are about the election only because I attach specific meanings to these words, in accordance with my knowledge of English. In this respect they are unlike Chinese symbols for me. Let me abbreviate this axiom as

AXIOM 2. HUMAN MINDS HAVE MENTAL CONTENTS (SEMANTICS).

Now let me add the point that the Chinese room demonstrated. Having the symbols by themselves—just having the syntax—is not sufficient for having the semantics. Merely manipulating symbols is not enough to guarantee knowledge of what they mean. I shall abbreviate this as

AXIOM 3. SYNTAX BY ITSELF IS NEITHER CONSTITUTIVE OF NOR SUFFICIENT FOR SEMANTICS.

At one level this principle is true by definition. One might, of course, define the terms syntax and semantics differently. The point is that there is a distinction between formal elements, which have no intrinsic meaning or content, and those phenomena that have intrinsic content. From these premises it follows that

CONCLUSION 1. PROGRAMS ARE NEITHER CONSTITUTIVE OF NOR SUFFICIENT FOR MINDS. AND THAT IS JUST ANOTHER WAY OF SAYING THAT STRONG AI IS FALSE.

It is important to see what is proved and not proved by this argument.

First, I have not tried to prove that "a computer cannot think." Since anything that can be simulated computationally can be described as a computer, and since our brains can at some levels be simulated, it follows trivially that our brains are computers and they certainly can think. But from the fact that a system can be simulated by symbol manipulation and the fact that it is thinking, it does not follow that the thinking is equivalent to formal symbol manipulation.

Second, I have not tried to show that only biologically based systems like our brains can think. Right now those are the only systems we know for a fact can think, but we might find other systems in the universe that can produce conscious thoughts, and we might even come to be able to create thinking systems artificially. I regard this issue as up for grabs.

Third, strong AI's thesis is not that, for all we know, computers with the right programs might be thinking, that they might have some as yet undetected psychological properties; rather it is that they must be thinking because that is all there is to thinking.

Fourth, I have tried to refute strong AI so defined. I have tried to demonstrate that the program by itself is not constitutive of thinking because the program is purely a matter of formal symbol manipulation—and we know independently that symbol manipulations by themselves are not sufficient to guarantee the presence of meanings. That is the principle on which the Chinese room argument works.

I emphasize these points here partly because it seems to me the Churchlands [see "Could a Machine Think?" in this volume] have not quite understood the issues. They think that strong AI is claiming that computers might turn out to think and I am denying this possibility on commonsense grounds. But that is not the claim of strong AI, and my argument against it has nothing to do with commonsense.

I will have more to say about their objections later. Meanwhile I should point out that, contrary to what the Churchlands suggest, the Chinese room argument also refutes any strong AI claims made for the new parallel technologies that are inspired by and modeled on neural networks. Unlike the traditional von Neumann computers, which proceed in a step-by-step fashion, these systems have many computational elements that operate in parallel and interact with one another according to rules inspired by neurobiology. Although the results are still modest, these "parallel distributed processing" or "connectionist" models raise useful questions about how the complex, parallel networks systems like those in brains might actually function in the production of intelligent behavior.

The parallel, "brainlike" character of the processing, however, is irrelevant to the purely computational aspects of the process. Any function that can be computed on a parallel machine can also be computed on a serial machine. Indeed, because parallel machines are still rare, connectionist programs are usually run on traditional serial machines. Parallel processing, then, does not afford a way around the Chinese room argument.

What is more, the connectionist system is subject even on its own terms to a variant of the objections presented by the original Chinese room argument. Imagine that instead of a Chinese room, I have a Chinese gym: a hall containing many monolingual, English-speaking men. These men would carry out the same operations as the nodes and synapses in a connectionist architecture as described by the Churchlands, and the outcome would be the same as having one man manipulate symbols according to a rule book. No one in the gym speaks a word of Chinese, and there is no way for the system as a whole to learn the meanings of any Chinese words. Yet with the appropriate adjustments, the system could give the correct answers to Chinese questions.

There are, as I suggested earlier, interesting properties of the connectionist nets that enable them to simulate brain processes more accurately than traditional serial architecture does. But the advantages of parallel architecture for weak AI are quite irrelevant to the issues between the Chinese room argument and strong AI.

The Churchlands miss this point when they say that a big enough Chinese gym might have higher-level mental features that emerge from the size and complexity of the system, just as whole brains have mental features that are not had by individual neurons. That is, of course, a possibility, but it has nothing to do with computation. Computationally, serial and parallel systems are equivalent: any computation that can be done in parallel can be done in serial. If the man in the Chinese room is computationally equivalent to both, then if he does not understand Chinese solely by virtue of doing the computations, neither do they. The Churchlands are correct in saying that the original Chinese room argument was designed with traditional AI in mind but wrong in thinking that connectionism is immune to the argument. It applies to any computational system. You can't get semantically loaded thought contents from formal computations alone, whether they are done in serial or parallel; that is why the Chinese room argument refutes strong AI in any form.

Many people who are impressed by this argument are nonetheless puzzled about the differences between people and computers. If humans are, at least in a trivial sense, computers, and if humans have semantics, then why couldn't we give semantics to other computers? Why couldn't we program a Vax or cray so that it too would have thoughts and feelings? Or why couldn't some new computer technology overcome the gulf between form and content, between syntax and semantics? What, in fact, are the differences between animal brains and computer systems that enable the Chinese room argument to work against computers but not against brains?

The most obvious difference is that the processes that define something as a computer—computational processes—are completely independent of any reference to a specific type of hardware implementation. One could make a computer out of old beer cans strung together with wires and powered by windmills.

But when it comes to brains, although science is largely ignorant of how brains function to produce mental states, one is struck by the extreme specificity of the anatomy and the physiology. Where some understanding exists of how brain processes produce mental phenomena—for example, pain, thirst, vision, smell—it is clear that specific neurobiological processes are involved. Thirst, at least of certain kinds, is caused by certain types of neuron firings in the hypothalamus, which in turn are caused by the action of a specific peptide, angiotensin II. The causation is from the "bottom up" in the sense that lower-level neuronal processes cause higher-level mental phenomena. Indeed, as far as we know, every "mental" event, ranging from feelings of thirst to thoughts of mathematical theorems and memories of childhood, is caused by specific neurons firing in specific neural architectures.

But why should this specificity matter? After all, neuron firings could be simulated on computers that had a completely different physics and chemistry from that of the brain. The answer is that the brain does not merely instantiate a formal pattern or program (it does that, too), but it also causes mental events by virtue of specific neurobiological processes. Brains are specific biological organs, and their specific biochemical properties enable them to cause consciousness and other sorts of mental phenomena. Computer simulation of brain processes provide models of the formal aspects of these processes. But the simulation should not be confused with duplication. The computational model of mental processes is no more real than the computational model of any other natural phenomenon.

One can imagine a computer simulation of the action of peptides in the hypothalamus that is accurate down to the last synapse. But equally one can imagine a computer simulation of the oxidation of hydrocarbons in a car engine or the action of digestive processes in a stomach when it is digesting pizza. And the simulation is no more the real thing in the case of the brain than it is in the case of the car or the stomach. Barring miracles, you could not run your car by doing a computer simulation of the oxidation of gasoline, and you could not digest pizza by running the program that simulates such digestion. It seems obvious that a simulation of cognition will not produce the effects of the neurobiology of cognition.

All mental phenomena, then, are caused by neurophysiological processes in the brain. Hence,

AXIOM 4. BRAINS CAUSE MINDS.

In conjunction with my earlier derivation, I immediately derive, trivially,

CONCLUSION 2: ANY OTHER SYSTEM CAPABLE OF CAUSING MINDS WOULD HAVE TO HAVE CAUSAL POWERS (AT LEAST) EQUIVALENT TO BRAINS.

This is like saying that if an electrical engine is to be able to run a car as fast as a gas engine, it must have (at least) an equivalent power output. This conclusion says nothing about the mechanisms. As a matter of fact, cognition is a biological phenomenon: mental states and processes are caused by brain processes. This does not imply that only a biological system could think, but it does imply that any alternative system, whether made of silicon, beer cans or whatever, would have to have the relevant causal capacity equivalent to those of brains. So now I can derive

CONCLUSION 3: ANY ARTIFACT THAT PRODUCED MENTAL PHENOMENA, ANY ARTIFICIAL BRAIN, WOULD HAVE TO BE ABLE TO DUPLICATE THE SPECIFIC CAUSAL POWERS OF BRAINS, AND IT COULD NOT DO JUST THAT BY RUNNING A FORMAL PROGRAM.

Furthermore, I can derive an important conclusion about human brains:

CONCLUSION 4: THE WAY THAT HUMAN BRAINS ACTUALLY PRODUCE MENTAL PHENOMENA CANNOT BE SOLELY BY VIRTUE OF RUNNING A COMPUTER PROGRAM.

I first presented the Chinese room parable in the pages of *Behavioral and Brain Sciences* in 1980, where it appeared, as is the practice of the journal, along with peer commentary, in this case, 26 commentaries. Frankly, I think the point it makes is rather obvious, but to my surprise the publication was followed by a further flood of objections that—more surprisingly—continues to the present day. The Chinese room argument clearly touched some sensitive nerve.

The thesis of strong AI is that any system whatsoever—whether it is made of beer cans, silicon chips or toilet paper—not only might have thoughts and feelings but *must* have thoughts and feelings, provided only that it implements the right program, with the right inputs and outputs. Now, that is a profoundly antibiological view, and one would think that people in AI would be glad to abandon it. Many of them, especially the younger generation, agree with me, but I am amazed at the number and vehemence of the defenders. Here are some of the common objections.

a. In the Chinese room you really do understand Chinese, even though you don't know it. It is, after all, possible to understand something without knowing that one understands it.
b. You don't understand Chinese, but there is an (unconscious) subsystem that does. It is, after all, possible to have unconscious mental states, and there is no reason why your understanding of Chinese should not be wholly unconscious.
c. You don't understand Chinese, but the whole room does. You are like a single neuron in the brain, and just as such a single neuron by itself cannot understand but only contributes to the understanding of the whole system, you don't understand, but the whole system does.
d. Semantics doesn't exist anyway; there is only syntax. It is a kind of pre-scientific illusion to suppose that there exist in the brain some mysterious "mental contents," "thought processes" or "semantics." All that exists in the brain is the same sort of syntactic symbol manipulation that goes on in computers. Nothing more.
e. You are not really running the computer program—you only think you are. Once you have a conscious agent going through the steps of the program, it ceases to be a care of implementing a program at all.
f. Computers would have semantics and not just syntax if their inputs and outputs were put in appropriate causal relation to the rest of the world. Imagine that we put the computer into a robot, attached television cameras to the robot's head, installed transducers connecting the television messages to the computer and had the computer output operate the robot's arms and legs. Then the whole system would have a semantics.
g. If the program simulated the operation of the brain of a Chinese speaker, then it would understand Chinese. Suppose that we simulated the brain of a Chinese person at the level of neurons. Then surely such a system would understand Chinese as well as any Chinese person's brain.

And so on.

All of these arguments share a common feature: they are all inadequate because they fail to come to grips with the actual Chinese room argument. That argument rests on the distinction between the formal symbol manipulation that is done by the computer and the mental contents biologically produced by the brain, a distinction I have abbreviated—I hope not misleadingly—as the distance between syntax and semantics. I will not repeat my answers to all of these objections, but it will help to clarify the issues if I explain the weaknesses of the most widely held objection, argument c—what I call the systems reply. (The brain simulator reply, argument g, is another popular one, but I have already addressed that one in the previous section.)

The systems reply asserts that of course you don't understand Chinese but the whole system—you, the room, the rule book, the bushel baskets full of symbols—does. When I first heard this explanation, I asked one of its proponents, "Do you mean the room understands Chinese?" His answer was yes. It is a daring move, but aside from its implausibility, it will not work on purely logical grounds. The point of the original argument was that symbol shuffling by itself does not give any access to the meanings of the symbols. But this is as much true of the whole room as it is of the person inside. One can see this point by extending the thought experiment. Imagine that I memorize the contents of the baskets and the rule book, and I do all the calculations in my head. You can even imagine that I work out in the open. There is nothing in the "system" that is not in me, and since I don't understand Chinese, neither does the system.

The Churchlands in their companion piece produce a variant of the systems reply by imagining an amusing analogy. Suppose that someone said that light could not be electromagnetic because if you shake a bar magnet in a dark room, the system still will not give off visible light. Now, the Churchlands ask, is not the Chinese room argument just like that? Does it not merely say that if you shake Chinese symbols in a semantically dark room, they will not give off the light of Chinese understanding? But just as later investigation showed that light was entirely constituted by electromagnetic radiation, could not later investigation also show that semantics are entirely constituted of syntax? Is this not a question for further scientific investigation?

Arguments from analogy are notoriously weak, because before one can make the argument work, one has to establish that the two cases are truly analogous. And there I think they are not.

The account of light in terms of electromagnetic radiation is a causal story right down to the ground. It is a causal account of the physics of electromagnetic radiation. But the analogy with formal symbols fails because formal symbols have no physical, causal powers. The only power that symbols have, qua symbols, is the power to cause the next step in the program when the machine is running. And there is no question of waiting on further research to reveal the physical, causal properties of 0's and 1's. The only relevant properties of 0's and 1's are abstract computational properties, and they are already well known.

The Churchlands complain that I am "begging the question" when I say that uninterpreted formal symbols are not identical to mental contents. Well I certainly did not spend much time arguing for it, because I take it as a logical truth. As with any logical truth, one can quickly see that it is true, because one gets inconsistencies if one tries to imagine the converse. So let us try it. Suppose that in the Chinese room some undetectable Chinese thinking really is going on. What exactly is supposed to make the manipulation of the syntactic elements into specifically Chinese thought contents? Well, after all, I am assuming that the programmers were Chinese speakers, programming the system to process Chinese information.

Fine. But now imagine that as I am sitting in the Chinese room shuffling the Chinese symbols, I get bored with just shuffling the—to me—meaningless symbols. So, suppose that I decide to interpret the symbols as standing for moves in a chess game. Which semantics is the system giving off now? Is it giving off a Chinese semantics or a chess semantics, or both simultaneously? Suppose there is a third person looking in through the window, and she decides that the symbol manipulations can all be interpreted as stock-market predictions. And so on. There is no limit to the number of semantic interpretations that can be assigned to the symbols because, to repeat, the symbols are purely formal. They have no intrinsic semantics.

Is there any way to rescue the Churchlands' analogy from incoherence? I said above that formal symbols do not have causal properties. But of course the program will always be implemented in some hardware or another, and the hardware will have specific physical, causal powers. And any real computer will give off various phenomena. My computers, for example, give off heat, and they make a humming noise and sometimes crunching sounds. So is there some logically compelling reason why they could not also give off consciousness? No. Scientifically, the idea is out of the question, but it is not something the Chinese room argument is supposed to refute, and it is not something that an adherent of strong AI would wish to defend, because any such giving off would have to derive from the physical features of the implementing medium. But the basic premise of strong AI is that the physical features of the implementing medium are totally irrelevant. What matters are programs, and programs are purely formal.

The Churchlands' analogy between syntax and electromagnetism, then, is confronted with a dilemma; either the syntax is construed purely formally in terms of its abstract mathematical properties, or it is not. If it is, then the analogy breaks down, because syntax so construed has no physical powers and hence no physical, causal powers. If, on the other hand, one is supposed to think in terms of the physics of the implementing medium, then there is indeed an analogy, but it is not one that is relevant to strong AI.

Because the points I have been making are rather obvious—syntax is not the same as semantics, brain processes cause mental phenomena—the question arises. How did we get into this mess? How could anyone have supposed that a computer simulation of a mental process must be the real thing? After all, the whole point of models is that they contain only certain features of the modeled domain and leave out the rest. No one expects to get wet in a pool filled with Ping-Pong ball models of water molecules. So why would anyone think a computer model of thought processes would actually think?

Part of the answer is that people have inherited a residue of behaviorist psychological theories of the past generation. The Turing test enshrines the temptation to think that if something behaves as if it had certain mental processes, then it must actually have those mental processes. And this is part of the behaviorists' mistaken assumption that in order to be scientific, psychology must confine its study to externally observable behavior. Paradoxically, this residual behaviorism is tied to a residual dualism. Nobody thinks that a computer simulation of digestion would actually digest anything, but where cognition is concerned, people are willing to believe in such a miracle because they fail to recognize that the mind is just as much a biological phenomenon as digestion. The mind, they suppose, is something formal and abstract, not a part of the wet and slimy stuff in our heads. The polemical literature in AI usually contains attacks on something the authors call dualism, but what they fail to see is that they themselves display dualism in a strong form, for unless one accepts the idea that the mind is completely independent of the brain or of any other physically specific system, one could not possibly hope to create minds just by designing programs.

Historically, scientific developments in the West that have treated humans as just a part of the ordinary physical, biological order have often been opposed by various rearguard actions. Copernicus and Galileo were opposed because they denied that the earth was the center of the universe; Darwin was opposed because he claimed that humans had descended from the lower animals. It is best to see strong AI as one of the last gasps of this antiscientific tradition, for it denies that there is anything essentially physical and biological about the human mind. The mind according to strong AI is independent of the brain.

NOTE

Reprinted by permission. Copyright © 1990 by Scientific American, Inc. All rights reserved.

Online resources:

John Searle
http://ist-socrates.berkeley.edu/~jsearle/

14

Could a Machine Think?

Paul and Patricia Churchland

Artificial intelligence research is undergoing a revolution, To explain how and why, and to put John R. Searle's argument in perspective, we first need a flashback.

By the early 1950's the old, vague question, Could a machine think? Had been replaced by the more approachable question, Could a machine that manipulated physical symbols according to structure-sensitive rules think? This question was an improvement because formal logic and computational theory had seen major developments in the preceding half-century. Theorists had come to appreciate the enormous power of abstract systems of symbols that undergo rule-governed transformations. If those systems could just be automated, then their abstract computational power, it seemed, would be displayed in a real physical system. This insight spawned a well-defined research program with deep theoretical underpinnings.

Could a machine think? There were many reasons for saying yes. One of the earliest and deepest reasons lay in two important results in computational theory. The first was Church's thesis, which states that every effectively computable function is recursively computable. Effectively computable means that there is a "rote" procedure for determining, in finite time, the output of the function for a given input. Recursively computable means more specifically that there is a finite set of operations that can be applied to a given input, and then applied again and again to the successive results of such applications, to yield the function's output in finite time. The notion of a rote procedure is nonformal and intuitive; thus, Church's thesis does not admit of a formal proof. But it does go to the heart of what it is to compute, and many lines of evidence converge in supporting it.

The second important result was Alan M. Turing's demonstration that any recursively computable function can be computed in finite time by a maximally simple sort of symbol manipulating machine that has come to be called a universal Turing machine. This machine is guided by a set of recursively applicable rules that are sensitive to the identity, order and arrangement of the elementary symbols it encounters as input.

These two results entail something remarkable, namely that a standard digital computer, given only the right program, a large enough memory and sufficient time, can compute any rule-governed input-output function. That is, it can display any systematic pattern of responses to the environment whatsoever.

More specifically, these results imply that a suitably programmed symbol-manipulating machine (hereafter, SM machine) should be able to pass the Turing test for conscious intelligence. The Turing test is a purely behavioral test for conscious intelligence, but it is a very demanding test even so. (Whether it is a fair test will be addressed below, where we shall also encounter a second and quite different "test" for conscious intelligence.) In the original version of the Turing test, the inputs to the SM machine are conversational questions and remarks typed into a console by you or me, and the outputs are typewritten responses from the SM machine. The machine passes this test for conscious intelligence if its responses cannot be discriminated from the typewritten responses of a real, intelligent person. Of course, at present no one knows the function that would produce the output behavior of a conscious person. But the Church and Turing results assure us that, whatever that (presumably effective) function might be, a suitable SM machine could compute it.

This is a significant conclusion, especially since Turing's portrayal of a purely teletyped interaction is an unnecessary restriction. The same conclusion follows even if the SM machine interacts with the world in more complex ways: by direct vision, real speech and so forth. After all, a more complex recursive function is still Turing-computable. The only remaining problem is to identify the undoubtedly complex function that governs the human pattern of response to the environment and then write the program (the set of recursively applicable rules) by which the SM machine will compute it. These goals form the fundamental research program of classical AI.

Initial results were positive. SM machines with clever programs performed a variety of ostensibly cognitive activities. They responded to complex instructions, solved complex arithmetic, algebraic and tactical problems, played checkers and chess, proved theorems and engaged in simple dialogue. Performance continued to improve with the appearance of larger memories and faster machines and with the use of longer and more cunning programs. Classical, or "program-writing," AI was a vigorous and successful research effort from almost every perspective. The occasional denial that an SM machine might eventually think appeared uninformed and ill motivated. The case for a positive answer to our title question was overwhelming.

There were a few puzzles, of course. For one thing SM machines were admittedly not very brainlike. Even here, however, the classical approach had a convincing answer. First, the physical material of any SM machine has nothing essential to do with what function it computes.

That is fixed by its program. Second, the engineering details of any machine's functional architecture are also irrelevant since different architectures running quite different programs can still be computing the same input-output function.

Accordingly, AI sought to find the input-output function characteristic of intelligence and the most efficient of the many possible programs for computing it. The idiosyncratic way in which the brain computes the function just doesn't matter, it was said. This completes the rationale for classical AI and for a positive answer to our title question. Could a machine think? There were also some arguments for saying no. Through the 1960's interesting negative arguments were relatively rare. The objection was occasionally made that thinking was a nonphysical process in an immaterial soul. But such dualistic resistance was neither revolutionarily nor explanatorily plausible. It had a negligible impact on AI research.

A quite different line of objection was more successful in gaining the AI community's attention. In 1972 Hubert L. Dreyfus published a book that was highly critical of the parade-case simulations of cognitive activity. He argued for their inadequacy as simulations of genuine cognition, and he pointed to a pattern of failure in these attempts. What they were missing, he suggested, was the vast store of inarticulate background knowledge every person possesses and the common-sense capacity for drawing on relevant aspects of that knowledge as changing circumstance demands. Dreyfus did not deny the possibility that an artificial physical system of some kind might think, but he was highly critical of the idea that this could be achieved solely by symbol manipulation at the hands of recursively applicable rules.

Dreyfus's complaints were broadly perceived within the AI community, and within the discipline of philosophy as well, as shortsighted and unsympathetic, as harping on the inevitable simplifications of a research effort still in its youth. These deficits might be real, but surely they were temporary. Bigger machines and better programs should repair them in due course. Time, it was felt, was on AI's side. Here again the impact on research was negligible.

Time was on Dreyfus's side as well: the rate of cognitive return on increasing speed and memory began to slacken in the late 1970s and early 1980s. The simulation of object recognition in the visual system, for example, proved computationally intensive to an unexpected degree. Realistic results required longer and longer periods of computer time, periods far in excess of what a real visual system requires. This relative slowness of the simulations was darkly curious; signal propagation in a computer is roughly a million times faster than in the brain, and the clock frequency of a computer's central processor is greater than any frequency found in the brain by a similarly dramatic margin. And yet, on realistic problems, the tortoise easily outran the hare. Furthermore, realistic performance required that the computer program have access to an extremely large knowledge base. Constructing the relevant knowledge base was problem enough, and it was compounded by the problem of how to access just the contextually relevant parts of that knowledge base in real time. As the knowledge base got bigger and better, the access problem got worse. Exhaustive search took too much time, and heuristics for relevance did poorly. Worries of the sort Dreyfus had raised finally began to take hold here and there even among AI researchers.

At about this time (1980) John Searle authored a new and quite different criticism aimed at the most basic assumption of the classical research program: the idea that the appropriate manipulation of structured symbols by the recursive application of structure-sensitive rules could constitute conscious intelligence.

Searle's argument is based on a thought experiment that displays two crucial features. First, he describes an SM machine that realizes, we are to suppose, an input-output function adequate to sustain a successful Turing test conversation conducted entirely in Chinese. Second, the internal structure of the machine is such that, however it behaves, an observer remains certain that neither the machine nor any part of it understands Chinese. All it contains is a monolingual English speaker following a written set of instructions for manipulating the Chinese symbols that arrive and leave through a mail slot. In short, the system is supposed to pass the Turing test, while the system itself lacks any genuine understanding of Chinese or real Chinese semantic content (see "Is the Brain's Mind a Computer Program?" by John R. Searle).

The general lesson drawn is that any system that merely manipulates physical symbols in accordance with structure-sensitive rules will be at best a hollow mock-up of real conscious intelligence, because it is impossible to generate "real semantics" merely by cranking away on "empty syntax". Here, we should point out, Searle is imposing a nonbehavioral test for consciousness: the elements of conscious intelligence must possess real semantic content. One is tempted to complain that Searle's thought experiment is unfair because his Rube Goldberg system will compute with absurd slowness. Searle insists, however, that speed is strictly irrelevant here. A slow thinker should still be a real thinker. Everything essential to the duplication of thoughts, as per classical AI, is said to be present in the Chinese room. Searle's paper provoked a lively reaction from AI researchers, psychologists and philosophers alike. On the whole, however, he was met with an even more hostile reception than Dreyfus had experienced. In his companion piece in this issue, Searle forthrightly lists a number of these critical responses. We think many of them are reasonable, especially those that "bite the bullet" by insisting that, although it is appallingly slow, the overall system of the room-plus contents does understand Chinese.

We think those are good responses, but not because we think that the room understands Chinese. We agree with Searle that it does not. Rather they are good responses because they reflect a refusal to accept the crucial third axiom of Searle's argument: "Syntax by itself is neither constitutive of nor sufficient for semantics". Perhaps this axiom is true, but Searle cannot rightly pretend to know that it is. Moreover, to assume its truth is tantamount to begging the question against the research program of classical AI, for that program is predicated on the very interesting assumption that if one can just set in motion an appropriately structured internal dance of syntactic elements, appropriately connected to inputs and outputs, it can produce the same cognitive states and achievements found in human beings.

The question-begging character of Searle's axiom 3 becomes clear when it is compared directly with his conclusion 1: "Programs are neither constitutive of nor sufficient for minds." Plainly, his third axiom is already carrying 90 percent of the weight of this almost identical conclusion. That is why Searle's thought experiment is devoted to shoring up axiom 3 specifically. That is the point of the Chinese room.

Although, the story of the Chinese room makes axiom 3 tempting to the unwary, we do not think it succeeds in establishing axiom 3, and we offer a parallel argument below in illustration of its failure. A single transparently fallacious instance of a disputed argument often provides far more insight than a book full of logic chopping.

Searle's style of skepticism has ample precedent in the history of science. The eighteenth-century Irish bishop George Berkeley found it unintelligible that compression waves in the air, by themselves, could constitute or be sufficient for objective sound. The English poet-artist William Blake and the German poet-naturalist Johann W. von Goethe found it inconceivable that small particles by themselves could constitute or be sufficient for the objective phenomenon of light. Even in this century, there have been people who found it beyond imagining that inanimate matter by itself, and however organized, could ever constitute or be sufficient for life. Plainly, what people can or cannot imagine often has nothing to do with what is or is not the case, even where the people involved are highly intelligent.

To see how this lesson applies to Searle's case, consider a deliberately manufactured parallel to his argument and its supporting thought experiment.

Axiom 1. Electricity and magnetism are forces.
Axiom 2. The essential property of light is luminance.
Axiom 3. Forces by themselves are neither constitutive of nor sufficient for luminance.

Conclusion 1. Electricity and magnetism are neither constitutive of nor sufficient for light. Imagine this argument raised shortly after James Clerk Maxwell's 1864 suggestion that light and electromagnetic waves are identical but before the world's full appreciation of the systematic parallels between the properties of light and the properties of electromagnetic waves. This argument could have served as a compelling objection to Maxwell's imaginative hypothesis, especially if it were accompanied by the following commentary in support of axiom 3. "Consider a dark room containing a man holding a bar magnet or charged object. If the man pumps the magnet up and down, then, according to Maxwell's theory of artificial luminance (AL), it will initiate a spreading circle of electromagnetic waves and will thus be luminous. But as all of us who have toyed with magnets or charged balls well know, their forces (or any other forces for that matter), even when set in motion, produce no luminance at all. It is inconceivable that you might constitute real luminance just by moving forces around!"

How should Maxwell respond to this challenge? He might begin by insisting that the "luminous room" experiment is a misleading display of the phenomenon of luminance because the frequency of oscillation of the magnet is absurdly low, too low by a factor of 10^{15}. This might well elicit the impatient response that frequency has nothing to do with it, that the room with the bobbing magnet already contains everything essential to light, according to Maxwell's own theory.

In response Maxwell might bite the bullet and claim, quite correctly, that the room really is bathed in luminance, albeit a grade or quality too feeble to appreciate. (Given the low frequency with which the man can oscillate the magnet, the wavelength of the electromagnetic waves produced is far too long and their intensity is much too weak for human retinas to respond to them.) But in the climate of understanding here contemplated—the 1860s—this tactic is likely to elicit laughter and hoots of derision. "Luminous room, my foot, Mr. Maxwell. It's pitch-black in there!"

Alas, poor Maxwell has no easy route out of this predicament. All he can do is insist on the following three points. First, axiom 3 of the above argument is false. Indeed, it begs the question despite its intuitive plausibility. Second, the luminous room experiment demonstrates nothing of interest one way or the other about the nature of light. And third, what is needed to settle the problem of light and the possibility of artificial luminance is an ongoing research program to determine whether under the appropriate conditions the behavior of electromagnetic waves does indeed mirror perfectly the behavior of light.

This is also the response that classical AI should give to Searle's argument. Even though Searle's Chinese room may appear to be "semantically dark," he is in no position to insist, on the strength of this appearance, that rule-governed symbol manipulation can never constitute semantic phenomena, especially when people have only an uninformed commonsense understanding of the semantic and cognitive phenomena that need to be explained. Rather than exploit one's understanding of these things, Searle's argument freely exploits one's ignorance of them.

With these criticisms of Searle's argument in place, we return to the question of whether the research program of classical AI has a realistic chance of solving the problem of conscious intelligence and of producing a machine that thinks. We believe that the prospects are poor, but we rest this opinion on reasons very different from Searle's. Our reasons derive from the specific performance failures of the classical research program in AI and from a variety of lessons learned from the biological brain and a new class of computational models inspired by its structure. We have already indicated some of the failures of classical AI regarding tasks that the brain performs swiftly and efficiently. The emerging consensus on these failures is that the functional architecture of classical SM machines is simply the wrong architecture for the very demanding jobs required.

What we need to know is this: How does the brain achieve cognition? Reverse engineering is a common practice in industry. When a new piece of technology comes on the market, competitors find out how it works by taking it apart and divining its structural rationale. In the case of the brain, this strategy presents an unusually stiff challenge. For the brain is the most complicated and sophisticated thing on the planet. Even so, the neurosciences have revealed much about the brain on a wide variety of structural levels. Three anatomic points will provide a basic contrast with the architecture of conventional electronic computers.

First, nervous systems are parallel machines, in the sense that signals are processed in millions of different pathways simultaneously. The retina, for example, presents its complex input to the brain not in chunks of eight, 16 or 32 elements, as in a desktop computer, but rather in the form of almost a million distinct signal elements arriving simultaneously at the target of the optic nerve (the lateral geniculate nucleus), there to be processed collectively, simultaneously and in one fell swoop. Second, the brain's basic processing unit, the neuron, is comparatively simple. Furthermore, its response to incoming signals is analog, not digital, inasmuch as its output spiking frequency varies continuously with its input signals. Third, in the brain axons projecting from one neuronal population to another are often matched by axons returning from their target population. These descending or recurrent projections allow the brain to modulate the character of its sensory processing. More important still, their existence makes the brain a genuine dynamical system whose continuing behavior is both highly complex and to some degree independent of its peripheral stimuli.

Highly simplified model networks have been useful in suggesting how real neural networks might work and in revealing the computational properties of parallel architectures. For example, consider a three-layer model consisting of neuronlike units fully connected by axonlike connections to the units at the next layer. An input stimulus produces some activation level in a given input unit, which conveys a signal of proportional strength along its "axon" to its many "synaptic" connections to the hidden units. The global effect is that a pattern of activations across the set of input units produces a distinct pattern of activations across the set of hidden units.

The same story applies to the output units. As before, an activation pattern across the hidden units produces a distinct activation pattern across the output units. All told, this network is a device for transforming any one of a great many possible input vectors (activation patterns) into a uniquely corresponding output vector. It is a device for computing a specific function. Exactly which function it computes is fixed by the global configuration of its synaptic weights.

There are various procedures for adjusting the weights so as to yield a network that computes almost any function—that is, any vector-to-vector transformation—that one might desire. In fact, one can even impose on it a function one is unable to specify, so long as one can supply a set of examples of the desired input-output pairs. This process, called "training up the network," proceeds by successive adjustment of the network's weights until it performs the input-output transformations desired.

Although this model network vastly oversimplifies the structure of the brain, it does illustrate several important ideas. First, a parallel architecture provides a dramatic speed advantage over a conventional computer, for the many synapses at each level perform many small computations simultaneously instead of in laborious sequence. This advantage gets larger as the number of neurons increases at each layer. Strikingly, the speed of processing is entirely independent of both the number of units involved in each layer and the complexity of the function they are computing. Each layer could have four units or a hundred million; as configuration of synaptic weights could be computing simple one-digit sums or second-order differential equations. It would make no difference. The computation time would be exactly the same.

Second, massive parallelism means that the system is fault-tolerant and functionally persistent; the loss of a few connections, even quite a few, has a negligible effect on the character of the overall transformation performed by the surviving network.

Third, a parallel system stores large amounts of information in a distributed fashion, any part of which can be accessed in milliseconds. That information is stored in the specific configuration of synaptic connection strengths, as shaped by past learning. Relevant information is "released" as the input vector passes through—and is transformed by that configuration of connections.

Parallel processing is not ideal for all types of computation. On tasks that require only a small input vector, but many millions of swiftly iterated recursive computations, the brain performs very badly, whereas classical SM machines excel. This class of computations is very large and important, so classical machines will always be useful, indeed, vital. There is, however, an equally large class of computations for which the brain's architecture is the superior technology. These are computations that typically confront living creatures; recognizing a predator's outline in a noisy environment; recalling instantly how to avoid its gaze, flee its approach or fend off its attack; distinguishing food from nonfood and mates from nonmates; navigating through a complex and ever-changing physical/social environment; and so on.

Finally, it is important to note that the parallel system described is not manipulating symbols according to structure sensitive rules. Rather, symbol manipulation appears to be just one of many cognitive skills that a network may or may not learn to display. Rule-governed symbol manipulation is not its basic mode of operation. Searle's argument against is directed against rule-governed SM machines; vector transformers of the kind we describe are therefore not threatened by his Chinese room argument even if it were sound, which we have found independent reason to doubt.

Searle is aware of parallel processors but thinks they too will be devoid of real semantic content. To illustrate their inevitable failure, he outlines a second thought experiment, the Chinese gym, which has a gymnasium full of people organized into a parallel network. From there his argument proceeds as in the Chinese room.

We find this second story far less responsive or compelling than his first. For one, it is irrelevant that no unit in his system understands Chinese, since the same is true of nervous systems; no neuron in my brain understands English, although my whole brain does. For another, Searle neglects to mention that his simulation (using one person per neuron, plus a fleet-footed child for each synaptic connection) will require at least 10 to the 14th people, since the human brain has 10 to the 11th neurons, each of which averages over 10 to the 3rd connections. His system will require the entire human populations of over 10,000 earths. One gymnasium will not begin to hold a fair simulation.

On the other hand, if such a system were to be assembled on a suitably cosmic scale, with all its pathways faithfully modeled on the human case, we might then have a large, slow, oddly made but still functional brain on our hands. In that case the default assumption is surely that, given proper inputs, it would think, not that it couldn't. There is no guarantee that its activity would constitute real thought, because the vector-processing theory sketched above may not be the correct theory of how brains work. But neither is there any a priori guarantee that it could not be thinking. Searle is once more mistaking the limits of his (or the reader's) current imagination for the limits on objective reality . . .

NOTE

Reprinted by permission. Copyright © 1990 by Scientific American, Inc. All rights reserved.

15

The Practical Requirements for Making a Conscious Robot

Daniel C. Dennett

1. ARE CONSCIOUS ROBOTS POSSIBLE "IN PRINCIPLE"?

It is unlikely, in my opinion, that anyone will ever make a robot that is conscious in just the way we human beings are. Presumably that prediction is less interesting than the reasons one might offer for it. They might be deep—conscious robots are in some way "impossible in principle"—or they might be trivial—for instance, conscious robots might simply cost too much to make. Nobody will ever synthesize a gall bladder out of atoms of the requisite elements, but I think it is uncontroversial that a gall bladder is nevertheless "just" a stupendous assembly of such atoms. Might a conscious robot be "just" a stupendous assembly of more elementary artifacts—silicon chips, wires, tiny motors and cameras—or would any such assembly, of whatever size and sophistication, have to leave out some special ingredient that is requisite for consciousness?

Let us briefly survey a nested series of reasons someone might advance for the impossibility of a conscious robot:

(1) Robots are purely material things, and consciousness requires immaterial mind-stuff. (Old-fashioned dualism.)

It continues to amaze me how attractive this position still is to many people. I would have thought a historical perspective alone would make this view seem ludicrous: over the centuries, every other phenomenon of initially "supernatural" mysteriousness has succumbed to an uncontroversial explanation within the commodious folds of physical science. Thales, the Pre-Socratic proto-scientist, thought the loadstone had a soul, but we now know better; magnetism is one of the best understood of physical phenomena, strange though its manifestations are. The "miracles" of life itself, and of reproduction, are now analyzed into the well-known intricacies of molecular biology. Why should consciousness be any exception? Why should the brain be the only complex physical object in the universe to have an interface with another realm of being? Besides, the notorious problems with the supposed transactions at that dualistic interface are as good as a reductio ad absurdum of the view. The phenomena of consciousness are an admittedly dazzling lot, but I suspect that dualism would never be seriously considered if there weren't such a strong undercurrent of desire to protect the mind from science, by supposing it composed of a stuff that is in principle uninvestigatable by the methods of the physical sciences.

But if you are willing to concede the hopelessness of dualism, and accept some version of materialism, you might still hold:

(2) Robots are inorganic (by definition), and consciousness can exist only in an organic brain.

Why might this be? Instead of just hooting this view off the stage as an embarrassing throwback to old-fashioned vitalism, we might pause to note that there is a respectable, if not very interesting, way of defending this claim. Vitalism is deservedly dead; as biochemistry has shown in matchless detail, the powers of organic compounds are themselves all mechanistically reducible and hence mechanistically reproducible at one scale or another in alternative physical media; but it is conceivable—if unlikely—that the sheer speed and compactness of biochemically engineered processes in the brain are in fact unreproducible in other physical media (Dennett, 1987). So there might be straightforward reasons of engineering that showed that any robot that could not make use of organic tissues of one sort or another within its fabric would be too ungainly to execute some task critical for consciousness. If making a conscious robot were conceived of as a sort of sporting event—like the America's Cup—rather than a scientific endeavor, this could raise a curious conflict over the official rules. Team A wants to use artificially constructed organic polymer "muscles" to move its robot's limbs, because otherwise the motor noise wreaks havoc with the robot's artificial ears. Should this be allowed? Is a robot with "muscles" instead of motors a robot within the meaning of the act? If muscles are allowed, what about lining the robot's artificial retinas with genuine organic rods and cones instead of relying on relatively clumsy color-tv technology?

I take it that no serious scientific or philosophical thesis links its fate to the fate of the proposition that a protein-free conscious robot can be made, for example. The standard understanding that a robot shall be made of metal, silicon chips, glass, plastic, rubber and such, is an expression of the willingness of theorists to bet on a simplification of the issues: their conviction is that the crucial functions of intelligence can be achieved by one high-level simulation or another, so that it would be no undue hardship to restrict themselves to these materials, the readily available cost-effective ingredients in any case. But if somebody were to invent some sort of cheap artificial neural network fabric that could usefully be spliced into various tight corners in a robot's control system, the embarrassing fact that this fabric was made of organic molecules would not and should not dissuade serious roboticists from using it—and simply taking on the burden of explaining to the uninitiated why this did not constitute "cheating" in any important sense.

I have discovered that some people are attracted by a third reason for believing in the impossibility of conscious robots.

(3) Robots are artifacts, and consciousness abhors an artifact; only something natural, born not manufactured, could exhibit genuine consciousness.

Once again, it is tempting to dismiss this claim with derision, and in some of its forms, derision is just what it deserves. Consider the general category of creed we might call origin essentialism: only wine made under the direction of the proprietors of Chateau Plonque counts as genuine Chateau Plonque; only a canvas every blotch on which was caused by the hand of Cézanne counts as a genuine Cézanne; only someone "with Cherokee blood" can be a real Cherokee. There are perfectly respectable reasons, eminently defensible in a court of law, for maintaining such distinctions, so long as they are understood to be protections of rights growing out of historical processes. If they are interpreted, however, as indicators of "intrinsic properties" that set their holders apart from their otherwise indistinguishable counterparts, they are pernicious nonsense. Let us dub origin chauvinism the category of view that holds out for some mystic difference (a difference of value, typically) due simply to such a fact about origin. Perfect imitation Chateau Plonque is exactly as good a wine as the real thing, counterfeit though it is, and the same holds for the fake Cézanne, if it is really indistinguishable by experts. And of course no person is intrinsically better or worse in any regard just for having or not having Cherokee (or Jewish, or African) "blood."

And to take a threadbare philosophical example, an atom-for-atom duplicate of a human being, an artifactual counterfeit of you, let us say, might not legally be you, and hence might not be entitled to your belongings, or

deserve your punishments, but the suggestion that such a being would not
be a feeling, conscious, alive person as genuine as any born of woman is pre-
posterous nonsense, all the more deserving of our ridicule because if taken
seriously it might seem to lend credibility to the racist drivel with which it
shares a bogus "intuition".

If consciousness abhors an artifact, it cannot be because being born gives
a complex of cells a property (aside from that historic property itself) that it
could not otherwise have "in principle". There might, however, be a question of practicality. We have just seen how, as a matter of exigent practicality,
it could turn out after all that organic materials were needed to make a conscious robot. For similar reasons, it could turn out that any conscious robot
had to be, if not born, at least the beneficiary of a longish period of infancy.
Making a fully-equipped conscious adult robot might just be too much
work. It might be vastly easier to make an initially unconscious or nonconscious "infant" robot and let it "grow up" into consciousness, more or less
the way we all do. This hunch is not the disreputable claim that a certain sort
of historic process puts a mystic stamp of approval on its product, but the
more interesting and plausible claim that a certain sort of process is the only
practical way of designing all the things that need designing in a conscious
being.

Such a claim is entirely reasonable. Compare it to the claim one might
make about the creation of Steven Spielberg's film, *Schindler's List*: it could
not have been created entirely by computer animation, without the filming
of real live actors. This impossibility claim must be false "in principle," since
every frame of that film is nothing more than a matrix of gray-scale pixels of
the sort that computer animation can manifestly create, at any level of detail
or "realism" you are willing to pay for. There is nothing mystical, however,
about the claim that it would be practically impossible to render the nuances
of that film by such a bizarre exercise of technology. How much easier it is,
practically, to put actors in the relevant circumstances, in a concrete simulation of the scenes one wishes to portray, and let them, via ensemble activity
and re-activity, provide the information to the cameras that will then fill in
all the pixels in each frame. This little exercise of the imagination helps to
drive home just how much information there is in a "realistic" film, but even
a great film, such as *Schindler's List*, for all its complexity, is a simple, non-
interactive artifact many orders of magnitude less complex than a conscious
being.

When robot-makers have claimed in the past that in principle they could
construct "by hand" a conscious robot, this was a hubristic overstatement
analogous to what Walt Disney might once have proclaimed: that his studio
of animators could create a film so realistic that no one would be able to tell
that it was a cartoon, not a "live action" film. What Disney couldn't do in
fact, computer animators still cannot do, but perhaps only for the time being.

Robot makers, even with the latest high-tech innovations, also fall far short of their hubristic goals, now and for the foreseeable future. The comparison serves to expose the likely source of the outrage so many skeptics feel when they encounter the manifestos of the Artificial Intelligencia. Anyone who seriously claimed that *Schindler's List* could in fact have been made by computer animation could be seen to betray an obscenely impoverished sense of what is conveyed in that film. An important element of the film's power is the fact that it is a film made by assembling human actors to portray those events, and that it is not actually the newsreel footage that its black-and-white format reminds you of. When one juxtaposes in one's imagination a sense of what the actors must have gone through to make the film with a sense of what the people who actually lived the events went through, this reflection sets up reverberations in one's thinking that draw attention to the deeper meanings of the film. Similarly, when robot enthusiasts proclaim the likelihood that they can simply construct a conscious robot, there is an understandable suspicion that they are simply betraying an infantile grasp of the subtleties of conscious life. (I hope I have put enough feeling into that condemnation to satisfy the skeptics.)

But however justified that might be in some instances as an ad hominem suspicion, it is simply irrelevant to the important theoretical issues. Perhaps no cartoon could be a great film, but they are certainly real films—and some are indeed good films; if the best the roboticists can hope for is the creation of some crude, cheesy, second-rate, artificial consciousness, they still win. Still, it is not a foregone conclusion that even this modest goal is reachable. If you want to have a defensible reason for claiming that no conscious robot will ever be created, you might want to settle for this:

(4) Robots will always just be much too simple to be conscious.

After all, a normal human being is composed of trillions of parts (if we descend to the level of the macromolecules), and many of these rival in complexity and design cunning the fanciest artifacts that have ever been created. We consist of billions of cells, and a single human cell contains within itself complex "machinery" that is still well beyond the artifactual powers of engineers. We are composed of thousands of different kinds of cells, including thousands of different species of symbiont visitors, some of whom might be as important to our consciousness as others are to our ability to digest our food! If all that complexity were needed for consciousness to exist, then the task of making a single conscious robot would dwarf the entire scientific and engineering resources of the planet for millennia. And who would pay for it?

If no other reason can be found, this may do to ground your skepticism about conscious robots in your future, but one shortcoming of this last reason is that it is scientifically boring. If this is the only reason there won't be conscious robots, then consciousness isn't that special, after all. Another shortcoming with this reason is that it is dubious on its face. Everywhere else we have looked, we have found higher-level commonalities of function that permit us to substitute relatively simple bits for fiendishly complicated bits. Artificial heart valves work really very well, but they are orders of magnitude simpler than organic heart valves, heart valves born of woman or sow, you might say. Artificial ears and eyes that will do a serviceable (if crude) job of substituting for lost perceptual organs are visible on the horizon, and anyone who doubts they are possible in principle is simply out of touch. Nobody ever said a prosthetic eye had to see as keenly, or focus as fast, or be as sensitive to color gradations as a normal human (or other animal) eye in order to "count" as an eye. If an eye, why not an optic nerve (or acceptable substitute thereof), and so forth, all the way in?

Some (Searle, 1992, Mangan, 1993) have supposed, most improbably, that this proposed regress would somewhere run into a non-fungible medium of consciousness, a part of the brain that could not be substituted on pain of death or zombiehood. Once the implications of that view are spelled out (Dennett, 1993a, 1993b), one can see that it is a non-starter. There is no reason at all to believe that some one part of the brain is utterly irreplaceable by prosthesis, provided we allow that some crudity, some loss of function, is to be expected in most substitutions of the simple for the complex. An artificial brain is, on the face of it, as "possible in principle" as an artificial heart, just much, much harder to make and hook up. Of course once we start letting crude forms of prosthetic consciousness—like crude forms of prosthetic vision or hearing—pass our litmus tests for consciousness (whichever tests we favor) the way is open for another boring debate, over whether the phenomena in question are too crude to count.

2. THE COG PROJECT: A HUMANOID ROBOT

A much more interesting tack to explore, in my opinion, is simply to set out to make a robot that is theoretically interesting independent of the philosophical conundrum about whether it is conscious. Such a robot would have to perform a lot of the feats that we have typically associated with consciousness in the past, but we would not need to dwell on that issue from the outset. Maybe we could even learn something interesting about what the truly hard problems are without ever settling any of the issues about consciousness.

Such a project is now underway at MIT. Under the direction of Professors Rodney Brooks and Lynn Andrea Stein of the AI Lab, a group of bright, hard-working young graduate students are laboring as I speak to create Cog, the most humanoid robot yet attempted, and I am happy to be a part of the

Cog team. Cog is just about life-size—that is, about the size of a human adult. Cog has no legs, but lives bolted at the hips, you might say, to its stand. It has two human-length arms, however, with somewhat simple hands on the wrists. It can bend at the waist and swing its torso, and its head moves with three degrees of freedom just about the way yours does. It has two eyes, each equipped with both a foveal high-resolution vision area and a low-resolution wide-angle parafoveal vision area, and these eyes saccade at almost human speed. That is, the two eyes can complete approximately three fixations a second, while you and I can manage four or five. Your foveas are at the center of your retinas, surrounded by the grainier low-resolution parafoveal areas; for reasons of engineering simplicity, Cog's eyes have their foveas mounted above their wide-angle vision areas.

This is typical of the sort of compromise that the Cog team is willing to make. It amounts to a wager that a vision system with the foveas moved out of the middle can still work well enough not to be debilitating, and the problems encountered will not be irrelevant to the problems encountered in normal human vision. After all, nature gives us examples of other eyes with different foveal arrangements. Eagles, for instance have two different foveas in each eye. Cog's eyes won't give it visual information exactly like that provided to human vision by human eyes (in fact, of course, it will be vastly degraded), but the wager is that this will be plenty to give Cog the opportunity to perform impressive feats of hand-eye coordination, identification, and search. At the outset, Cog will not have color vision.

Since its eyes are video cameras mounted on delicate, fast-moving gimbals, it might be disastrous if Cog were inadvertently to punch itself in the eye, so part of the hard-wiring that must be provided in advance is an "innate" if rudimentary "pain" or "alarm" system to serve roughly the same protective functions as the reflex eye-blink and pain-avoidance systems hard-wired into human infants.

Cog will not be an adult at first, in spite of its adult size. It is being designed to pass through an extended period of artificial infancy, during which it will have to learn from experience, experience it will gain in the rough-and-tumble environment of the real world. Like a human infant, however, it will need a great deal of protection at the outset, in spite of the fact that it will be equipped with many of the most crucial safety-systems of a living being. It has limit switches, heat sensors, current sensors, strain gauges and alarm signals in all the right places to prevent it from destroying its many motors and joints. It has enormous "funny bones"—motors sticking out from its elbows in a risky way. These will be protected from harm not by being shielded in heavy armor, but by being equipped with patches of exquisitely sensitive piezo-electric membrane "skin" which will trigger alarms when they make contact with anything. The goal is that Cog will quickly "learn" to keep its funny bones from being bumped—if Cog cannot learn this in short order, it will have to have this high-priority policy hard-wired in. The same sensitive membranes will be used on its fingertips and elsewhere, and, like human tactile nerves, the "meaning" of the signals sent along the attached wires will depend more on what the central control system "makes of them" than on their "intrinsic" characteristics. A gentle touch, signaling sought-for contact with an object to be grasped, will not differ, as an information packet, from a sharp pain, signaling a need for rapid countermeasures. It all depends on what the central system is designed to do with the packet, and this design is itself indefinitely revisable—something that can be adjusted either by Cog's own experience or by the tinkering of Cog's artificers.

One of its most interesting "innate" endowments will be software for visual face recognition. Faces will "pop out" from the background of other objects as items of special interest to Cog. It will further be innately designed to "want" to keep its "mother's" face in view, and to work hard to keep "mother" from turning away. The role of mother has not yet been cast, but several of the graduate students have been tentatively tapped for this role. Unlike a human infant, of course, there is no reason why Cog can't have a whole team of mothers, each of whom is innately distinguished by Cog as a face to please if possible. Clearly, even if Cog really does have a Lebenswelt, it will not be the same as ours.

Decisions have not yet been reached about many of the candidates for hard-wiring or innate features. Anything that can learn must be initially equipped with a great deal of unlearned design. That is no longer an issue; no tabula rasa could ever be impressed with knowledge from experience. But it is also not much of an issue which features ought to be innately fixed, for there is a convenient trade-off. I haven't mentioned yet that Cog will actually be a multi-generational series of ever improved models (if all goes well!), but of course that is the way any complex artifact gets designed. Any feature that is not innately fixed at the outset, but does get itself designed into Cog's control system through learning, can then often be lifted whole (with some revision, perhaps) into Cog-II, as a new bit of innate endowment designed by Cog itself—or rather by Cog's history of interactions with its environment. So even in cases in which we have the best of reasons for thinking that human infants actually come innately equipped with pre-designed gear, we may choose to try to get Cog to learn the design in question, rather than be born with it. In some instances, this is laziness or opportunism—we don't really know what might work well, but maybe Cog can train itself up. This insouciance about the putative nature/nurture boundary is already a familiar attitude among neural net modelers, of course. Although Cog is not specifically intended to demonstrate any particular neural net thesis, it should come as no surprise that Cog's nervous system is a massively parallel architecture capable of simultaneously training up an indefinite number of special-purpose networks or circuits, under various regimes.

How plausible is the hope that Cog can retrace the steps of millions of years of evolution in a few months or years of laboratory exploration? Notice first that what I have just described is a variety of Lamarckian inheritance that no organic lineage has been able to avail itself of. The acquired design innovations of Cog-I can be immediately transferred to Cog-II, a speed-up of evolution of tremendous, if incalculable, magnitude. Moreover, if you bear in mind that, unlike the natural case, there will be a team of overseers ready to make patches whenever obvious shortcomings reveal themselves, and to jog the systems out of ruts whenever they enter them, it is not so outrageous a hope, in our opinion. But then, we are all rather outrageous people.

One talent that we have hopes of teaching to Cog is a rudimentary capacity for human language. And here we run into the fabled innate language organ or Language Acquisition Device made famous by Noam Chomsky. Is there going to be an attempt to build an innate LAD for our Cog? No. We are going to try to get Cog to build language the hard way, the way our ancestors must have done, over thousands of generations. Cog has ears (four, because it's easier to get good localization with four microphones than with carefully shaped ears like ours!) and some special-purpose signal-analyzing software is being developed to give Cog a fairly good chance of discriminating human speech sounds, and probably the capacity to distinguish different human voices. Cog will also have to have speech synthesis hardware and software, of course, but decisions have not yet been reached about the details. It is important to have Cog as well-equipped as possible for rich and natural interactions with human beings, for the team intends to take advantage of as much free labor as it can. Untrained people ought to be able to spend time—hours if they like, and we rather hope they do—trying to get Cog to learn this or that. Growing into an adult is a long, time-consuming business, and Cog—and the team that is building Cog—will need all the help it can get.

Obviously this will not work unless the team manages somehow to give Cog a motivational structure that can be at least dimly recognized, responded to, and exploited by naive observers. In short, Cog should be as human as possible in its wants and fears, likes and dislikes. If those anthropomorphic terms strike you as unwarranted, put them in scare-quotes or drop them altogether and replace them with tedious neologisms of your own choosing: Cog, you may prefer to say, must have goal-registrations and preference-functions that map in rough isomorphism to human desires. This is so for many reasons, of course. Cog won't work at all unless it has its act together in a daunting number of different regards. It must somehow delight in learning, abhor error, strive for novelty, recognize progress. It must be vigilant in some regards, curious in others, and deeply unwilling to engage in self-destructive activity. While we are at it, we might as well try to make it crave human praise and company, and even exhibit a sense of humor.

Let me switch abruptly from this heavily anthropomorphic language to a brief description of Cog's initial endowment of information-processing hardware. The computer-complex that has been built to serve as the development platform for Cog's artificial nervous system consists of four backplanes, each with 16 nodes; each node is basically a Mac-II computer—a 68332 processor with a megabyte of RAM. In other words, you can think of Cog's brain as roughly equivalent to sixty-four Mac-IIs yoked in a custom parallel architecture. Each node is itself a multiprocessor, and instead of running Mac software, they all run a special version of parallel Lisp developed by Rodney Brooks, and called, simply, L. Each node has an interpreter for L in its ROM, so it can execute L files independently of every other node.

Each node has 6 assignable input-output ports, in addition to the possibility of separate i-o (input-output) to the motor boards directly controlling the various joints, as well as the all-important i-o to the experimenters' monitoring and control system, the Front End Processor or FEP (via another unit known as the Interfep). On a bank of separate monitors, one can see the current image in each camera (two foveas, two parafoveas), the activity in each of the many different visual processing areas, or the activities of any other nodes. Cog is thus equipped at birth with the equivalent of chronically implanted electrodes for each of its neurons; all its activities can be monitored in real time, recorded and debugged. The FEP is itself a Macintosh computer in more conventional packaging. At startup, each node is awakened by a FEP call that commands it to load its appropriate files of L from a file server. These files configure it for whatever tasks it has currently been designed to execute. Thus the underlying hardware machine can be turned into any of a host of different virtual machines, thanks to the capacity of each node to run its current program. The nodes do not make further use of disk memory, however, during normal operation. They keep their transient memories locally, in their individual megabytes of RAM. In other words, Cog stores both its genetic endowment (the virtual machine) and its long term memory on disk when it is shut down, but when it is powered on, it first configures itself and then stores all its short term memory distributed one way or another among its 64 nodes.

The space of possible virtual machines made available and readily explorable by this underlying architecture is huge, of course, and it covers a volume in the space of all computations that has not yet been seriously explored by artificial intelligence researchers. Moreover, the space of possibilities it represents is manifestly much more realistic as a space to build brains in than is the space heretofore explored, either by the largely serial architectures of GOFAI ("Good Old Fashioned AI", Haugeland, 1985), or by parallel architectures simulated by serial machines. Nevertheless, it is arguable that every

one of the possible virtual machines executable by Cog is minute in comparison to a real human brain. In short, Cog has a tiny brain. There is a big
wager being made: the parallelism made possible by this arrangement will
be sufficient to provide real-time control of importantly humanoid activities
occurring on a human time scale. If this proves to be too optimistic by as
little as an order of magnitude, the whole project will be forlorn, for the
motivating insight for the project is that by confronting and solving actual,
real time problems of self-protection, hand-eye coordination, and interaction with other animate beings, Cog's artificers will discover the sufficient
conditions for higher cognitive functions in general—and maybe even for a
variety of consciousness that would satisfy the skeptics.

It is important to recognize that although the theoretical importance of
having a body has been appreciated ever since Alan Turing (1950) drew specific attention to it in his classic paper, "Computing Machines and Intelligence," within the field of Artificial Intelligence there has long been a
contrary opinion that robotics is largely a waste of time, money and effort.
According to this view, whatever deep principles of organization make cognition possible can be as readily discovered in the more abstract realm of
pure simulation, at a fraction of the cost. In many fields, this thrifty attitude
has proven to be uncontroversial wisdom. No economists have asked for the
funds to implement their computer models of markets and industries in tiny
robotic Wall Streets or Detroits, and civil engineers have largely replaced
their scale models of bridges and tunnels with computer models that can do
a better job of simulating all the relevant conditions of load, stress and strain.
Closer to home, simulations of ingeniously oversimplified imaginary organisms foraging in imaginary environments, avoiding imaginary predators and
differentially producing imaginary offspring are yielding important insights
into the mechanisms of evolution and ecology in the new field of Artificial
Life. So it is something of a surprise to find this AI group conceding, in
effect, that there is indeed something to the skeptics' claim (e.g., Dreyfus
and Dreyfus, 1986) that genuine embodiment in a real world is crucial to
consciousness. Not, I hasten to add, because genuine embodiment provides
some special vital juice that mere virtual-world simulations cannot secrete,
but for the more practical reason—or hunch—that unless you saddle your-
self with all the problems of making a concrete agent take care of itself in
the real world, you will tend to overlook, underestimate, or misconstrue the
deepest problems of design.

Besides, as I have already noted, there is the hope that Cog will be able to
design itself in large measure, learning from infancy, and building its own
representation of its world in the terms that it innately understands. Nobody
doubts that any agent capable of interacting intelligently with a human being
on human terms must have access to literally millions if not billions of logically independent items of world knowledge. Either these must be hand-

coded individually by human programmers—a tactic being pursued, notoriously, by Douglas Lenat (Lenat and Guha, 1990) and his CYC team in Dal-
las—or some way must be found for the artificial agent to learn its world
knowledge from (real) interactions with the (real) world. The potential vir-
tues of this shortcut have long been recognized within AI circles (e.g., Waltz,
1988). The unanswered question is whether taking on the task of solving the
grubby details of real-world robotics will actually permit one to finesse the
task of hand-coding the world knowledge. Brooks, Stein and their team—
myself included—are gambling that it will.

At this stage of the project, most of the problems being addressed would
never arise in the realm of pure, disembodied AI. How many separate
motors might be used for controlling each hand? They will have to be
mounted somehow on the forearms. Will there then be room to mount
the motor boards directly on the arms, close to the joints they control, or
would they get in the way? How much cabling can each arm carry before
weariness or clumsiness overcome it? The arm joints have been built to be
compliant—springy, like your own joints. This means that if Cog wants to
do some fine-fingered manipulation, it will have to learn to "burn" some of
the degrees of freedom in its arm motion by temporarily bracing its elbows
or wrists on a table or other convenient landmark, just as you would do.
Such compliance is typical of the mixed bag of opportunities and problems
created by real robotics. Another is the need for self-calibration or re-
calibration in the eyes. If Cog's eyes jiggle away from their preset aim,
thanks to the wear and tear of all that sudden saccading, there must be ways
for Cog to compensate, short of trying continually to adjust its camera-eyes
with its fingers. Software designed to tolerate this probable sloppiness in the
first place may well be more robust and versatile in many other ways than
software designed to work in a more "perfect" world.

Earlier I mentioned a reason for using artificial muscles, not motors, to
control a robot's joints, and the example was not imaginary. Brooks is concerned that the sheer noise of Cog's skeletal activities may seriously interfere
with the attempt to give Cog humanoid hearing. There is research underway
at the AI Lab to develop synthetic electro-mechanical muscle tissues, which
would operate silently as well as being more compact, but this will not be
available for early incarnations of Cog. For an entirely different reason,
thought is being given to the option of designing Cog's visual control software as if its eyes were moved by muscles, not motors, building in a software
interface that amounts to giving Cog a set of virtual eye-muscles. Why might
this extra complication in the interface be wise? Because the "opponent-
process" control system exemplified by eye-muscle controls is apparently a
deep and ubiquitous feature of nervous systems, involved in control of attention generally and disrupted in such pathologies as unilateral neglect. If we
are going to have such competitive systems at higher levels of control, it

might be wise to build them in "all the way down," concealing the final translation into electric-motor-talk as part of the backstage implementation, not the model.

Other practicalities are more obvious, or at least more immediately evocative to the uninitiated. Three huge red "emergency kill" buttons have already been provided in Cog's environment, to ensure that if Cog happens to engage in some activity that could injure or endanger a human interactor (or itself), there is a way of getting it to stop. But what is the appropriate response for Cog to make to the KILL button? If power to Cog's motors is suddenly shut off, Cog will slump, and its arms will crash down on whatever is below them. Is this what we want to happen? Do we want Cog to drop whatever it is holding? What should "Stop!" mean to Cog? This is a real issue about which there is not yet any consensus.

There are many more details of the current and anticipated design of Cog that are of more than passing interest to those in the field, but on this occasion, I want to use the little remaining time to address some overriding questions that have been much debated by philosophers, and that receive a ready treatment in the environment of thought made possible by Cog. In other words, let's consider Cog merely as a prosthetic aid to philosophical thought-experiments, a modest but by no means negligible role for Cog to play.

3. THREE PHILOSOPHICAL THEMES ADDRESSED

A recent criticism of "strong AI" that has received quite a bit of attention is the so-called problem of "symbol grounding" (Harnad, 1990). It is all very well for large AI programs to have data structures that purport to refer to Chicago, milk, or the person to whom I am now talking, but such imaginary reference is not the same as real reference, according to this line of criticism. These internal "symbols" are not properly "grounded" in the world, and the problems thereby eschewed by pure, non-robotic, AI are not trivial or peripheral. As one who discussed, and ultimately dismissed, a version of this problem many years ago (Dennett, 1969, p.182ff), I would not want to be interpreted as now abandoning my earlier view. I submit that Cog moots the problem of symbol grounding, without having to settle its status as a criticism of "strong AI". Anything in Cog that might be a candidate for symbolhood will automatically be "grounded" in Cog's real predicament, as surely as its counterpart in any child, so the issue doesn't arise, except as a practical problem for the Cog team, to be solved or not, as fortune dictates. If the day ever comes for Cog to comment to anybody about Chicago, the question of whether Cog is in any position to do so will arise for exactly the same reasons, and be resolvable on the same considerations, as the parallel question about the reference of the word "Chicago" in the idiolect of a young child.

Another claim that has often been advanced, most carefully by Haugeland (1985), is that nothing could properly "matter" to an artificial intelligence, and mattering (it is claimed) is crucial to consciousness. Haugeland restricted his claim to traditional GOFAI systems, and left robots out of consideration. Would he concede that something could matter to Cog? The question, presumably, is how seriously to weigh the import of the quite deliberate decision by Cog's creators to make Cog as much as possible responsible for its own welfare. Cog will be equipped with some "innate" but not at all arbitrary preferences, and hence provided of necessity with the concomitant capacity to be "bothered" by the thwarting of those preferences, and "pleased" by the furthering of the ends it was innately designed to seek. Some may want to retort: "This is not real pleasure or pain, but merely a simulacrum." Perhaps, but on what grounds will they defend this claim? Cog may be said to have quite crude, simplistic, one-dimensional pleasure and pain, cartoon pleasure and pain if you like, but then the same might also be said of the pleasure and pain of simpler organisms—clams or houseflies, for instance. Most, if not all, of the burden of proof is shifted by Cog, in my estimation. The reasons for saying that something does matter to Cog are not arbitrary; they are exactly parallel to the reasons we give for saying that things matter to us and to other creatures. Since we have cut off the dubious retreats to vitalism or origin chauvinism, it will be interesting to see if the skeptics have any good reasons for declaring Cog's pains and pleasures not to matter—at least to it, and for that very reason, to us as well. It will come as no surprise, I hope, that more than a few participants in the Cog project are already musing about what obligations they might come to have to Cog, over and above their obligations to the Cog team.

Finally, J. R. Lucas has raised the claim (at this meeting) that if a robot were really conscious, we would have to be prepared to believe it about its own internal states. I would like to close by pointing out that this is a rather likely reality in the case of Cog. Although equipped with an optimal suite of monitoring devices that will reveal the details of its inner workings to the observing team, Cog's own pronouncements could very well come to be a more trustworthy and informative source of information on what was really going on inside it. The information visible on the banks of monitors, or gathered by the gigabyte on hard disks, will be at the outset almost as hard to interpret, even by Cog's own designers, as the information obtainable by such "third-person" methods as MRI and CT scanning in the neurosciences. As the observers refine their models, and their understanding of their models, their authority as interpreters of the data may grow, but it may also suffer eclipse. Especially since Cog will be designed from the outset to redesign itself as much as possible, there is a high probability that the designers will simply lose the standard hegemony of the artificer ("I made it, so I know what it is supposed to do, and what it is doing now!"). Into this epistemological vacuum Cog may very well thrust itself. In fact, I would gladly defend the conditional prediction: if Cog develops to the point where it can conduct what appear to be robust and well-controlled conversations in something like a natural language, it will certainly be in a position to rival its own monitors (and the theorists who interpret them) as a source of knowledge about what it is doing and feeling, and why.

NOTE

"The Practical Requirements for Making a Conscious Robot." *Philosophical Transactions of the Royal Society of London, Series A: Physical Sciences and Engineering* (October 15, 1994), 349(1689): 133–46. Reprinted with permission.

REFERENCES

Dennett, Daniel C., 1969, *Content and Consciousness*, London: Routledge & Kegan Paul.

Dennett, Daniel C., 1987, "Fast Thinking," in Dennett, *The Intentional Stance*, Cambridge, MA: MIT Press, pp. 323–37.

Dennett, Daniel C., 1993a, Review of John Searle, "The Rediscovery of the Mind," in *J.Phil.* 90, pp. 193–205.

Dennett, Daniel C., 1993b, "Caveat Emptor," *Consciousness and Cognition*, 2, pp. 48–57.

Dreyfus, Hubert & Dreyfus, Stuart, 1986, *Mind Over Machine*, New York: Macmillan.

Harnad, Stevan, 1990, "The Symbol Grounding Problem," *Physica D*, 42, pp. 335–46.

Haugeland, John, 1985, *Artificial Intelligence: The Very Idea*, Cambridge MA: MIT Press.

Lenat, Douglas B., and Guha, R. V., 1990, Building Large Knowledge-Based Systems: Representation and Inference in the CYC Project, Reading, MA: Addison-Wesley.

Mangan, Bruce, "Dennett, Consciousness, and the Sorrows of Functionalism," *Consciousness and Cognition*, 2, pp. 1–17.

Searle, John, 1992, *The Redisovery of the Mind*, Cambridge, MA: MIT Press.

Turing, Alan, 1950, "Computing Machinery and Intelligence," *Mind*, 59, pp. 433–60.

Waltz, David, 1988, "The Prospects for Building Truly Intelligent Machines," *Daedalus*, 117, pp. 191–222.

IV

CONSCIOUSNESS

Readings in this section present views regarding what is arguably the most intriguing subject in philosophy of mind—consciousness. The meaning of the term "consciousness" is notoriously difficult to define, especially if we wish to avoid **begging the question** about what the nature of consciousness is from the start. When we speak of a person being conscious, we may mean that they are awake (as opposed to being asleep). Yet being awake, simply responsive to stimuli, could describe animals or even robots. There appears to be more to consciousness than being awake. More often, when we speak of someone being conscious, we mean to indicate that she is not simply awake but also aware of what she is doing. She is conscious of something, and, perhaps, aware (in some way) that she herself is in this state. Philosophers seem to agree that consciousness has a special status involving some form of awareness, yet disagree over whether consciousness is so special as to defy scientific explanation. The subsequent readings explore ways to define and understand consciousness.

Subjectivity/Objectivity

In the first set of readings, we find that consciousness is understood as a **subjective** phenomenon. The question that arises is whether the subjective character of conscious experience poses an obstacle to the development of a scientific and physical theory of the mind. According to Thomas Nagel in his paper "What Is It Like to Be a Bat," consciousness is defined as "what it's like" to be in a certain mental state. There is something that it is like, for instance, to taste a cherry, to listen to a song, or to be a bat. Conscious experience is subjective—there is something it's like to eat an orange from a particular, individual point of view. Therein lies the problem. Scientific explanation is, by definition, **objective** in character. This objective character of scientific explanation seems to rule out, in principle, explanations that are subjective and individual. We do not have the conceptual resources to relate subjective conscious experience to objective, scientific theories of the mind. Keith Gunderson does not agree that subjectivity poses this kind of obstacle to objective inquiry. In his article "Asymmetries and Mind-Body Perplexities," Keith Gunderson addresses the issue of this apparent **asymmetry** between scientific descriptions and our own subjective points of view. He argues that parallel cases involving similar asymmetries, such as the eye that cannot see itself and a periscope that cannot find itself in its own crosshairs, do not pose obstacles to objective theoretical descriptions. David Lewis addresses the problem that subjective qualities of conscious experience (what it's like) raise for materialists and functionalists in his brief piece, "Knowing What It's Like." While agreeing that there are subjective experiences, he denies that these experiences provide information—information that an objective scientific inquiry would necessarily leave out of its account. Instead, he claims that subjective experiences, such as what it's like to taste Vegemite, are abilities. Much like Gilbert Ryles' notion of **"Knowing How,"** Lewis suggests that subjective experiences should be understood as providing us with abilities to recognize, discriminate different experiences, and imagine and predict them, and should not be considered as cases of **"Knowing That,"** which lessons or theories could never teach us.

Two representative theories of consciousness are presented in this subsection. David Armstrong provides a **materialist** view in a selection, "What is Consciousness?" from his book, *The Nature of Mind* (1981). David Chalmers provides an **Anti-reductionist** theory in his article "Facing Up to the Problem of Consciousness." A materialist about consciousness holds that this **phenomenon** is physical and can be accounted for in purely physical terms. It is **reductionist,** not in the sense that conscious experience is made less or "reduced" to nothing but in the sense that the mental quality of consciousness can be fully explained as a physical phenomenon. Of course, the materialist must provide an account of what consciousness is, and this is precisely where Armstrong begins. He is upfront in distinguishing his view as "Anti-Cartesian," rejecting the idea that a mental state is essentially conscious if it is to be considered a mental state at all. This idea, which Descartes presented in the *Principles of Philosophy*, is one that Armstrong strongly disagrees with, and his selection explains an alternative way for us to understand how consciousness is a part of our mental life that is the "icing on the cake." In other words, mental states do not necessarily have to be conscious in terms of one's being aware that one is in a certain mental state to qualify as mental states. Descartes holds that consciousness is a kind of self-consciousness, but for Armstrong this misleadingly restricts what can be understood about mental states in general. Armstrong holds what is called a "Causal Theory of the Mind," and in this theory he shows how different levels of conscious mental states play causal roles in our behavior as well as in relations to other mental states. He sets out his view, presenting what he calls "**causally quiescent**" mental states—Minimal Consciousness. These are mental states that we possess, for example, even while sleeping, such as beliefs and memories. These mental states are causally quiescent in that they are inactive and are not affecting other mental states or our behavior. Mental activity above Minimal Consciousness, such as Perceptual Consciousness and **Introspective** Consciousness, is causally active in that it produces other mental effects. Yet Introspective Consciousness is not required for us to be Minimally or Perceptually Conscious. Armstrong illustrates this condition with a case of long-distance truck drivers who experience a "coming to" while driving, realizing that they have not been fully self-aware for a time, yet have been successfully driving for some distance. The driver has been Minimally and Perceptually Conscious without being Introspectively Conscious. There is no reason, Armstrong thinks, to hold that the driver has not had mental states altogether (because he was not self-aware), or that the driver was completely unconscious (he had minimal consciousness—his intentions, beliefs—and was perceiving). Introspective Consciousness of our own mental states is a sophisticated component of human mental life that, according to Armstrong, evolved to organize our perceptions and beliefs and desires with respect to the world around us in relation to ourselves. It permits us to become aware (self-aware) of the mental states that we possess at any given time. It does not surprise Armstrong that in the past Introspective Consciousness had been given pride of place in views about the mind and was mistaken for the whole of conscious experience, since it plays a determining role in how we, as persons, account for ourselves.

In the selection, "Facing Up to the Problem of Consciousness," David Chalmers presents a theory of consciousness that resonates with many of the criticisms of materialism and functionalism presented earlier, since for him a theory of consciousness must be "**anti-reductive**." Chalmers also terms his view "**Naturalistic Dualism**," by which he means that in the tradition of Descartes and following Thomas Nagel, his view accepts the idea that there truly is a hard problem that theorists confront when explaining the mind. This hard problem is explaining why our mental functions give rise to conscious experience. There is something it's like to experience things like tasting an apple or seeing a sunset, and unlike the easy problems of explaining mental functions, conscious experience cannot be explained by way of functional and neuro-biological explanations. The question, "Why does experience arise?" can be asked of any of these explanations of our minds. The answer, according to Chalmers, must lie in an "extra ingredient," with which we can bridge functional/neuro-biological explanation and an explanation of consciousness. Chalmers thus finds he is committed to a form of **dualism** about the mind. Some non-physical entity or entities must be assumed in a theory of consciousness to provide an explanation to this "Why Question" that he finds unanswerable. Chalmer's dualism, unlike Cartesian dualism, is "**naturalistic**" or open to scientific inquiry and investigation. This is because the extra ingredient that he believes is required in a theory of consciousness should be considered akin to the entities or **primitive terms** that physicists utilize in their theories, terms that are assumed without further explanation for the development of a theory. Conscious experience will need to have the role of a primitive term in a theory of consciousness. Chalmers' **naturalism** continues in that he believes that a theory of consciousness such as the one he suggests will prove to be compatible with other scientific theories. Consciousness, too, will be governed by laws, and a theory of consciousness will show how conscious phenomena coheres with all other natural phenomena. His point is that although a theory of consciousness requires an extra ingredient that is non-physical, the theory, when worked out, will show that this extra ingredient is not at odds with what we can understand about the physical world.

Chalmers does not leave his theory of consciousness as a critical evaluation of materialist views but concludes with positive suggestions as to the laws with which an anti-reductive theory of consciousness might begin. He determines some basic **psycho-physical** principles that connect conscious experience with the physical world, including "Structural Coherence," "Organizational Invariance," and the "Double Aspect Theory of Information." Each of these principles would help determine lawful regularities in conscious experience and it can be studied in its own right like any other natural phenomenon. Chalmers finds that his view neither eliminates conscious experience nor renders it a complete mystery. Further work on this anti-reductive theory of consciousness must be undertaken, but according to Chalmers, we are in a position to begin such work.

This section concludes with Barbara Montero's paper, "Rethinking the

Mind-Body Problem." This paper will be of interest to those wondering while reading these debates on the nature of the mind, "What is the physical?" Both **materialists** and **anti-reductionists** have been using this term, debating if the mind can be fully explained in physical or non-physical terms, but what is "physical" and how does it contrast with what is "non-physical?" Montero investigates this question, especially since it is so pertinent to the mind-body debate, and shows that claims about what is physical (and how things like the mind might be) are harder to grasp than we might initially believe. Science has not yet determined the nature of all matter, and discoveries continue to challenge our understanding of the fundamental features of the world. A materialist about the mind cannot rely on science as an article of faith. Perhaps the very question, "Is the Mind Physical" is not helpful. We might find more productive questions to ask and investigate. Montero suggests that the question we might ask is whether the mental is non-mental. This may appear to be a strange question to ask—aren't these ideas mutually exclusive! But if we consider the debate between Armstrong and Chalmers regarding consciousness, we may recognize that the essence of their disagreement lies in how different kinds of mental phenomena might be related and, perhaps, build upon each other. A strong theory of mind would best explain why mental processes arose in the physical world, and distinguish these processes from those we understand to be non-mental.

16

What Is It Like to Be a Bat?

Thomas Nagel

Consciousness is what makes the mind-body problem really intractable. Perhaps that is why current discussions of the problem give it little attention or get it obviously wrong. The recent wave of reductionist euphoria has produced several analyses of mental phenomena and mental concepts designed to explain the possibility of some variety of materialism, psychophysical identification, or reduction.[1] But the problems dealt with are those common to this type of reduction and other types, and what makes the mind-body problem unique, and unlike the water-H2O problem or the Turing machine-IBM machine problem or the lightning-electrical discharge problem or the gene-DNA problem or the oak tree-hydrocarbon problem, is ignored.

Every reductionist has his favorite analogy from modern science. It is most unlikely that any of these unrelated examples of successful reduction will shed light on the relation of mind to brain. But philosophers share the general human weakness for explanations of what is incomprehensible in terms suited for what is familiar and well understood, though entirely different. This has led to the acceptance of implausible accounts of the mental largely because they would permit familiar kinds of reduction. I shall try to explain why the usual examples do not help us to understand the relation between mind and body—why, indeed, we have at present no conception of what an explanation of the physical nature of a mental phenomenon would be. Without consciousness the mind-body problem would be much less interesting. With consciousness it seems hopeless. The most important and characteristic feature of conscious mental phenomena is very poorly understood. Most reductionist theories do not even try to explain it. And careful examination will show that no currently available concept of reduction is applicable to it. Perhaps a new theoretical form can be devised for the purpose, but such a solution, if it exists, lies in the distant intellectual future.

Conscious experience is a widespread phenomenon. It occurs at many levels of animal life, though we cannot be sure of its presence in the simpler organisms, and it is very difficult to say in general what provides evidence of it. (Some extremists have been prepared to deny it even of mammals other than man.) No doubt it occurs in countless forms totally unimaginable to us, on other planets in other solar systems throughout the universe. But no matter how the form may vary, the fact that an organism has conscious experience *at all* means, basically, that there is something it is like to be that organism. There may be further implications about the form of the experience; there may even (though I doubt it) be implications about the behavior of the organism. But fundamentally an organism has conscious mental states if and only if there is something that it is to be that organism—something it is like *for* the organism.

We may call this the subjective character of experience. It is not captured by any of the familiar, recently devised reductive analyses of the mental, for all of them are logically compatible with its absence. It is not analyzable in terms of any explanatory system of functional states, or intentional states, since these could be ascribed to robots or automata that behaved like people though they experienced nothing.[2] It is not analyzable in terms of the causal role of experiences in relation to typical human behavior—for similar reasons.[3] I do not deny that conscious mental states and events cause behavior, nor that they may be given functional characterizations. I deny only that this kind of thing exhausts their analysis. Any reductionist program has to be based on an analysis of what is to be reduced. If the analysis leaves something out, the problem will be falsely posed. It is useless to base the defense of materialism on any analysis of mental phenomena that fails to deal explicitly with their subjective character. For there is no reason to suppose that a reduction which seems plausible when no attempt is made to account for consciousness can be extended to include consciousness. With out some idea, therefore, of what the subjective character of experience is, we cannot know what is required of physicalist theory.

While an account of the physical basis of mind must explain many things, this appears to be the most difficult. It is impossible to exclude the phenomenological features of experience from a reduction in the same way that one excludes the phenomenal features of an ordinary substance from a physical or chemical reduction of it—namely, by explaining them as effects on the minds of human observers.[4] If physicalism is to be defended, the phenomenological features must themselves be given a physical account. But when we examine their subjective character it seems that such a result is impossible. The reason is that every subjective phenomenon is essentially connected with a single point of view, and it seems inevitable that an objective, physical theory will abandon that point of view.

Let me first try to state the issue somewhat more fully than by referring to the relation between the subjective and the objective, or between the *pour-soi* and the *en-soi*. This is far from easy. Facts about what it is like to be an X are very peculiar, so peculiar that some may be inclined to doubt their reality, or the significance of claims about them. To illustrate the connection between subjectivity and a point of view, and to make evident the importance of subjective features, it will help to explore the matter in relation to an example that brings out clearly the divergence between the two types of conception, subjective and objective.

I assume we all believe that bats have experience. After all, they are mammals, and there is no more doubt that they have experience than that mice or pigeons or whales have experience. I have chosen bats instead of wasps or flounders because if one travels too far down the phylogenetic tree, people gradually shed their faith that there is experience there at all. Bats, although more closely related to us than those other species, nevertheless present a range of activity and a sensory apparatus so different from ours that the problem I want to pose is exceptionally vivid (though it certainly could be raised with other species). Even without the benefit of philosophical reflection, anyone who has spent some time in an enclosed space with an excited bat knows what it is to encounter a fundamentally *alien* form of life.

I have said that the essence of the belief that bats have experience is that there is something that it is like to be a bat. Now we know that most bats (the microchiroptera, to be precise) perceive the external world primarily by sonar, or echolocation, detecting the reflections, from objects within range, of their own rapid, subtly modulated, high-frequency shrieks. Their brains are designed to correlate the outgoing impulses with the subsequent echoes, and the information thus acquired enables bats to make precise discriminations of distance, size, shape, motion, and texture comparable to those we make by vision. But bat sonar, though clearly a form of perception, is not similar in its operation to any sense that we possess, and there is no reason to suppose that it is subjectively like anything we can experience or imagine. This appears to create difficulties for the notion of what it is like to be a bat. We must consider whether any method will permit us to extrapolate to the inner life of the bat from our own case,[5] and, if not, what alternative methods there may be for understanding the notion.

Our own experience provides the basic material for our imagination, whose range is therefore limited. It will not help to try to imagine that one has webbing on one's arms, which enables one to fly around at dusk and dawn catching insects in one's mouth; that one has very poor vision and perceives the surrounding world by a system of reflected high-frequency sound signals; and that one spends the day hanging upside down by one's feet in an attic. In so far as I can imagine this (which is not very far), it tells me only what it would be like for *me* to behave as a bat behaves. But that is not the question. I want to know what it is like for a bat to be a bat. Yet if I try to imagine this, I am restricted to the resources of my own mind, and those resources are inadequate to the task. I cannot perform it either by imagining additions to my present experience, or by imagining segments gradually subtracted from it, or by imagining some combination of additions, subtractions, and modifications.

To the extent that I could look and behave like a wasp or a bat without changing my fundamental structure, my experiences would not be anything like the experiences of those animals. On the other hand, it is doubtful that any meaning can be attached to the supposition that I should possess the internal neurophysiological constitution of a bat. Even if I could by gradual degrees be transformed into a bat, nothing in my present constitution enables me to imagine what the experiences of such a future stage of myself thus metamorphosed would be like. The best evidence would come from the experiences of bats, if we only knew what they were like.

So if extrapolation from our own case is involved in the idea of what it is like to be a bat, the extrapolation must be incompletable. We cannot form more than a schematic conception of what it *is* like. For example, we may ascribe general *types* of experience on the basis of the animal's structure and behavior. Thus we describe bat sonar as a form of three-dimensional forward perception; we believe that bats feel some versions of pain, fear, hunger, and lust, and that they have other, more familiar types of perception besides sonar. But we believe that these experiences also have in each case a specific subjective character, which it is beyond our ability to conceive. And if there's conscious life elsewhere in the universe, it is likely that some of it will not be describable even in the most general experiential terms available to us.[6] (The problem is not confined to exotic cases, however, for it exists between one person and another. The subjective character of the experience of a person deaf and blind from birth is not accessible to me, for example, nor presumably is mine to him. This does not prevent us each from believing that the other's experience has such a subjective character.)

If anyone is inclined to deny that we can believe in the existence of facts like this whose exact nature we cannot possibly conceive, he should reflect that in contemplating the bats we are in much the same position that intelligent bats or Martians[7] would occupy if they tried to form a conception of what it was like to be us. The structure of their own minds might make it impossible for them to succeed, but we know they would be wrong to conclude that there is not anything precise that it is like to be us: that only certain general types of mental state could be ascribed to us (perhaps perception and appetite would be concepts common to us both; perhaps not). We know they would be wrong to draw such a skeptical conclusion because we know what it is like to be us. And we know that while it includes an enormous amount of variation and complexity, and while we do not possess the vocabulary to describe it adequately, its subjective character is highly specific, and in some respects describable in terms that can be understood only by creatures like us. The fact that we cannot expect ever to accommodate in our language a detailed description of Martian or bat phenomenology should not lead us to dismiss as meaningless the claim that bats and Martians have experiences fully comparable in richness of detail to our own. It would be fine if someone were to develop concepts and a theory that enabled us to think about those things; but such an understanding may be permanently denied to us by the limits of our nature. And to deny the reality or logical significance of what we can never describe or understand is the crudest form of cognitive dissonance.

This brings us to the edge of a topic that requires much more discussion than I can give it here: namely, the relation between facts on the one hand and conceptual schemes or systems of representation on the other. My realism about the subjective domain in all its forms implies a belief in the existence of facts beyond the reach of human concepts. Certainly it is possible for a human being to believe that there are facts which humans never *will* possess the requisite concepts to represent or comprehend. Indeed, it would be foolish to doubt this, given the finiteness of humanity's expectations. After all there would have been transfinite numbers even if everyone had been wiped out by the Black Death before Cantor discovered them. But one might also believe that there are facts which *could* not ever be represented or comprehended by human beings, even if the species lasted forever—simply because our structure does not permit us to operate with concepts of the requisite type. This impossibility might even be observed by other beings, but it is not clear that the existence of such beings, or the possibility of their existence, is a precondition of the significance of the hypothesis that there are humanly inaccessible facts. (After all, the nature of beings with access to humanly inaccessible facts is presumably itself a humanly inaccessible fact.) Reflection on what it is like to be a bat seems to lead us, therefore, to the conclusion that there are facts that do not consist in the truth of propositions expressible in a human language. We can be compelled to recognize the existence of such facts without being able to state or comprehend them.

I shall not pursue this subject, however. Its bearing on the topic before us (namely, the mind-body problem) is that it enables us to make a general observation about the subjective character of experience. Whatever may be the status of facts about what it is like to be a human being, or a bat, or a Martian, these appear to be facts that embody a particular point of view.

I am not adverting here to the alleged privacy of experience to its possessor. The point of view in question is not one accessible only to a single individual. Rather it is a *type*. It is often possible to take up a point of view other than one's own, so the comprehension of such facts is not limited to one's own case. There is a sense in which phenomenological facts are perfectly objective: one person can know or say of another what the quality of the other's experience is. They are subjective, however, in the sense that even this objective ascription of experience is possible only for someone sufficiently similar to the object of ascription to be able to adopt his point of view—to understand the ascription in the first person as well as in the third, so to speak. The more different from oneself the other experiencer is, the less success one can expect with this enterprise. In our own case we occupy the relevant point of view, but we will have as much difficulty understanding our own experience properly if we approach it from another point of view as we would if we tried to understand the experience of another species without taking up *its* point of view.[8]

This bears directly on the mind-body problem. For if the facts of experience—facts about what it is like *for* the experiencing organism—are accessible only from one point of view, then it is a mystery how the true character of experiences could be revealed in the physical operation of that organism. The latter is a domain of objective facts par excellence—the kind that can be observed and understood from many points of view and by individuals with differing perceptual systems. There are no comparable imaginative obstacles to the acquisition of knowledge about bat neurophysiology by human scientists, and intelligent bats or Martians might learn more about the human brain than we ever will.

This is not by itself an argument against reduction. A Martian scientist with no understanding of visual perception could understand the rainbow, or lightning, or clouds as physical phenomena, though he would never be able to understand the human concepts of rainbow, lightning, or cloud, or the place these things occupy in our phenomenal world. The objective nature of the things picked out by these concepts could be apprehended by him because, although the concepts themselves are connected with a particular point of view and a particular visual phenomenology, the things apprehended from that point of view are not: they are observable—from the point of view but external to it; hence they can be comprehended from other points of view also, either by the same organisms or by others. Lightning has an objective character that is not exhausted by its visual appearance, and this can be investigated by a Martian without vision. To be precise, it has a *more* objective character than is revealed in its visual appearance. In speaking of the move from subjective to objective characterization, I wish to remain noncommittal about the existence of an end point, the completely objective intrinsic nature of the thing, which one might or might not be able to reach. It may be more accurate to think of objectivity as a direction in which the understanding can travel. And in understanding a phenomenon like lightning, it is legitimate to go as far away as one can from a strictly human view-point.[9]

In the case of experience, on the other hand, the connection with a partic-ular point of view seems much closer. It is difficult to understand what could be meant by the *objective* character of an experience, apart from the particu-lar point of view from which its subject apprehends it. After all, what would be left of what it was like to be a bat if one removed the viewpoint of the bat? But if experience does not have, in addition to its subjective character, an objective nature that can be apprehended from many different points of view, then how can it be supposed that a Martian investigating my brain might be observing physical processes which were my mental processes (as he might observe physical processes which were bolts of lightning), only from a different point of view? How, for that matter, could a human physi-ologist observe them from another point of view?[10]

We appear to be faced with a general difficulty about psychophysical reduction. In other areas the process of reduction is a move in the direction of greater objectivity, toward a more accurate view of the real nature of things. This is accomplished by reducing our dependence on individual or species-specific points of view toward the object of investigation. We describe it not in terms of the impressions it makes on our senses, but in terms of its more general effects and of properties detectable by means other than the human senses. The less it depends on a specifically human view-point, the more objective is our description. It is possible to follow this path because although the concepts and ideas we employ in thinking about the external world are initially applied from a point of view that involves our perceptual apparatus, they are used by us to refer to things beyond them-selves—toward which we *have* the phenomenal point of view. Therefore we can abandon it in favor of another, and still be thinking about the same things.

Experience itself however, does not seem to fit the pattern. The idea of moving from appearance to reality seems to make no sense here. What is the analogue in this case to pursuing a more objective understanding of the same phenomena by abandoning the initial subjective viewpoint toward them in favor of another that is more objective but concerns the same thing? Cer-tainly it *appears* unlikely that we will get closer to the real nature of human experience by leaving behind the particularity of our human point of view and striving for a description in terms accessible to beings that could not imagine what it was like to be us. If the subjective character of experience is fully comprehensible only from one point of view, then any shift to greater objectivity—that is, less attachment to a specific viewpoint—does not take us nearer to the real nature of the phenomenon: it takes us farther away from it.

In a sense, the seeds of this objection to the reducibility of experience are already detectable in successful cases of reduction; for in discovering sound to be, in reality, a wave phenomenon in air or other media, we leave behind one viewpoint to take up another, and the auditory, human or animal viewpoint that we leave behind remains unreduced. Members of radically different species may both understand the same physical events in objective terms, and this does not require that they understand the phenomenal forms in which those events appear to the senses of members of the other species. Thus it is a condition of their referring to a common reality that their more particular viewpoints are not part of the common reality that they both apprehend. The reduction can succeed only if the species-specific viewpoint is omitted from what is to be reduced.

But while we are right to leave this point of view aside in seeking a fuller understanding of the external world, we cannot ignore it permanently, since it is the essence of the internal world, and not merely a point of view on it. Most of the neobehaviorism of recent philosophical psychology results from the effort to substitute an objective concept of mind for the real thing, in order to have nothing left over which cannot be reduced. If we acknowledge that a physical theory of mind must account for the subjective character of experience, we must admit that no presently available conception gives us a clue how this could be done. The problem is unique. If mental processes are indeed physical processes, then there is something it is like, intrinsically,[11] to undergo certain physical processes. What it is for such a thing to be the case remains a mystery.

What moral should be drawn from these reflections, and what should be done next? It would be a mistake to conclude that physicalism must be false. Nothing is proved by the inadequacy of physicalist hypotheses that assume a faulty objective analysis of mind. It would be truer to say that physicalism is a position we cannot understand because we do not at present have any conception of how it might be true. Perhaps it will be thought unreasonable to require such a conception as a condition of understanding. After all, it might be said, the meaning of physicalism is clear enough: mental states are states of the body; mental events are physical events. We do not know *which* physical states and events they are, but that should not prevent us from understanding the hypothesis. What could be clearer than the words 'is' and 'are'?

But I believe it is precisely this apparent clarity of the word 'is' that is deceptive. Usually, when we are told that X is Y we know *how* it is supposed to be true, but that depends on a conceptual or theoretical background and is not conveyed by the 'is' alone. We know how both "X" and "Y" refer, and the kinds of things to which they refer, and we have a rough idea how the two referential paths might converge on a single thing, be it an object, a person, a process, an event or whatever. But when the two terms of the identification are very disparate it may not be so clear how it could be true.

We may not have even a rough idea of how the two referential paths could converge, or what kind of things they might converge on, and a theoretical framework may have to be supplied to enable us to understand this. Without the framework, an air of mysticism surrounds the identification.

This explains the magical flavor of popular presentations of fundamental scientific discoveries, given out as propositions to which one must subscribe without really understanding them. For example, people are now told at an early age that all matter is really energy. But despite the fact that they know what 'is' means, most of them never form a conception of what makes this claim true, because they lack the theoretical background.

At the present time the status of physicalism is similar to that which the hypothesis that matter is energy would have had if uttered by a pre-Socratic philosopher. We do not have the beginnings of a conception of how it might be true. In order to understand the hypothesis that a mental event is a physical event, we require more than an understanding of the word 'is'. The idea of how a mental and a physical term might refer to the same thing is lacking, and the usual analogies with theoretical identification in other fields fail to supply it. They fail because if we construe the reference of mental terms to physical events on the usual model, we either get a reappearance of separate subjective events as the effects through which mental reference to physical events is secured, or else we get a false account of how mental terms refer (for example, a causal behaviorist one).

Strangely enough, we may have evidence for the truth of something we cannot really understand. Suppose a caterpillar is locked in a sterile safe by someone unfamiliar with insect metamorphosis, and weeks later the safe is reopened, revealing a butterfly. If the person knows that the safe has been shut the whole time, he has reason to believe that the butterfly is or was once the caterpillar, without having any idea in what sense this might be so. (One possibility is that the caterpillar contained a tiny winged parasite that devoured it and grew into the butterfly.)

It is conceivable that we are in such a position with regard to physicalism. Donald Davidson has argued that if mental events have physical causes and effects, they must have physical descriptions. He holds that we have reason to believe this even though we do not—and in fact *could* not—have a general psychophysical theory.[12] His argument applies to intentional mental events, but I think we also have some reason to believe that sensations are physical processes, without being in a position to understand how. Davidson's position is that certain physical events have irreducibly mental properties, and perhaps some view describable in this way is correct. But nothing of which we can now form a conception corresponds to it; nor have we any idea what a theory would be like that enabled us to conceive of it.[13]

Very little work has been done on the basic question (from which mention of the brain can be entirely omitted) whether any sense can be made of experiences' having an objective character at all. Does it make sense, in other words, to ask what my experiences are really like, as opposed to how they appear to me? We cannot genuinely understand the hypothesis that their nature is captured in a physical description unless we understand the more fundamental idea that they *have* an objective nature (or that objective processes can have a subjective nature).[14]

I should like to close with a speculative proposal. It may be possible to approach the gap between subjective and objective from another direction. Setting aside temporarily the relation between the mind and the brain, we can pursue a more objective understanding of the mental in its own right. At present we are completely unequipped to think about the subjective character of experience without relying on the imagination—without taking up the point of view of the experiential subject. This should be regarded as a challenge to form new concepts and devise a new method—an objective phenomenology not dependent on empathy or the imagination. Though presumably it would not capture everything, its goal would be to describe, at least in part, the subjective character of experiences in a form comprehensible to beings incapable of having those experiences.

We would have to develop such a phenomenology to describe the sonar experiences of bats; but it would also be possible to begin with humans. One might try, for example, to develop concepts that could be used to explain to a person blind from birth what it was like to see. One would reach a blank wall eventually, but it should be possible to devise a method of expressing in objective terms much more than we can at present, and with much greater precision. The loose intermodal analogies—for example, "Red is like the sound of a trumpet"—which crop up in discussions of this subject are of little use. That should be clear to anyone who has both heard a trumpet and seen red. But structural features of perception might be more accessible to objective description, even though something would be left out. And concepts alternative to those we learn in the first person may enable us to arrive at a kind of understanding even of our own experience which is denied us by the very ease of description and lack of distance that subjective concepts afford.

Apart from its own interest, a phenomenology that is in this sense objective may permit questions about the physical[15] basis of experience to assume a more intelligible form. Aspects of subjective experience that admitted this kind of objective description might be better candidates for objective explanations of a more familiar sort. But whether or not this guess is correct, it seems unlikely that any physical theory of mind can be contemplated until more thought has been given to the general problem of subjective and objective. Otherwise we cannot even pose the mind-body problem without side-stepping it.

NOTES

1. Examples are J. J. C. Smart, *Philosophy and Scientific Realism* (London: Routledge & Kegan Paul, 1963); David K. Lewis, 'An Argument for the Identity Theory', *Journal of Philosophy*, LXIII (1966), reprinted with addenda in David M. Rosenthal, *Materialism & the Mind-Body Problem* (Engelwood Cliffs, N.J.: Prentice-Hall, 1971); Hilary Putnam, "Psychological Predicates", in *Art, Mind, & Religion*, ed. W. H. Capitan and D. D. Merrill (Pittsburgh: University of Pittsburgh Press, 1967), reprinted in *Materialism*, ed. Rosenthal, as "The Nature of Mental States"; D. M. Armstrong, *A Materialist Theory of the Mind* (London: Routledge & Kegan Paul, 1968); D. C. Dennett, *Content and Consciousness* (London: Routledge & Kegan Paul, 1969). I have expressed earlier doubts in "Armstrong on the Mind," *Philosophical Review*, LXXIX (1970), 394–403; a review of Dennett, *Journal of Philosophy*, LXIX (1972); and chapter 11 above. See also Saul Kripke, 'Naming and Necessity,' in *Semantics of Natural Language*, ed. D. Davidson and G. Harman (Dordrecht: Reidel, 1972), esp. pp. 334–42; and M. T. Thornton, "Ostensive Terms and Materialism", *The Monist*, LVI (1972), 193–214.

2. Perhaps there could not actually be such robots. Perhaps anything complex enough to behave like a person would have experiences. But that, if true, is a fact which cannot be discovered merely by analyzing the concept of experience.

3. It is not equivalent to that about which we are incorrigible, both because we are not incorrigible about experience and because experience is present in animals lacking language and thought, who have no beliefs at all about their experiences.

4. Cf. Richard Rorty, "Mind-Body Identity, Privacy, and Categories," *Review of Metaphysics*, XIX (1965), esp. 37–8.

5. By "our own case" I do not mean just "my own case", but rather the mentalistic ideas that we apply unproblematically to ourselves and other human beings.

6. Therefore the analogical form of the English expression "what it is like" is misleading. It does not mean "what (in our experience) it resembles", but rather "how it is for the subject himself."

7. Any intelligent extraterrestrial beings totally different from us.

8. It may be easier than I suppose to transcend inter-species barriers with the aid of the imagination. For example, blind people are able to detect objects near them by a form of sonar, using vocal clicks or taps of a cane. Perhaps if one knew what that was like, one could by extension imagine roughly what it was like to possess the much more refined sonar of a bat. The distance between oneself and other persons and other species can fall anywhere on a continuum. Even for other persons the understanding of what it is like to be them is only partial, and when one moves to species very different from oneself, a lesser degree of partial understanding may still be available. The imagination is remarkably flexible. My point, however, is not that we cannot know what it is like to be a bat. I am not raising that epistemological problem. My point is rather that even to form a conception of what it is like to be a bat (and a fortiori to know what it is like to be a bat) one must take up the bat's point of view. If one can take it up roughly, or partially, then one's conception will also be rough or partial. Or so it seems in our present state of understanding.

9. The problem I am going to raise can therefore be posed even if the distinction between more subjective and more objective descriptions or viewpoints can itself be

made only within a larger human point of view. I do not accept this kind of conceptual relativism, but it need not be refuted to make the point that psychophysical reduction cannot be accommodated by the subjective-to-objective model from other cases.

10. The problem is not just that when I look at the Mona Lisa, my visual experience has a certain quality, no trace of which is to be found by someone looking into my brain. For even if he did observe there a tiny image of the Mona Lisa, he would have no reason to identify it with the experience.

11. The relation would therefore not be a contingent one, like that of a cause and its distinct effect. It would be necessarily true that a physical state felt a certain way. Saul Kripke in *Semantics of Natural Language* (ed. Davidson and Harman) argues that causal behaviorist and related analyses of the mental fail because they construe, e.g., "pain" as a merely contingent name of pains. The subjective character of an experience ("its immediate phenomenolocal quality" Kripke calls it [p. 340]) is the essential property left out by such analyses, and the one in virtue of which it is, necessarily, the experience it is. My view is closely related to his. Like Kripke, I find the hypothesis that a certain brain state should necessarily have a certain subjective character incomprehensible without further explanation. No such explanation emerges from theories which view the mind-brain relation as contingent, but perhaps there are other alternatives, not yet discovered.

A theory that explained how the mind-brain relation was necessary would still leave us with Kripke's problem of explaining why it nevertheless appears contingent. That difficulty seems to me surmountable, in the following way. We may imagine something by representing it to ourselves either perceptually, sympathetically, or symbolically. I shall not try to say how symbolic imagination works, but part of what happens in the other two cases is this. To imagine something perceptually, we put ourselves in a conscious state resembling the state we would be in if we perceived it. To imagine something sympathetically, we put ourselves in a conscious state resembling the thing itself. (This method can be used only to imagine mental events and stares—our own or another's.) When we try to imagine a mental state occurring without its associated brain state, we first sympathetically imagine the occurrence of the mental state: that is, we put ourselves into a state that resembles it mentally. At the same time, we attempt perceptually to imagine the nonoccurrence of the associated physical state, by putting ourselves into another state unconnected with the first; one resembling that which we would be in if we perceived the nonoccurrence of the physical state. Where the imagination of physical features is perceptual and the imagination of mental features is sympathetic, it appears to us that we can imagine any experience occurring without its associated brain state, and vice versa. The relation between them will appear contingent even if it is necessary, because of the independence of the disparate types of imagination. (Solipsism incidentally, results if one misinterprets sympathetic imagination as if it worked like perceptual imagination: it then seems impossible to imagine any experience that is not one's own.)

12. See "Mental Events" in *Experience and Theory*, ed. Lawrence Foster and J. W. Swanson (Amherst: University of Massachusetts Press, 1970); though I do not understand the argument against psychophysical laws.

13. Similar remarks apply to my paper "Physicalism", *Philosophical Review*,

LXXIV (1965), 339–56, reprinted with postscript in *Modern Materialism*, ed. John O'Connor (New York: Harcourt Brace Jovanovich, 1969).

14. This question also lies at the heart of the problem of other minds, whose close connection with the mind-body problem is often overlooked. If one understood how subjective experience could have an objective nature, one would understand the existence of subjects other than oneself.

15. I have not defined the term "physical." Obviously it does not apply just to what can be described by the concepts of contemporary physics, since we expect further developments. Some may think there is nothing to prevent mental phenomena from eventually being recognized as physical in their own right. But whatever else may be said of the physical, it has to be objective. So if our idea of the physical ever expands to include mental phenomena, it will have to assign them an objective character—whether or not this is done by analyzing them in terms of other phenomena already regarded as physical. It seems to me more likely, however, that mental-physical relations will eventually be expressed in a theory whose fundamental terms cannot be placed clearly in either category.

Online resources:

Thomas Nagel
http://philosophy.fas.nyu.edu/object/thomasnagel

17

Asymmetries and Mind-Body Perplexities

Keith Gunderson

> O wad some Pow'r the giftie gie us
> To see oursels as others see us!"
>
> —From "To a Louse" by Robert Burns

I

Any satisfactory solution to the mind-body problem must include an account of why the so-called "I," "subjective self," or "self as subject of experiences" seems so adept at slipping through the meshes of every nomological net of physical explanation which philosophers have been able to imagine science someday bestowing upon them. Until this agility on the part of the self is either curtailed or shown to be ontologically benign the mind-body problem is not going to go away. Unless the self itself, however characterized, can be shown to be comfortably at home within the domain of the physical, many of its putative attributes—thoughts, feelings, and sensations—will not seem to be at rest there either.

Nor will it do to attempt to pre-empt the playing out of these perplexities by launching a frontal attack a la Hume or Ryle on allegedly quixotic views as to the nature of the self. The problem I am alluding to does not arise because of quixotic views of the self. It is just the reverse: philosophers find themselves forced to endorse quixotic views of the self primarily because they systematically fail to show how a human being might conceive of himself as being completely in the world.

Some kind of thoroughgoing physicalism seems intuitively plausible mainly because of a dramatic absence of reasons for supposing that were we to dissect, dismantle, and exhaustively inspect any other person we would discover anything more than a complicated organization of physical things, properties, processes, and events. Furthermore, as has been emphasized recently, we have a strong sense of many of our mental features as being embodied.[1] On the other hand there's a final persuasiveness physicalism lacks which can be traced to the conceptual hardship each person faces when trying to imagine himself being completely accounted for by any such dissection, dismantling, or inspection. It is not so much that one boggles at conceiving of any aspect of his self, person, or consciousness being described in physicalistic terms; it is rather that one boggles at conceiving of *every* aspect of being simultaneously so describable. For convenience of exposition I shall sometimes use the word "self" to refer to whatever there is (or isn't!) which seems to resist such description. Such reference to a self or aspect thereof will not commit me to any positive characterization of it. Neither to the view that one's self remains unchanged from moment to moment, nor to the view that it doesn't, nor to the view that it is a thing, process, or bundle of events. What I am committed to is phrasing and unpicking the following problem: If a thoroughgoing physicalism (or any kind of monism) is true, why should it even seem so difficult for me to view my mind or self as an item wholly in the world? And this independently of how I may construe that mind or self: whether as a substance or as a cluster of properties, processes, or events. The paradox becomes: a physicalistic (or otherwise monistic) account of the mind at the outset seems quite convincing so long as I consider anyone except myself. If, however, physicalism provides an adequate account of the minds or selves of others, why should it not, then, provide an adequate account of the nature of my mind or self so long as I lack any reason to suppose that I am utterly unique?[2] But if I am unable to see how physicalism could account for the nature of my mind or self, why then should it not seem equally implausible as a theory about the mind or self of anyone else, again assuming that I lack reasons for supposing that I am unique? In this way we teeter-totter between the problem of viewing our self as wholly in the world, or physical, and the problem of viewing other people who seem wholly in the world as being somewhat mental. But if the mental is after all physical, why should this be so? Although I may not initially believe that in my or anyone else's investigation of the world I or they will find need to riddle our explanations with references to immaterial selves or spirits, it still remains easy to believe that I will never turn up the whole of my self as something co-habiting with items in the natural world. Hence the presumptuousness of assuming I really do find other selves in the world.

II

Thomas Nagel in his recent article, "Physicalism," writes:

> The feeling that physicalism leaves out of account the essential subjectivity of psychological states is the feeling that nowhere in the description of the state of a human body could there be room for a physical equivalent of the fact that I (or any self), and not just the body, am the subject of those states.[3]

No doubt (as Nagel himself intimates) such puzzlements are to some extent reflected in (perhaps in some sense caused by?) the peculiar linguistic role played by indexical expressions such as 'I" ("now," "this," and so on. . . .) Even so, what then needs to be shown is that the pragmatic conditions underlying the difference in use between the indexical "I" and nonindexicals do not add up to a metaphysical difference between whatever the indexical "I" denotes when it is used and the sorts of things which nonindexicals might refer to or characterize.

In brief, I believe that a major temptation to reject a physicalistic theory of mentality, *or any monistic doctrine,* and by default flirt with some variety of Cartesianism or mind/body dualism derives from the as yet inadequately assessed asymmetry between (a) how I am able to view myself as a potential object of investigation (within a spatio-temporal setting) and (b) how at first sight it seems one would be able to investigate virtually anything else including (supposedly) other people within such a setting. Given this asymmetry it is cold comfort to be told that my sensations and feelings may be identical with certain brain processes *in the way that* a lightning flash is identical with an electrical discharge or a cloud is identical with a mass of tiny particles in suspension.[4] Such comparisons may serve to assuage whatever logical qualms had been felt concerning the compatibility of an identity statement ("Sensations are identical with brain processes") with the supposedly synthetic empirical character of the mind-body identity thesis. (For we have learned that although a lightning flash is identical with an electrical discharge we had to make empirical discoveries to disclose it.) But as long as we seem systematically unable to view our own mind or self as something which can be wholly investigated in the way in which lightning flashes or electrical discharges or, as it seems, other people can be wholly investigated, illustrations involving lightning flashes, electrical discharges (and the like) will seem less than illustrative. It is for this reason that the seeming duality of the phenomenal and the physical does not comprise an analogue to the "complementarity" involved in the Copenhagen interpretation of Quantum Mechanics. For both particles and waves are, *in some sense,* equally at home *in* or "out of" the world.

An invisible bull in the china shop of the physicalist's analogies is the ominous absence of whatever those arguments might be which would show one that his own self is as wholly amenable to physical investigation as are *either* clouds or molecules *or* lightning flashes or electrical discharges. The identity-analogies usually engaged in the service of physicalism involve only identities between entities rather obviously susceptible to eventual specification and characterization by expressions which conveniently locate them within a spatio-temporal framework and describe them in physicalistic ways. The question of whether my mind or self is wholly amenable to even roughly this sort of description is one of the major points at issue. It is not sufficient to argue that if other minds seem to consist of nothing other than that which can be physically located and characterized then my mind must be too, unless I suppose it is unique; for the failure to suppose it's unique can be utilized to show that other minds cannot be accounted for in a purely physicalistic way.

Should the above diagnosis be correct, any solution to the mind-body problem must proceed through (at least) two stages: At the first stage what must be overcome is a natural resistance to viewing one's own mind or self as *the sort of thing* which can be wholly investigated in a way in which other things, events, objects, (people?) can be imagined as being wholly investigated by one's own mind or self. I shall refer to the difficulties encountered at this first stage as *The Investigational Asymmetries Problem.*[5] Once such difficulties have been dissolved one may go on to attempt to answer the question of whether one's mind (and hence other minds) which is amenable to such investigation can best be characterized after such an investigation as "a certain kind of information processing system," "a coalition of computer-like routines and subroutines," or instead as "a certain type of entelechy" or as "a certain sort of vital force" and so on. I shall refer to the difficulties encountered at this second stage as *The Characterization Problem.*

So the problem I wish to focus on is not simply that my self seems so private to me and hence could not be a physical object of scientific investigations carried out by others, but rather that it seems in some part so unpublic to me, and hence cannot be viewed by me at any given time as an item wholly susceptible even in principle to scientific investigations by me. (We might call this the problem of empirically "underprivileged access" to ourselves.) But if my self could never be wholly public to me in the way that cogs or pulleys, dendrites or axons seem to be, it is easy to be persuaded that it is not really wholly public to anyone else either. Hence a thesis such as physicalism which certainly ought to be committed to the view that my mental states are public in virtue of their being physical states or processes which are incontestably public still seems implausible.

What I hope to show is that the asymmetry between how I am able to investigate my self (and thereby the subjects of my thoughts, feelings, and sensations) and how it is I can investigate what I regard as other selves and other things within some spatio-temporal scheme is structurally similar to other ontologically benign asymmetries. By seeing why it is that these analogous asymmetries fail to thrust upon us any dualistic ontology of things, processes, or features. I think it will be shown that there is no need to suppose that the *Investigational Asymmetries* underlying the mind-body problem forces upon us a dualistic ontology of things, processes, or features.

III

Case 1: The My Eyes Problem

How can I tell what both my eyes look like (at one time)? Not in the same way I can tell what someone else's eyes look like, not simply by observing them. Only by looking in mirrors, or at photographs, or at movies of me, or by asking others to tell me what my eyes look like.

There are two ways of finding out what a person's two eyes look like at one time: (1) a way of finding out about the eyes of others, and (2) a way of finding out about my own.

A familiar division. Here we have a kind of other minds problem in reverse. I can know by directly looking at them what other people's eyes look like, but I can never know what my own eyes look like by looking at them—except with the aid of mirrors, photographs, and so on. (I shall hereafter rule out the latter).

I can imagine what it would be like to be in a position to see what anybody else's eyes look like, but I cannot imagine what it would be like to be in a position to see with my present eyes what my present eyes look like. At least I cannot imagine being in a position to see what my eyes look like, without, say imagining something like the case where I have my current eyes removed and replaced by a different pair of eyes. But this changes the case. By "my eyes", I mean to mean "the eyes which I now possess in my body and which I now see through."

But is there any reason to suppose that the general characteristics which my eyes have differ in kind from the sorts of features which other people's eyes have and which I can see that they have by looking at them? That is to say, are we in the least bit tempted here to propagate a double ontology concerning eyes: (1) the sorts of features my eyes have and which from my point of view seem non-visible and (2) the sorts of features (or looks) everybody else's eyes have and which I am aware of whenever I look at them? Are we to imagine that there is more (or, better still, less) to other people's eyes than meets my eye since I have no reason to suppose I am unique, and seemingly every reason to suppose there is something in eyes which cannot be investigated since I cannot investigate my own?

Consider the complications which arise if we tried to refute the testimony of mirrors, photographs, and other people as wholly adequate for our own case. We would have to assume that though we know what everyone else's eyes looked like, and know that they looked just as they looked in the mirror, ours do not look as they look in the mirror to everyone else. Ours, we might insist, have non-visible features. If we were to do this we would also have to assume that the looks of our eyes differ from any other part of the body with respect to their reflections in a mirror. We know our hands look like our hands look in the mirror; we know our stomachs look like our stomachs look in the mirror; and so on. But eyes, well, no, or maybe, or we can't tell whether they do look like they look in the mirror or that they are even the sorts of things of which it makes sense to say "they look a certain way," and so on. We would have to believe that everybody else lies with respect to our eyes, and that mirrors "lie" with respect to our eyes, though they "tell the truth" with respect to every other reflectable feature of us.

I do not conclude that my eyes look as they look in the mirror, because I adopt a simple "reverse" argument from analogy: "Since other people's eyes look like what they look like in the mirror, therefore my eyes must look like what they look like in the mirror." Rather, it is because it would take an immensely complicated and implausible theory to try to explain my eyes not looking like they look in the mirror, given that my hands do, given that my feet do, given that other people's eyes do, given that I have no reason for thinking other people are lying when they tell me what my eyes look like, and so on. Lacking a special theory for my own case, I not only accept what other people say about the looks of my eyes, and what is shown in the mirror, I have excellent reasons for accepting this. And certainly I do not conclude that my eyes are, say "featureless." This latter absurdity, however, is one we could be needled into accepting were we to decide to "start from our own case" and reason by analogy to the nature of the eyes of others. We would be forced to submit to the conclusion, even in the face of other faces, that the eyes of others have no visible features, for our own eyes seem to us to have none. But we never seemed pressed to such calamitous conclusions, and this is because we have a perfectly good explanation of why we could never be in a position to see the features of our own eyes in the way we are in a good position (potentially) for seeing the features of anyone else's eyes. And the explanation is that in order for me to see my eyes with my eyes, my own eyes would have to be in two (actually four) places at once: in front of themselves to be looked at as well as at the point from which they are being looked at. Note too the conceptual absurdity involved in supposing we know how eyes (in general) look by "starting from our own case" and then reasoning by analogy that other eyes are as ours seem to us, i.e. featureless. What possible sense could be given to the claim that our eyes seem to us to have or lack features of any sort whatsoever if we suppose there are no mirrors about and so on?

Wittgenstein remarked in the Tractatus . . . If I wrote a book called The World as I found it, I should have to include a report on my body and should have to say which parts were subordinate to my will, and which were not, etc. this being a method of isolating the subject, or rather of showing that in an important sense there is no subject; for it alone could not be mentioned in that book.

Surely Wittgenstein here has his eye on what I have called The Investigational Asymmetries Problem. In other words, just as the eye does not, cannot, see itself in its own visual field, so too, the self will never, in its inventory-taking of the world, find itself in the world in the manner in which it finds other people and things. But Wittgenstein wrongly concludes from this that the self ("the subject") in "an important sense" does not exist. What I am arguing is that there's no more reason to suppose the self does not exist because it is unable to observe itself, than there is reason to suppose eyes have no visible features since one is unable to observe them in his own case. (Compare: "There is no meaning to my own utterance tokens because only items which require some degree of interpretation or disambiguation can have meaning, and I don't [generally can't] disambiguate my own remarks!") Note: Wittgenstein anticipates this move, but seems willing to accept the consequences: "You will say that this is exactly like the case of the eye and the visual field. But really you do not see the eye."[6] Of course. But we really do see eyes, and (1) have an explanation of why it is we cannot observe our own, and (2) have no reason to assume our case is unlike the case of other eyes which we do observe. But if our having eyes does not guarantee that we ourselves be able to inspect their looks, their visible natures, why should we suppose that our being or having selves should guarantee that we will be in a position fully to inspect their natures, and so on? The way back into the world for the self which seems to itself not to be there, is simply its coming to realize that it is to other people what other people are to it.

The case of "my eyes," though it is a kind of other minds problem in reverse, is exactly parallel to that problem of the self which has concerned me here. For the problem of convincing myself that the looks of my eyes are (more or less) exactly like the looks of other eyes, is parallel to the problem of becoming convinced that the nature of my self is (more or less) exactly like the selves of others which, it seems, can be exhaustively described by reference to their behavior and physiology.

But another case will help to consolidate and further clarify the conceptual theses advanced in the first case. It might be noted that nowhere in this second case is any mention of a living organism involved. This should serve to erase any suggestion that the form which the *Investigational Asymmetries Problem* takes is peculiar to sentient agents.

Case II: The Self-Scanning Scanner Problem

Suppose, we have a non-conscious scanning mechanism, call it SM 1, which is able to scan what we shall call its communication cell, CC 1, somewhat after the manner in which current computing machines are able to scan symbols in their communication cells. We shall imagine CC 1, to be a cell of rather flexible size. It shall be able to expand and contract. We shall suppose that SM 1, could scan CC 1, for the appearance of symbols, or the presence of objects, say a bug or a watch or a feather. Let us also imagine that SM 1 could scan other scanners, SM 2, SM 3, . . . SMn, all of which would differ only from SM 1 in that they'd be smaller than SM 1, during the time at which they were being scanned. Whenever a scanner such as SM 1 scans another scanner, the scanner being scanned will have to shrink suitably in order for it to appear in CC 1. We shall also suppose that SM 1 could scan other scanners while they were in the state of scanning things. Scanners SM 1, SM 2, . . . SMn, will be similar in all interesting respects: in design and structure, and in the sorts of inputs, outputs, and so on which are possible for them. So now let us suppose that SM 1 is able to perform what we shall call a "complete scan" of the workings of SM 2, while SM 2 is scanning its communication cell CC 2 in which there appears some symbol or thing. Thus the nature of SM 2, its program, its actual operation while scanning CC 2, will be made available to SM 1 in the form of descriptions. Each scanner we shall suppose to be endowed with certain pattern recognition or generalization capacities. For example, each scanner will be able to recognize various instances of triangles as triangles, apples of different sizes and color, all as being apples, and so on. Thus a scanner will be equipped to answer simple questions as to how a certain item is classified. Let us imagine that such information could be stored as an entry to a list contained in some storage system which is an appendage of SM 1. Let us call this list SM 1's "World List." And let us call the list of all possible World Lists (of scanners SM 1, SM 2, . . . SMn) "The World List." So now let us imagine that SM 1 goes on to scan SM 3, SM 4, . . . SMn while each is in a state of scanning a symbol or a bug or a watch or a feather. Thus a description of each scanner scanning would be potentially available to SM 1 and could be stored in SM 1's storage system on its "World List." And if we imagine the universe in which SM 1 exists as being a universe in which there are only other scanners SM 2, SM 3, . . . SMn and a few objects and events-feathers, bugs, watches, scanners scanning—then we can imagine SM 1 being able to describe virtually everything in its universe. That is, it could in principle scan most everything in its universe and store a description of each item on its World List. But obviously there is going to be one description which SM 1 will never be able to insert on its own World List: namely, any complete description of SM 1 while it is in a state of scanning. SM 1 is, of course, not able to obtain information about itself while scanning in the same way that it is able to gain information about SM 2, SM

3, . . . SMn. In order for SM 1 to obtain information about itself scanning an X, say, in the way that it obtains information about SM 2 scanning an X, SM 1 would have to be in two places at once: where it is, and inside its own communication cell.

Nevertheless, a description of SM 1 in a state of scanning will be available to the World List of some other scanner—say SM 27. Hence, such a description could appear on The World List. All descriptions of scanners in a state of scanning could appear on The World List. So if we think of scanners SM 1, SM 2, . . . SMn as all being of a comparable nature, and the descriptions of them in a state of scanning as depicting that nature, then we can see that SM 1 in a state of scanning is the same in nature as the other scanning scanners it scans, though it will never be able to locate a description which depicts its nature of other scanners scanning which are descriptions on its (SM 1's) World List. In other words it would be utterly wrong to conclude from SM 1's failure to find a description of its own state of scanning on its World List (or for SM 1 somehow to report on the basis of this) that SM 1 possessed features different in nature from the features which other scanners scanning had and which could be revealed to SM 1. For this would be to suggest that a comparison between SM 1's features and the features of other scanners made available to SM 1 while scanning had been made and that radical differences had been found. Although scanner SM 1 is in principle unable to construe itself on the model of other scanners in a state of scanning in the restricted sense that it cannot construct a list of information about itself comparable to the lists of information it can compile about other scanners, there is no reason for it to report or for us to suppose that some kind of scanning dualism is in order. In other words, there is no reason to assert that SM 1 while in the state of scanning differs in nature from the sorts of features it finds other scanners to possess while in a state of scanning X. Hence, there is also no reason to suppose that there is more to other scanners in a state of scanning than that which could be revealed to SM 1.

The scanning mechanism may be compared to a periscope which is able to sight other ships, even parts of the ship to which it belongs, but which is unable to place itself in its own crosshairs.

The import of such examples for the mind-body problem should by now be transparent: the difficulty in construing our self at any given moment as an item wholly susceptible to third-person physicalistic and behavioristic descriptions is comparable to the difficulty a periscope would face in attempting to place itself between its own crosshairs.

IV

On the basis of the forgoing cases, I think it is correct to conclude that the following statements are true: (1) Even though I can never be in a position to look at them, the visual appearances which my eyes possess are identical in kind with members of the class of visual features to which the visual features of the eyes of others belong, which features are revealed to me simply by looking at other eyes (sans mirrors, photographs, et al.). (2) Whenever scanner SM 1 is in a state of scanning its communication cell, it is in a state identical in kind with the sorts of states other scanners in a state of scanning are in, and which are revealed to SM 1 whenever other scanners scanning are placed in SM 1's communication cell. (A periscope 1 is identical in kind with members of the class of periscopes 2 . . . any one of which periscope 1 can place between its crosshairs.)

The two foregoing statements might all be called "metaphysically neutral." For even though it can be shown that X, say, is identical in kind with Y's, it leaves open the question as to what kind of things Y's are. Yet such a "metaphysically neutral" identity statement is, I believe, exactly what must first be shown to be true of a theory such as physicalism is to seem justified. The statement which the above analogies are designed to support is: "I am identical in kind with what I find other people to be" where by "what I find other people to be" is meant as they are (or might be) revealed to be on the basis of empirical investigation, etc. (which could in principle be found out by me). This latter qualification must be made in order to distinguish our case from the case where a mind/body dualist accepts the claim that he is identical in kind with other people but asserts that other people all have private selves not amenable to empirical investigation and derives this conclusion from the belief that his self is not amenable to being treated by himself as an object for investigation lying within the world.[7] That is I am assuming that what we find other people to be will no longer be colored by the assumption that since I cannot wholly investigate myself, then since there is no reason to assume I am unique, there is something for all people which does not yield to empirical investigation either. In other words, "what I find other people to be" will be construed as "what I find them to be *sans* use of the just mentioned assumption." This again, as argued earlier, does not load the dice in favor of physicalism. It simply seems that way, since it is obvious at the moment that unless we resort to such an assumption there is no reason to suppose other people are not wholly physical beings.

It is easy to unwittingly saddle oneself with the view that if I am an object wholly amenable to scientific investigation, I had better be able to imagine myself as being an object which I myself could wholly investigate. This I have argued is an absurd demand. And for the same reason that it's absurd to demand that I be able to see my own eyes if I am to credit them with the same sorts of features I ascribe to the eyes of others. Yet, the self-centered insistence that if I am an item susceptible to empirical investigation I ought to be able, at least in principle, to carry out the complete investigation is quite understandable. For what this really adds up to is the insistence that anyone, myself or others, be able to demonstrate to my satisfaction that I am such an item. And the insistence that it be possible to demonstrate *to my satisfaction* that I am such an item slips into seeming comparable to the demand that I be in a position to appreciate the demonstrations. (Compare: I must be the sort of creature which can never die, since I cannot imagine being in a position to observe my own death. And since I'm not unique, perhaps we are all immortal.)

V

Non-physicalism according to my story has an initially plausible ring which echoes from the fact that I cannot be in two places at the same time, and the tendency to wish to be in as good a position to investigate myself (empirically) as I am in (at least potentially) with respect to others. Curiously enough the failure to be able to be in two places at once in this case forces us to feel that we, as minds, or consciousness, are not in any place at all.

And it is this sense of non-location which tends to reinforce the view that the mind is only contingently connected with the physical. But the foregoing arguments, if correct, should rid us of any temptation to adopt either view.

The solution to stage one of the mind-body question, on the above analysis, turns out to be nothing more than coming to an acceptance of the fact that although we will never be in as good a position to investigate ourselves as we are to investigate others, objects, things, events, etc. this makes no more difference (ontologically) than the fact that a submarine's periscope cannot locate itself in its own crosshairs makes an ontological difference between the nature of the periscope doing the sighting and the things it can sight.

NOTES

Keith Gunderson, "Asymmetries and Mind-Body Perplexities," in M. Radner and S. Winokur (eds.), *Minnesota Studies in the Philosophy of Science*, vol. IV, *Analyses of Theories and Methods of Physics and Psychology*, University of Minnesota Press. Copyright © 1970. Reprinted by permission of the University of Minnesota Press.

1. Vesey, G. A., *The Embodied Mind*, London: Allen & Unwin, 1965.

2. Cf. Paul Ziff's "The Simplicity of Other Minds," *The Journal of Philosophy*, Vol. LXII, No. 20: October 21, 1965, pp. 575–584.

3. In *Philosophical Review*, Vol. LXXIV, No. 3, July 1965, p. 354.

4. Cf. J. J. C. Smart's "Sensations and Brain Processes," in *The Philosophy of Mind*, edited by V. C. Chappell, Prentice-Hall, 1962. Such analogies are, of course, scattered throughout the writings of proponents of the identity thesis.

5. These asymmetries can be phrased either in terms of (1) how we find out about the minds of others as distinct from the way in which we find out about our own

mind, or (2) the problem we have in finding ourselves in the world as distinct from the way we can at least imagine finding anything else in the world. Here I restrict myself to (2).

6. *Tractatus Logico-Philosophicus*, trans. by D. F. Pears and B. F. McGuiness, Routledge and Kegan Paul, 1961, p. 117.

7. This latter belief may itself be derived from the more radical notion that the self cannot treat itself as an object for investigation period.

Online resources:

Keith Gunderson
www.philosophy.umn.edu/people/faculty/gunderson.html

18

Knowing What It's Like

David Lewis

The most formidable challenge to any sort of materialism and functionalism comes from the friend of phenomenal qualia. He says we leave out the phenomenal aspect of mental life: we forget that pain is a feeling, that there is something it is like to hold one's hand in a flame, that we are aware of something when we suffer pain, that we can recognize that something when it comes again. So far, our proper reply is the one sketched in Section VIII: we deny none of that! We say to the friend of qualia that, beneath his tendentious jargon, he is just talking about pain and various aspects of its functional role. We have already said what we take pain to be; and we do not doubt that part of its causal role is to give rise to judgments that one is in pain, and part is to enable one to recognize pain (the same realizer of the same role) when it comes again.

So far, so good. But if he persists, the friend of qualia can succeed in escaping our unwelcome agreement; and when he does, we must reverse our strategy. Suppose he makes his case as follows.[1]

You have not tasted Vegemite (a celebrated yeast-based condiment). So you do not know what it is like to taste Vegemite. And you never will, unless you taste Vegemite. (Or unless the same experience, or counterfeit traces of it, are somehow produced in you by artificial means.) No amount of the information whereof materialists and functionalists speak will help you at all. But if you taste Vegemite, then you will know what it is like. So you will have gained a sort of information that the materialists and functionalists overlook entirely. Call this phenomenal information. By qualia I mean the special subject matter of this phenomenal information.

211

Now we must turn eliminative. We dare not grant that there is a sort of information we overlook; or, in other words, that there are possibilities exactly alike in the respects we know of, yet different in some other way. That would be defeat. Neither can we credibly claim that lessons in physics, physiology could teach the inexperienced what it is like to taste Vegemite. Our proper answer, I think, is that knowing what it's like is not the possession of information at all. It isn't the elimination of any hitherto open possibilities. Rather, knowing what it's like is the possession of abilities: abilities to recognize, abilities to imagine, abilities to predict one's behavior by means of imaginative experiments. (Someone who knows what it's like to taste Vegemite can easily and reliably predict whether he would eat a second helping of Vegemite ice cream.) Lessons cannot impart these abilities—who would have thought that they could? There is a state of knowing what it's like, sure enough. And Vegemite has a special power to produce that state. But phenomenal information and its special subject matter do not exist.[2]

Imagine a smart data bank. It can be told things, it can store the information it is given, it can reason with it, it can answer questions on the basis of its stored information. Now imagine a pattern-recognizing device that works as follows. When exposed to a pattern it makes a sort of template, which is then applied to patterns presented to it in future. Now imagine one device with both faculties, rather like a clock radio. There is no reason to think that any such device must have a third faculty: a faculty of making templates for patterns it has never been exposed to, using its stored information about these patterns. If it has a full description about a pattern but no template for it, it lacks ability but it doesn't lack information. (Rather, it lacks information in usable form.) When it is shown the pattern it makes a template and gains abilities, but it gains no information. We might be rather like that.

NOTES

    1. This is the "knowledge argument" of Frank Jackson, "Epiphenomenal Qualia." *Philosophical Quarterly* 32 (1982): 127–36. It appears also, in less purified form, in Thomas Nagel, "What Is It Like To Be a Bat?" *Philosophical Review* 83 (1974): 435–50, and in Paul Meehl, "The Compleat Autocerebroscopist," in Paul Feyerabend and Grover Maxwell, eds., *Mind, Matter and Method: Essays in Philosophy and Science in Honor of Herbert Feigl* (Minneapolis: University of Minnesota Press, 1966).

    2. This defense against the knowledge argument is presented in detail in Laurence Nemirow, *Functionalism and the Subjective Quality of Experience* (Ph.D. dissertation, Stanford University, 1979), chapter 2; and more briefly in his review of Thomas Nagel's "Mortal Questions," *Philosophical Review* 89 (1980): 473–77.

Theories of Consciousness: Materialist and Anti-Reductionist

19

What is Consciousness?

David M. Armstrong

The notion of consciousness is notoriously obscure. It is difficult to analyze, and some philosophers and others have thought it unanalysable. It is not even clear that the word 'consciousness' stands for just one sort of entity, quality, process, or whatever. There is, however, one thesis about consciousness that I believe can be confidently rejected: Descartes' doctrine that consciousness is the essence of mentality. That view assumes that we can explain mentality in terms of consciousness. I think that the truth is in fact the other way round. Indeed, in the most interesting sense of the word 'consciousness', consciousness is the cream on the cake of mentality, a special and sophisticated development of mentality. It is not the cake itself. In what follows, I develop an anti-Cartesian account of consciousness.

MINIMAL CONSCIOUSNESS

In thinking about consciousness, it is helpful to begin at the other end and consider a totally unconscious person. Somebody in a sound, dreamless sleep may be taken as an example. It has been disputed whether unconsciousness is really ever total. There is some empirical evidence that a person in dreamless sleep, or even under a total anaesthetic, still has some minimal awareness. Minimal behavioural reactions to sensory stimuli have been observed under these conditions. But let us take it, if only as a simplifying and perhaps unrealistic assumption, that we are dealing with total unconsciousness.

Notice first that we are perfectly happy to concede that such a person, while in this state of total unconsciousness, has a mind. Furthermore, although by hypothesis this mind is in no way active—no mental events take place, no mental processes occur within it—we freely allow that this mind is in various states.

The totally unconscious person does not lack knowledge and beliefs. Suppose him to be a historian of the mediaeval period. We will not deny him a great deal of knowledge of and beliefs about the Middle Ages just because he is sound asleep. He cannot give current expression to his knowledge and his beliefs, but he does not lack them. The totally unconscious person also may be credited with memories. He also can be said to have skills, including purely mental skills such as an ability for mental arithmetic. The ability is not lost during sound sleep just because it then cannot be exercised, any more than an athlete loses his athletic abilities during sound sleep, when he cannot exercise them. A totally unconscious person may be credited with likes and dislikes, attitudes and emotions, current desires and current aims and purposes. He may be said to have certain traits of character and temperament. He may be said to be in certain moods: 'He has been depressed all this week.'

How are we to conceive of these mental states (it seems natural to call them 'states') we attribute to the unconscious person? Some decades ago, under the influence of positivistic and phenomentalistic modes of thought, such attributions of mental states to an unconscious person would not have been taken very seriously, ontologically. It would have been thought that to say that the currently unconscious person A believes that p, is simply to refer to various ways in which A's mind works, or would work in suitable circumstances, before and/or after he wakes up. (The same positivist spirit might try further to reduce the way that A's mind works to A's peripheral bodily behaviour or to the behaviour A would exhibit in suitable circumstances.)

In historical perspective, we can see clearly how unsatisfactory such a view is. Consider two persons, A and B, unconscious at the same time, where it is true of A that he believes that p, but false of B. Must there not be a difference between A and B at that time to constitute this difference in belief-state? What else in the world could act as a truth-maker (the ground in the world) for the different conditional statements that are true of A and B? The mind of the unconscious person cannot be dissolved into statements about what would be true of the person if the situation were other than it was; if, in particular he were not unconscious.

In considering this point, I find very helpful the analogy between an unconscious person and a computer that has been programmed in various ways, that perhaps has partially worked through certain routines and is ready to continue with them, but is not currently operating. (I do not think that anything in the analogy turns on the material, physical nature of the computer. Even if the mind has to be conceived of in some immaterial way, the analogy will still hold.) The computer, perhaps, will have a certain amount of information stored in its memory-banks. This stored information may be compared to the knowledge, beliefs and memories the unconscious person still has during unconsciousness. If a Materialist account of the mind is correct, then, of course, knowledge, belief and memory will be physically encoded in the brain in some broadly similar way to the way in which information is stored in the computer. But the Dualist, say, will equally require the conception of immaterial storage of knowledge, belief and memory.

What we can say both of the knowledge, beliefs, etc. possessed by the totally unconscious person, and also of the information stored in the switched-off-computer, is that they are causally quiescent. Of course, nothing is causally quiescent absolutely: while a thing exists, it has effects upon its environment. But the information stored in the switched-off computer is causally quiescent with respect to the computing operations of the computer, and for our purposes this may be called causal quiescence. (The information may remain causally quiescent even after the computer has been switched on, unless that piece of information is required for current calculations.) In the same way, knowledge and beliefs may be said to be causally quiescent while they are not producing any mental effect in the person. The mental states of a totally unconscious person are thus causally quiescent (if they are not, we may stipulate that the person is not totally unconscious). Knowledge, beliefs, and so on may remain causally quiescent in this sense even when the mind is operational, for instance, where there is no call to use a particular piece of knowledge.

It seems, then, that we attribute mental states of various sorts to a totally unconscious person. But there are certain mental attributions we do not make. The totally unconscious person does not perceive, has no sensations, feelings or pangs of desire. He cannot think, contemplate or engage in any sort of deliberation. (He can have purposes, because purposes are capable of causal quiescence, but he cannot be engaged in carrying them out.) This is because perception, sensation and thinking are mental activities in a way that knowledge and beliefs are not. The distinction appears, roughly at any rate, to be the distinctions between events and occurrences on the one hand, and states on the other. When a mental state is producing mental effects, the comings-to-be of such effects are mental events and so mental activity is involved.

We now have a first sense for the word 'consciousness'. If there is mental activity occurring in the mind, if something mental is actually happening, then that mind is not totally unconscious. It is therefore conscious. A single faint sensation is not much, but if it occurs, to that extent there is consciousness. Unconsciousness is not total. I call consciousness in this sense 'minimal' consciousness.

It is alleged that it sometimes occurs that someone wakes up knowing the solution to, say, a mathematical problem, which they did not know when they went to sleep. If we rule out magical explanations, then there must have been mental activity during sleep. To that extent, there was minimal consciousness. This is compatible with the completest 'unconsciousness' in a sense still to be identified.

PERCEPTUAL CONSCIOUSNESS

Among the mental activities, however, it appears that we make a special link between consciousness and perception. In perception, there is consciousness of what is currently going on in one's environment and one's body. (Of course, the 'consciousness' may involve illusion.) There is an important sense in which, if a person is not perceiving, then he is not conscious, but if he is perceiving, then he is conscious. Suppose somebody to be dreaming. Since there is mental activity going on, the person is not totally unconscious. He is minimally conscious. Yet is there not some obvious sense in which he is unconscious? Now suppose that this person starts to perceive his environment and bodily state (I do not want to say 'suppose he wakes up', because perhaps there is more to waking up than just starting to perceive again). I think that we would be inclined to say that the person was now conscious in a way that he had not been before, while merely dreaming. Let us say, therefore, that he has regained 'perceptual' consciousness. This is a second sense of the word 'consciousness'. Perceptual consciousness entails minimal consciousness, but minimal consciousness does not entail perceptual consciousness.

INTROSPECTIVE CONSCIOUSNESS

Let us suppose, now, that there is mental activity going on in a person, and that this activity includes perception. If what has been said so far is accepted, then there are two senses in which such a person can be said to be conscious. He or she has minimal consciousness and has perceptual consciousness. There is, nevertheless, a third sense, in which such a person may still 'lack consciousness'. Various cases may be mentioned here. My own favourite is the case of the long-distance truck-driver. It has the advantage that many people have experienced the phenomenon.

After driving for long periods of time, particularly at night, it is possible to 'come to' and realize that for some time past one has been driving without being aware of what one has been doing. The coming-to is an alarming experience. It is natural to describe what went on before one came to by saying that during that time one lacked consciousness. Yet it seems clear that, in the two senses of the word that we have so far isolated, consciousness was present. There was mental activity, and as part of that mental activity, there was perception. That is to say, there was minimal consciousness and perceptual consciousness. If there is an inclination to doubt this, then consider the extraordinary sophistication of the activities successfully undertaken during the period of 'unconsciousness'.

A purpose was successfully advanced during that time: that of driving a car along a road. This purpose demanded that various complex sub-routines be carried out, and carried out at appropriate points (for instance, perhaps the brake or the clutch was used). Were not these acts purposeful? Above all, how is it possible to drive a car for kilometers along a road if one cannot perceive that road? One must be able to see where one is going, in order to adjust appropriately. It would have to be admitted, at the very least, that in such a case, eyes and brain have to be stimulated in just the same way as they are in ordinary cases of perception. Why then deny that perception takes place? So it seems that minimal consciousness and perceptual consciousness are present. But something else is lacking: consciousness in the most interesting sense of the word.

The case of the long-distance truck-driver appears to be a very special and spectacular one. In fact, however, I think it presents us with what is a relatively simple, and in evolutionary terms relatively primitive, level of mental functioning. Here we have more or less skilled purposive action, guided by perception, but apparently no other mental activity, and in particular no consciousness in some sense of 'consciousness', which differs from minimal and perceptual consciousness. It is natural to surmise that such relatively simple sorts of mental functioning came early in the course of evolutionary development. I imagine that many animals, particularly those whose central nervous system is less developed than ours, are continually, or at least normally, in the state in which the long-distance truck-driver is in temporarily. The third sort of consciousness, I surmise, is a late evolutionary development.

What is it that the long-distance truck-driver lacks? I think it is an additional form of perception, or, a little more cautiously, it is something that resembles perception. But unlike sense-perception, it is not directed towards our current environment and/or our current bodily state. It is perception of the mental. Such 'inner' perception is traditionally called introspection, or introspective awareness. We may therefore call this third sort of consciousness 'introspective' consciousness. It entails minimal consciousness. If perceptual consciousness is restricted to sense-perception, then introspective consciousness does not entail perceptual consciousness.

Introspective consciousness, then, is a perception-like awareness of current states and activities in our own mind. The current activities will include sense-perception: which latter is the awareness of current states and activities of our environment and our body. And (an important and interesting complication) since introspection is itself a mental activity, it too may become the object of introspective awareness.

Sense-perception is not a total awareness of the current states and activities of our environment and body. In the same way, introspective consciousness is not a total awareness of the current states and activities of our mind. At any time there will be states and activities of our mind of which we are not introspectively aware. These states and activities may be said to be unconscious mental states and activities in one good sense of the word 'unconscious'. (It is close to the Freudian sense, but there is no need to maintain that it always involves the mechanism of repression.) Such unconscious mental states and activities of course may involve minimal and/or perceptual consciousness, indeed the activities involve minimal consciousness by definition.

Just as perception is selective—not all-embracing—so it also may be mistaken. Perceptions may fail to correspond, more or less radically, to reality. In the same way, introspective consciousness may fail to correspond, more or less radically, to the mental reality of which it is a consciousness. (The indubitability of consciousness is a Cartesian myth, which has been an enemy of progress in philosophy and psychology.)

Following Locke, Kant spoke of introspection as 'inner sense', and it is essentially Kant's view I am defending here. By 'outer sense', Kant understood sense-perception. There is, however, one particular form of 'outer sense' that bears a particularly close formal resemblance to introspection. This is bodily perception or proprioception, the perception of our own current bodily states and activities. If we consider the objects of sight, sound, touch, taste and smell, then we notice that such objects are intersubjectively available. Each of us is capable of seeing or touching numerically the very same physical surface, hearing numerically the very same sound, tasting numerically the same tastes or smelling numerically the same smell. But the objects of proprioception are not intersubjectively available in this way.

Consider, for instance, kinaesthetic perception, which is one mode of proprioception. Each person kinaesthetically perceives (or, in some unusual cases, misperceives) the motion of his own limbs and those of nobody else. There is no overlap of kinaesthetic objects. This serves as a good model for, and at the same time it seems to demystify, the privacy of the objects of introspection. Each of us perceives current states and activities in our own mind and that of nobody else. The privacy is simply a little more complete than in the kinaesthetic case. There are other ways to perceive the motion of my limbs besides kinaesthetic perception for instance, by seeing and touching. These other ways are intersubjective. But, by contrast nobody else can have the direct awareness of my mental states and activities that I have. This privacy, however, is contingent only. We can imagine that somebody else should have the same direct consciousness of my mental states and activities that I enjoy. (They would not have those states, but they would be directly aware of them.)

Perception is a causal affair. If somebody perceives something, then it is involved in the perception: it is even involved in the concept of perception: that the thing perceived acts upon the perceiver, causing the perception of the object. If introspective consciousness is to be compared to perception, then it will be natural to say that the mental objects of introspection act within our mind so as to produce our introspective awareness of these states. Indeed, it is not easy to see what other naturalistic account of the coming-to-be of introspections could be given. If introspection is a causal process, then it will follow, incidentally, from our earlier definition of causal quiescence that whenever we are introspectively aware of one of our mental states, then that state is not at that time causally quiescent.

TYPES OF INTROSPECTIVE CONSCIOUSNESS

Perhaps we still have not drawn enough distinctions. Sometimes the distinction is drawn between mere 'reflex' consciousness, which is normally always present while we are awake (but which is lost by the long-distance truck-driver), and consciousness of a more explicit, self-conscious sort.

This difference appears to be parallel to the difference between mere 'reflex' seeing, which is always going on while we are awake and our eyes are open, and the careful scrutinizing of the visual environment that may be undertaken in the interest of some purpose we have. The eyes have a watching brief at all times that we are awake and have our eyes open; in special circumstances, they are used in a more attentive manner. (In close scrutiny by human beings, introspective consciousness is often, although not invariably, also called into play. We not only give the object more attention but have a heightened awareness of so doing. But presumably in lower animals such attentive scrutiny does not have this accompaniment.) Similarly, introspective consciousness normally has only a watching brief with respect to our mental states. Only sometimes do we carefully scrutinize our own current state of mind. We can mark the distinction by speaking of 'reflex' introspective awareness and opposing it to 'introspection proper'. It is a plausible hypothesis that the latter will normally involve not only introspective awareness of mental states and activities but also introspective awareness of the introspective awareness. It is in any case a peculiarly sophisticated sort of mental process.

WHAT IS SO SPECIAL ABOUT
INTROSPECTIVE CONSCIOUSNESS?

There remains the feeling that there is something quite special about introspective consciousness. The long-distance truck-driver has minimal and perceptual consciousness. But there is an important sense, we are inclined to
think, in which he has no experiences, indeed is not really a person, during
his period of introspective unconsciousness. Introspective consciousness
seems like a light switched on, which illuminates utter darkness. It has
seemed to many that with consciousness in this sense, a wholly new thing
enters the universe.

I now will attempt to explain why introspective consciousness seems to
have, but does not necessarily actually have, a quite special status in the
world. I proceed by calling attention to two points, which will then be
brought together at the end of the section.

First, it appears that introspective consciousness is bound up in a quite
special way with consciousness of self. I do not mean that the self is one of
the particular objects of introspective awareness alongside our mental states
and activities. This view was somewhat tentatively put forward by Russell in
The Problems of Philosophy (1912: Ch. 5) but had already been rejected by
Hume and by Kant. It involves accepting the extraordinary view that what
seems most inward to us, our mental states and activities, are not really us.
What I mean rather is that we take the states and activities of which we are
introspectively aware to be states and activities of a single continuing thing.

In recent years, we have often been reminded, indeed admonished, that
there is a great deal of theory involved even in quite unsophisticated perceptual judgments. To see that there is a tomato before our body is already to
go well beyond anything that can be said to be 'given', even where we do not
make excessive demands (such as indubitability) upon the notion of the
given. Consider knowingly perceiving a tomato. A tomato, to be a tomato,
must have sides and back, top and bottom, a certain history, certain causal
powers; and these things certainly do not seem to be given in perception. If
we consider the causal situation, it is only the shape, size and colour of some
portions of the surface of the tomato (the facing portions) that actually
determine the nature of the stimulation that reaches our eyes. This suggests
that, at best, it is only these properties that are in any way 'given' to us. The
rest is, in some sense, a matter of theory, although I do not think that we
should take this to mean that the perceptual judgment that there is a tomato
before us is a piece of risky speculation.

It is therefore natural to assume that the perceptions of 'inner sense'
involve a theory, involve going beyond the 'given', in the same general way
that the perceptions of 'outer sense' do. In particular, whatever may be the
case with other animals, or with small children, or with those who, like the

Wild Boy of Aveyron, have not been socialized, for ordinary persons, their mental states and activities are introspected as the states and activities of a single thing.

Once again, the comparison with proprioception seems to be instructive. We learn to organize our proprioceptions so that they yield us perceptions of a single unitary, physical object, our body, concerning which our proprioceptions give us certain information: its current posture, temperature, the movement of its limbs, and so on. This is clearly a theoretical achievement of some sophistication.

In the same way, we learn to organize what we introspect as being states of, and activities in, a single continuing entity: our self. Mere introspective consciousness, of course, is not at all clear just what this self is. At a primitive level perhaps, no distinction is made between the self and the body. Identification of the thing that is introspected as, say, a spiritual substance, or as the central nervous system, goes far beyond the level of theorizing involved in ordinary introspection. But the idea that the states and activities observed are states and activities of a unitary thing is involved. Introspective consciousness is consciousness of self.

If it is asked why introspection is theory-laden in this particular way, then an answer can be suggested. It is always worth asking the question about any human or animal organ or capacity: "What is its biological function?" It is therefore worth asking what is the biological function of introspective consciousness. Once the question is asked, then the answer is fairly obvious: it is to sophisticate our mental process in the interests of more sophisticated action.

Inner perception makes the sophistication of our mental processes possible in the following way. If we have a faculty that can make us aware of current mental states and activities, then it will be much easier to achieve integration of the states and activities, to get them working together in the complex and sophisticated ways necessary to achieve complex and sophisticated ends.

Current computer technology provides an analogy, though I would stress that it is no more than an analogy. In any complex computing operation, many different processes must go forward simultaneously: in parallel. There is need, therefore, for an overall plan for these activities, so that they are properly co-ordinated. This cannot be done simply in the manner in which a 'command economy' is supposed to be run: by a series of instructions from above. The co-ordination can only be achieved if the portion of the computing space made available for administering the overall plan is continuously made 'aware' of the current mental state of play with respect to the lower-level operations that are running in parallel. Only with this feedback is control possible. Equally, introspective consciousness provides the feedback (of a far more sophisticated sort than anything available in current computer technology) in the mind that enables 'parallel processes' in our mind to be integrated in a way that they could not be integrated otherwise. It is no accident that fully alert introspective consciousness characteristically arises in problem situations, situations that standard routines cannot carry one through.

We now can understand why introspection so naturally gives rise to the notion of the self. If introspective consciousness is the instrument of mental integration, then it is natural that what is perceived by that consciousness should be assumed to be something unitary.

There is nothing necessary about the assumption. It may even be denied on occasion. Less sophisticated persons than ourselves, on becoming aware of a murderous impulse springing up, may attribute it not to a hitherto unacknowledged and even dissociated part of themselves, but to a devil who has entered them. In Dickens' *Hard Times*, the dying Mrs. Gradgrind says that there seems to be a pain in the room, but she is not prepared to say that it is actually she that got it. In her weakened condition, she has lost her grip upon the idea that whatever she introspects is a state of one unitary thing: herself.

But although the assumption of unity is not necessary, it is one we have good reason to think true. A Physicalist in particular will take the states and activities introspected to be all physical states and activities of a continuing physical object: a brain.

That concludes the first step in my argument: to show that, and in what sense, introspective awareness is introspective awareness of self. The second step is to call attention to the special connection between introspective consciousness and event-memory, that is, memory of individual happenings. When the long-distance truck-driver recovers introspective consciousness, he has no memory of what happened while it was lacking. One sort of memory-processing cannot have failed him. His successful navigation of his vehicle depended upon him being able to recognize various things for what they were and treat them accordingly. He must have been able to recognize a certain degree of curve in the road, a certain degree of pressure on the accelerator, for what they were. But the things that happened to him during introspective unconsciousness were not stored in his event-memory. He lived solely in the present.

It is tempting to suppose, therefore, as a psychological hypothesis, that unless mental activity is monitored by introspective consciousness, then it is not remembered to have occurred, or at least it is unlikely that it will be remembered. It is obvious that introspective consciousness is not sufficient for event-memory. But perhaps it is necessary, or at least generally necessary. It is notoriously difficult, for instance, to remember dreams, and it is clear that, in almost all dreaming, introspective consciousness is either absent or is at a low ebb.

So it may be that introspective consciousness is essential or nearly essential for event-memory, that is, memory of the past as past. A fortiori, it will be essential or nearly essential for memory of the past of the self.

The two parts of the argument now may be brought together. If introspective consciousness involves (in reasonably mature human beings) consciousness of self, and if without introspective consciousness there would be little or no memory of the past history of the self, the apparent special illumination and power of introspective consciousness is explained. Without introspective consciousness, we would not be aware that we existed—our self would not be self to itself. Nor would we be aware of what the particular history of that self had been, even its very recent history. Now add just one more premise: the overwhelming interest that human beings have in themselves. We can then understand why introspective consciousness can come to seem a condition of anything mental existing, or even of anything existing at all.

Online resources:

David M. Armstrong
www.ditext.com/armstrong/armstrong.html
An Interview with Professor Armstrong by Andrew Churcky
www.ditext.com/armstrong/inter2.html

20

Facing Up to the Problem of Consciousness

David Chalmers

1: INTRODUCTION

Consciousness poses the most baffling problems in the science of the mind. There is nothing that we know more intimately than conscious experience, but there is nothing that is harder to explain. All sorts of mental phenomena have yielded to scientific investigation in recent years, but consciousness has stubbornly resisted. Many have tried to explain it, but the explanations always seem to fall short of the target. Some have been led to suppose that the problem is intractable, and that no good explanation can be given.

To make progress on the problem of consciousness, we have to confront it directly. In this paper, I first isolate the truly hard part of the problem, separating it from more tractable parts and giving an account of why it is so difficult to explain. I critique some recent work that uses reductive methods to address consciousness, and argue that such methods inevitably fail to come to grips with the hardest part of the problem. Once this failure is recognized, the door to further progress is opened. In the second half of the paper, I argue that if we move to a new kind of nonreductive explanation, a naturalistic account of consciousness can be given. I put forward my own candidate for such an account: a nonreductive theory based on principles of structural coherence and organizational invariance and a double-aspect view of information.

2: THE EASY PROBLEMS AND
THE HARD PROBLEM

There is not just one problem of consciousness. "Consciousness" is an ambiguous term, referring to many different phenomena. Each of these phenomena needs to be explained, but some are easier to explain than others. At the start, it is useful to divide the associated problems of consciousness into "hard" and "easy" problems. The easy problems of consciousness are those that seem directly susceptible to the standard methods of cognitive science, whereby a phenomenon is explained in terms of computational or neural mechanisms. The hard problems are those that seem to resist those methods.

The easy problems of consciousness include those of explaining the following phenomena:

the ability to discriminate, categorize, and react to environmental stimuli;
the integration of information by a cognitive system;
the reportability of mental states;
the ability of a system to access its own internal states;
the focus of attention;
the deliberate control of behavior;
the difference between wakefulness and sleep.

All of these phenomena are associated with the notion of consciousness. For example, one sometimes says that a mental state is conscious when it is verbally reportable, or when it is internally accessible. Sometimes a system is said to be conscious of some information when it has the ability to react on the basis of that information, or, more strongly, when it attends to that information, or when it can integrate that information and exploit it in the sophisticated control of behavior. We sometimes say that an action is conscious precisely when it is deliberate. Often, we say that an organism is conscious as another way of saying that it is awake.

There is no real issue about whether these phenomena can be explained scientifically. All of them are straightforwardly vulnerable to explanation in terms of computational or neural mechanisms. To explain access and reportability, for example, we need only specify the mechanism by which information about internal states is retrieved and made available for verbal report. To explain the integration of information, we need only exhibit mechanisms by which information is brought together and exploited by later processes. For an account of sleep and wakefulness, an appropriate neurophysiological account of the processes responsible for organisms' contrasting behavior in those states will suffice. In each case, an appropriate cognitive or neurophysiological model can clearly do the explanatory work.

If these phenomena were all there was to consciousness, then consciousness would not be much of a problem. Although we do not yet have anything close to a complete explanation of these phenomena, we have a clear idea of how we might go about explaining them. This is why I call these problems the easy problems. Of course, "easy" is a relative term. Getting the details right will probably take a century or two of difficult empirical work. Still, there is every reason to believe that the methods of cognitive science and neuroscience will succeed.

The really hard problem of consciousness is the problem of experience. When we think and perceive, there is a whir of information-processing, but there is also a subjective aspect. As Nagel (1974) has put it, there is something it is like to be a conscious organism. This subjective aspect is experience. When we see, for example, we experience visual sensations: the felt quality of redness, the experience of dark and light, the quality of depth in a visual field. Other experiences go along with perception in different modalities: the sound of a clarinet, the smell of mothballs. Then there are bodily sensations, from pains to orgasms; mental images that are conjured up internally; the felt quality of emotion, and the experience of a stream of conscious thought. What unites all of these states is that there is something it is like to be in them. All of them are states of experience.

It is undeniable that some organisms are subjects of experience. But the question of how it is that these systems are subjects of experience is perplexing. Why is it that when our cognitive systems engage in visual and auditory information-processing, we have visual or auditory experience: the quality of deep blue, the sensation of middle C? How can we explain why there is something it is like to entertain a mental image, or to experience an emotion? It is widely agreed that experience arises from a physical basis, but we have no good explanation of why and how it so arises. Why should physical processing give rise to a rich inner life at all? It seems objectively unreasonable that it should, and yet it does.

If any problem qualifies as the problem of consciousness, it is this one. In this central sense of "consciousness", an organism is conscious if there is something it is like to be that organism, and a mental state is conscious if there is something it is like to be in that state. Sometimes terms such as "phenomenal consciousness" and "qualia" are also used here, but I find it more natural to speak of "conscious experience" or simply "experience". Another useful way to avoid confusion (used by e.g. Newell 1990, Chalmers 1996) is to reserve the term "consciousness" for the phenomena of experience, using the less loaded term "awareness" for the more straightforward phenomena described earlier. If such a convention were widely adopted, communication would be much easier; as things stand, those who talk about "consciousness" are frequently talking past each other.

The ambiguity of the term "consciousness" is often exploited by both philosophers and scientists writing on the subject. It is common to see a paper on consciousness begin with an invocation of the mystery of consciousness, noting the strange intangibility and ineffability of subjectivity, and worrying that so far we have no theory of the phenomenon. Here, the topic is clearly the hard problem—the problem of experience. In the second half of the paper, the tone becomes more optimistic, and the author's own theory of consciousness is outlined. Upon examination, this theory turns out to be a theory of one of the more straightforward phenomena—of reportability, of introspective access, or whatever. At the close, the author declares that consciousness has turned out to be tractable after all, but the reader is left feeling like the victim of a bait-and-switch. The hard problem remains untouched.

3: FUNCTIONAL EXPLANATION

Why are the easy problems easy, and why is the hard problem hard? The easy problems are easy precisely because they concern the explanation of cognitive abilities and functions. To explain a cognitive function, we need only specify a mechanism that can perform the function. The methods of cognitive science are well-suited for this sort of explanation, and so are well-suited to the easy problems of consciousness. By contrast, the hard problem is hard precisely because it is not a problem about the performance of functions. The problem persists even when the performance of all the relevant functions is explained. (Here "function" is not used in the narrow teleological sense of something that a system is designed to do, but in the broader sense of any causal role in the production of behavior that a system might perform.)

To explain reportability, for instance, is just to explain how a system could perform the function of producing reports on internal states. To explain internal access, we need to explain how a system could be appropriately affected by its internal states and use information about those states in directing later processes. To explain integration and control, we need to explain how a system's central processes can bring information contents together and use them in the facilitation of various behaviors. These are all problems about the explanation of functions.

How do we explain the performance of a function? By specifying a mechanism that performs the function. Here, neurophysiological and cognitive modeling are perfect for the task. If we want a detailed low-level explanation, we can specify the neural mechanism that is responsible for the function. If we want a more abstract explanation, we can specify a mechanism in computational terms. Either way, a full and satisfying explanation will result. Once we have specified the neural or computational mechanism that performs the function of verbal report, for example, the bulk of our work in explaining reportability is over.

In a way, the point is trivial. It is a conceptual fact about these phenomena that their explanation only involves the explanation of various functions, as the phenomena are functionally definable. All it means for reportability to be instantiated in a system is that the system has the capacity for verbal reports of internal information. All it means for a system to be awake is for it to be appropriately receptive to information from the environment and for it to be able to use this information in directing behavior in an appropriate way. To see that this sort of thing is a conceptual fact, note that someone who says "you have explained the performance of the verbal report function, but you have not explained reportability" is making a trivial conceptual mistake about reportability. All it could possibly take to explain reportability is an explanation of how the relevant function is performed; the same goes for the other phenomena in question.

Throughout the higher-level sciences, reductive explanation works in just this way. To explain the gene, for instance, we needed to specify the mechanism that stores and transmits hereditary information from one generation to the next. It turns out that DNA performs this function; once we explain how the function is performed, we have explained the gene. To explain life, we ultimately need to explain how a system can reproduce, adapt to its environment, metabolize, and so on. All of these are questions about the performance of functions, and so are well-suited to reductive explanation. The same holds for most problems in cognitive science. To explain learning, we need to explain the way in which a system's behavioral capacities are modified in light of environmental information, and the way in which new information can be brought to bear in adapting a system's actions to its environment. If we show how a neural or computational mechanism does the job, we have explained learning. We can say the same for other cognitive phenomena, such as perception, memory, and language. Sometimes the relevant functions need to be characterized quite subtly, but it is clear that insofar as cognitive science explains these phenomena at all, it does so by explaining the performance of functions.

When it comes to conscious experience, this sort of explanation fails. What makes the hard problem hard and almost unique is that it goes beyond problems about the performance of functions. To see this, note that even when we have explained the performance of all the cognitive and behavioral functions in the vicinity of experience—perceptual discrimination, categorization, internal access, verbal report—there may still remain a further unanswered question: Why is the performance of these functions accompanied by experience? A simple explanation of the functions leaves this question open.

There is no analogous further question in the explanation of genes, or of life, or of learning. If someone says "I can see that you have explained how

DNA stores and transmits hereditary information from one generation to the next, but you have not explained how it is a gene", then they are making a conceptual mistake. All it means to be a gene is to be an entity that performs the relevant storage and transmission function. But if someone says "I can see that you have explained how information is discriminated, integrated, and reported, but you have not explained how it is experienced", they are not making a conceptual mistake. This is a nontrivial further question.

This further question is the key question in the problem of consciousness. Why doesn't all this information-processing go on "in the dark", free of any inner feel? Why is it that when electromagnetic waveforms impinge on a retina and are discriminated and categorized by a visual system, this discrimination and categorization is experienced as a sensation of vivid red? We know that conscious experience does arise when these functions are performed, but the very fact that it arises is the central mystery. There is an explanatory gap (a term due to Levine 1983) between the functions and experience, and we need an explanatory bridge to cross it. A mere account of the functions stays on one side of the gap, so the materials for the bridge must be found elsewhere.

This is not to say that experience has no function. Perhaps it will turn out to play an important cognitive role. But for any role it might play, there will be more to the explanation of experience than a simple explanation of the function. Perhaps it will even turn out that in the course of explaining a function, we will be led to the key insight that allows an explanation of experience. If this happens, though, the discovery will be an extra explanatory reward. There is no cognitive function such that we can say in advance that explanation of that function will automatically explain experience.

To explain experience, we need a new approach. The usual explanatory methods of cognitive science and neuroscience do not suffice. These methods have been developed precisely to explain the performance of cognitive functions, and they do a good job of it. But as these methods stand, they are only equipped to explain the performance of functions. When it comes to the hard problem, the standard approach has nothing to say.

4: SOME CASE-STUDIES

In the last few years, a number of works have addressed the problems of consciousness within the framework of cognitive science and neuroscience. This might suggest that the analysis above is faulty, but in fact a close examination of the relevant work only lends the analysis further support. When we investigate just which aspects of consciousness these studies are aimed at, and which aspects they end up explaining, we find that the ultimate target of explanation is always one of the easy problems. I will illustrate this with two representative examples.

The first is the "neurobiological theory of consciousness" outlined by Crick and Koch (1990; see also Crick 1994). This theory centers on certain 35–75 hertz neural oscillations in the cerebral cortex; Crick and Koch hypothesize that these oscillations are the basis of consciousness. This is partly because the oscillations seem to be correlated with awareness in a number of different modalities—within the visual and olfactory systems, for example—and also because they suggest a mechanism by which the binding of information contents might be achieved. Binding is the process whereby separately represented pieces of information about a single entity are brought together to be used by later processing, as when information about the color and shape of a perceived object is integrated from separate visual pathways. Following others (e.g., Eckhorn et al. 1988), Crick and Koch hypothesize that binding may be achieved by the synchronized oscillations of neuronal groups representing the relevant contents. When two pieces of information are to be bound together, the relevant neural groups will oscillate with the same frequency and phase.

The details of how this binding might be achieved are still poorly understood, but suppose that they can be worked out. What might the resulting theory explain? Clearly it might explain the binding of information contents, and perhaps it might yield a more general account of the integration of information in the brain. Crick and Koch also suggest that these oscillations activate the mechanisms of working memory, so that there may be an account of this and perhaps other forms of memory in the distance. The theory might eventually lead to a general account of how perceived information is bound and stored in memory, for use by later processing.

Such a theory would be valuable, but it would tell us nothing about why the relevant contents are experienced. Crick and Koch suggest that these oscillations are the neural correlates of experience. This claim is arguable—does not binding also take place in the processing of unconscious information?—but even if it is accepted, the explanatory question remains: Why do the oscillations give rise to experience? The only basis for an explanatory connection is the role they play in binding and storage, but the question of why binding and storage should themselves be accompanied by experience is never addressed. If we do not know why binding and storage should give rise to experience, telling a story about the oscillations cannot help us. Conversely, if we knew why binding and storage gave rise to experience, the neurophysiological details would be just the icing on the cake. Crick and Koch's theory gains its purchase by assuming a connection between binding and experience, and so can do nothing to explain that link.

I do not think that Crick and Koch are ultimately claiming to address the hard problem, although some have interpreted them otherwise. A published interview with Koch gives a clear statement of the limitations on the theory's ambitions.

> Well, let's first forget about the really difficult aspects, like subjective feelings, for they may not have a scientific solution. The subjective state of play, of pain, of pleasure, of seeing blue, of smelling a rose—there seems to be a huge jump between the materialistic level, of explaining molecules and neurons, and the subjective level. Let's focus on things that are easier to study—like visual awareness. You're now talking to me, but you're not looking at me, you're looking at the cappuccino, and so you are aware of it. You can say, 'It's a cup and there's some liquid in it.' If I give it to you, you'll move your arm and you'll take it—you'll respond in a meaningful manner. That's what I call awareness. ("What is Consciousness", *Discover*, November 1992, p. 96.)

The second example is an approach at the level of cognitive psychology. This is Baars' global workspace theory of consciousness, presented in his book *A Cognitive Theory of Consciousness*. According to this theory, the contents of consciousness are contained in a global workspace, a central processor used to mediate communication between a host of specialized nonconscious processors. When these specialized processors need to broadcast information to the rest of the system, they do so by sending this information to the workspace, which acts as a kind of communal blackboard for the rest of the system, accessible to all the other processors.

Baars uses this model to address many aspects of human cognition, and to explain a number of contrasts between conscious and unconscious cognitive functioning. Ultimately, however, it is a theory of cognitive accessibility, explaining how it is that certain information contents are widely accessible within a system, as well as a theory of informational integration and reportability. The theory shows promise as a theory of awareness, the functional correlate of conscious experience, but an explanation of experience itself is not on offer.

One might suppose that according to this theory, the contents of experience are precisely the contents of the workspace. But even if this is so, nothing internal to the theory explains why the information within the global workspace is experienced. The best the theory can do is to say that the information is experienced because it is globally accessible. But now the question arises in a different form: why should global accessibility give rise to conscious experience? As always, this bridging question is unanswered.

Almost all work taking a cognitive or neuroscientific approach to consciousness in recent years could be subjected to a similar critique. The "Neural Darwinism" model of Edelman (1989), for instance, addresses questions about perceptual awareness and the self-concept, but says nothing about why there should also be experience. The "multiple drafts" model of Dennett (1991) is largely directed at explaining the reportability of certain mental contents. The "intermediate level" theory of Jackendoff (1988) provides an account of some computational processes that underlie consciousness, but Jackendoff stresses that the question of how these "project" into conscious experience remains mysterious.

Researchers using these methods are often inexplicit about their attitudes to the problem of conscious experience, although sometimes they take a clear stand. Even among those who are clear about it, attitudes differ widely. In placing this sort of work with respect to the problem of experience, a number of different strategies are available. It would be useful if these strategic choices were more often made explicit.

The first strategy is simply to explain something else. Some researchers are explicit that the problem of experience is too difficult for now, and perhaps even outside the domain of science altogether. These researchers instead choose to address one of the more tractable problems such as reportability or the self-concept. Although I have called these problems the "easy" problems, they are among the most interesting unsolved problems in cognitive science, so this work is certainly worthwhile. The worst that can be said of this choice is that in the context of research on consciousness it is relatively unambitious, and the work can sometimes be misinterpreted.

The second choice is to take a harder line and deny the phenomenon. (Variations on this approach are taken by Allport 1988, Dennett 1991, and Wilkes 1988.) According to this line, once we have explained the functions such as accessibility, reportability, and the like, there is no further phenomenon called "experience" to explain. Some explicitly deny the phenomenon, holding for example that what is not externally verifiable cannot be real. Others achieve the same effect by allowing that experience exists, but only if we equate "experience" with something like the capacity to discriminate and report. These approaches lead to a simpler theory, but are ultimately unsatisfactory. Experience is the most central and manifest aspect of our mental lives, and indeed is perhaps the key explanandum in the science of the mind. Because of this status as an explanandum, experience cannot be discarded like the vital spirit when a new theory comes along. Rather, it is the central fact that any theory of consciousness must explain. A theory that denies the phenomenon "solves" the problem by ducking the question.

In a third option, some researchers claim to be explaining experience in the full sense. These researchers (unlike those above) wish to take experience very seriously; they lay out their functional model or theory, and claim that it explains the full subjective quality of experience (e.g. Flohr 1992, Humphrey 1992). The relevant step in the explanation is usually passed over quickly, however, and usually ends up looking something like magic. After some details about information processing are given, experience suddenly enters the picture, but it is left obscure how these processes should suddenly give rise to experience. Perhaps it is simply taken for granted that it does, but then we have an incomplete explanation and a version of the fifth strategy below.

A fourth, more promising approach appeals to these methods to explain the structure of experience. For example, it is arguable that an account of the discriminations made by the visual system can account for the structural relations between different color experiences, as well as for the geometric structure of the visual field (see e.g., Clark 1992 and Hardin 1992). In general, certain facts about structures found in processing will correspond to and arguably explain facts about the structure of experience. This strategy is plausible but limited. At best, it takes the existence of experience for granted and accounts for some facts about its structure, providing a sort of nonreductive explanation of the structural aspects of experience (I will say more on this later). This is useful for many purposes, but it tells us nothing about why there should be experience in the first place.

A fifth and reasonable strategy is to isolate the substrate of experience. After all, almost everyone allows that experience arises one way or another from brain processes, and it makes sense to identify the sort of process from which it arises. Crick and Koch put their work forward as isolating the neural correlate of consciousness, for example, and Edelman (1989) and Jackendoff (1988) make related claims. Justification of these claims requires a careful theoretical analysis, especially as experience is not directly observable in experimental contexts, but when applied judiciously this strategy can shed indirect light on the problem of experience. Nevertheless, the strategy is clearly incomplete. For a satisfactory theory, we need to know more than which processes give rise to experience; we need an account of why and how. A full theory of consciousness must build an explanatory bridge.

5: THE EXTRA INGREDIENT

We have seen that there are systematic reasons why the usual methods of cognitive science and neuroscience fail to account for conscious experience. These are simply the wrong sort of methods: nothing that they give to us can yield an explanation. To account for conscious experience, we need an extra ingredient in the explanation. This makes for a challenge to those who are serious about the hard problem of consciousness: What is your extra ingredient, and why should that account for conscious experience?

There is no shortage of extra ingredients to be had. Some propose an injection of chaos and nonlinear dynamics. Some think that the key lies in nonalgorithmic processing. Some appeal to future discoveries in neurophysiology. Some suppose that the key to the mystery will lie at the level of quantum mechanics. It is easy to see why all these suggestions are put forward. None of the old methods work, so the solution must lie with something new. Unfortunately, these suggestions all suffer from the same old problems.

Nonalgorithmic processing, for example, is put forward by Penrose (1989; 1994) because of the role it might play in the process of conscious mathematical insight. The arguments about mathematics are controversial, but even if they succeed and an account of nonalgorithmic processing in the human brain is given, it will still only be an account of the functions involved in mathematical reasoning and the like. For a nonalgorithmic process as much as an algorithmic process, the question is left unanswered: why should this process give rise to experience? In answering this question, there is no special role for nonalgorithmic processing.

The same goes for nonlinear and chaotic dynamics. These might provide a novel account of the dynamics of cognitive functioning, quite different from that given by standard methods in cognitive science. But from dynamics, one only gets more dynamics. The question about experience here is as mysterious as ever. The point is even clearer for new discoveries in neurophysiology. These new discoveries may help us make significant progress in understanding brain function, but for any neural process we isolate, the same question will always arise. It is difficult to imagine what a proponent of new neurophysiology expects to happen, over and above the explanation of further cognitive functions. It is not as if we will suddenly discover a phenomenal glow inside a neuron!

Perhaps the most popular "extra ingredient" of all is quantum mechanics (e.g. Hameroff 1994). The attractiveness of quantum theories of consciousness may stem from a Law of Minimization of Mystery: consciousness is mysterious and quantum mechanics is mysterious, so maybe the two mysteries have a common source. Nevertheless, quantum theories of consciousness suffer from the same difficulties as neural or computational theories. Quantum phenomena have some remarkable functional properties, such as nondeterminism and nonlocality. It is natural to speculate that these properties may play some role in the explanation of cognitive functions, such as random choice and the integration of information, and this hypothesis cannot be ruled out a priori. But when it comes to the explanation of experience, quantum processes are in the same boat as any other. The question of why these processes should give rise to experience is entirely unanswered.

(One special attraction of quantum theories is the fact that on some interpretations of quantum mechanics, consciousness plays an active role in "collapsing" the quantum wave function. Such interpretations are controversial, but in any case they offer no hope of explaining consciousness in terms of quantum processes. Rather, these theories assume the existence of consciousness, and use it in the explanation of quantum processes. At best, these theories tell us something about a physical role that consciousness may play. They tell us nothing about how it arises.)

At the end of the day, the same criticism applies to any purely physical account of consciousness. For any physical process we specify there will be an unanswered question: Why should this process give rise to experience? Given any such process, it is conceptually coherent that it could be instantiated in the absence of experience. It follows that no mere account of the physical process will tell us why experience arises. The emergence of experience goes beyond what can be derived from physical theory.

Purely physical explanation is well-suited to the explanation of physical structures, explaining macroscopic structures in terms of detailed microstructural constituents; and it provides a satisfying explanation of the performance of functions, accounting for these functions in terms of the physical mechanisms that perform them. This is because a physical account can entail the facts about structures and functions: once the internal details of the physical account are given, the structural and functional properties fall out as an automatic consequence. But the structure and dynamics of physical processes yield only more structure and dynamics, so structures and functions are all we can expect these processes to explain. The facts about experience cannot be an automatic consequence of any physical account, as it is conceptually coherent that any given process could exist without experience. Experience may arise from the physical, but it is not entailed by the physical.

The moral of all this is that you can't explain conscious experience on the cheap. It is a remarkable fact that reductive methods—methods that explain a high-level phenomenon wholly in terms of more basic physical processes—work well in so many domains. In a sense, one can explain most biological and cognitive phenomena on the cheap, in that these phenomena are seen as automatic consequences of more fundamental processes. It would be wonderful if reductive methods could explain experience, too; I hoped for a long time that they might. Unfortunately, there are systematic reasons why these methods must fail. Reductive methods are successful in most domains because what needs explaining in those domains are structures and functions, and these are the kind of thing that a physical account can entail. When it comes to a problem over and above the explanation of structures and functions, these methods are impotent.

This might seem reminiscent of the vitalist claim that no physical account could explain life, but the cases are disanalogous. What drove vitalist skepticism was doubt about whether physical mechanisms could perform the many remarkable functions associated with life, such as complex adaptive behavior and reproduction. The conceptual claim that explanation of functions is what is needed was implicitly accepted, but lacking detailed knowledge of biochemical mechanisms, vitalists doubted whether any physical process could do the job and put forward the hypothesis of the vital spirit as an alternative explanation. Once it turned out that physical processes could perform the relevant functions, vitalist doubts melted away.

With experience, on the other hand, physical explanation of the functions is not in question. The key is instead the conceptual point that the explanation of functions does not suffice for the explanation of experience. This basic conceptual point is not something that further neuroscientific investigation will affect. In a similar way, experience is disanalogous to the élan vital. The vital spirit was put forward as an explanatory posit, in order to explain the relevant functions, and could therefore be discarded when those functions were explained without it. Experience is not an explanatory posit but an explanandum in its own right, and so is not a candidate for this sort of elimination.

It is tempting to note that all sorts of puzzling phenomena have eventually turned out to be explainable in physical terms. But each of these were problems about the observable behavior of physical objects, coming down to problems in the explanation of structures and functions. Because of this, these phenomena have always been the kind of thing that a physical account might explain, even if at some points there have been good reasons to suspect that no such explanation would be forthcoming. The tempting induction from these cases fails in the case of consciousness, which is not a problem about physical structures and functions. The problem of consciousness is puzzling in an entirely different way. An analysis of the problem shows us that conscious experience is just not the kind of thing that a wholly reductive account could succeed in explaining.

6: NONREDUCTIVE EXPLANATION

At this point some are tempted to give up, holding that we will never have a theory of conscious experience. McGinn (1989), for example, argues that the problem is too hard for our limited minds; we are "cognitively closed" with respect to the phenomenon. Others have argued that conscious experience lies outside the domain of scientific theory altogether.

I think this pessimism is premature. This is not the place to give up; it is the place where things get interesting. When simple methods of explanation are ruled out, we need to investigate the alternatives. Given that reductive explanation fails, nonreductive explanation is the natural choice.

Although a remarkable number of phenomena have turned out to be explicable wholly in terms of entities simpler than themselves, this is not universal. In physics, it occasionally happens that an entity has to be taken as fundamental. Fundamental entities are not explained in terms of anything simpler. Instead, one takes them as basic, and gives a theory of how they relate to everything else in the world. For example, in the nineteenth century it turned out that electromagnetic processes could not be explained in terms of the wholly mechanical processes that previous physical theories appealed to, so Maxwell and others introduced electromagnetic charge and electromagnetic forces as new fundamental components of a physical theory. To explain electromagnetism, the ontology of physics had to be expanded. New basic properties and basic laws were needed to give a satisfactory account of the phenomena.

Other features that physical theory takes as fundamental include mass and space-time. No attempt is made to explain these features in terms of anything simpler. But this does not rule out the possibility of a theory of mass or of space-time. There is an intricate theory of how these features interrelate, and of the basic laws they enter into. These basic principles are used to explain many familiar phenomena concerning mass, space, and time at a higher level.

I suggest that a theory of consciousness should take experience as fundamental. We know that a theory of consciousness requires the addition of something fundamental to our ontology, as everything in physical theory is compatible with the absence of consciousness. We might add some entirely new nonphysical feature, from which experience can be derived, but it is hard to see what such a feature would be like. More likely, we will take experience itself as a fundamental feature of the world, alongside mass, charge, and space-time. If we take experience as fundamental, then we can go about the business of constructing a theory of experience.

Where there is a fundamental property, there are fundamental laws. A nonreductive theory of experience will add new principles to the furniture of the basic laws of nature. These basic principles will ultimately carry the explanatory burden in a theory of consciousness. Just as we explain familiar high-level phenomena involving mass in terms of more basic principles involving mass and other entities, we might explain familiar phenomena involving experience in terms of more basic principles involving experience and other entities.

In particular, a nonreductive theory of experience will specify basic principles telling us how experience depends on physical features of the world. These psychophysical principles will not interfere with physical laws, as it seems that physical laws already form a closed system. Rather, they will be a supplement to a physical theory. A physical theory gives a theory of physical processes, and a psychophysical theory tells us how those processes give rise to experience. We know that experience depends on physical processes, but we also know that this dependence cannot be derived from physical laws alone. The new basic principles postulated by a nonreductive theory give us the extra ingredient that we need to build an explanatory bridge.

Of course, by taking experience as fundamental, there is a sense in which this approach does not tell us why there is experience in the first place. But this is the same for any fundamental theory. Nothing in physics tells us why there is matter in the first place, but we do not count this against theories of matter. Certain features of the world need to be taken as fundamental by any scientific theory. A theory of matter can still explain all sorts of facts about matter, by showing how they are consequences of the basic laws. The same goes for a theory of experience.

This position qualifies as a variety of dualism, as it postulates basic properties over and above the properties invoked by physics. But it is an innocent version of dualism, entirely compatible with the scientific view of the world. Nothing in this approach contradicts anything in physical theory; we simply need to add further bridging principles to explain how experience arises from physical processes. There is nothing particularly spiritual or mystical about this theory—its overall shape is like that of a physical theory, with a few fundamental entities connected by fundamental laws. It expands the ontology slightly, to be sure, but Maxwell did the same thing. Indeed, the overall structure of this position is entirely naturalistic, allowing that ultimately the universe comes down to a network of basic entities obeying simple laws, and allowing that there may ultimately be a theory of consciousness cast in terms of such laws. If the position is to have a name, a good choice might be naturalistic dualism.

If this view is right, then in some ways a theory of consciousness will have more in common with a theory in physics than a theory in biology. Biological theories involve no principles that are fundamental in this way, so biological theory has a certain complexity and messiness to it; but theories in physics, insofar as they deal with fundamental principles, aspire to simplicity and elegance. The fundamental laws of nature are part of the basic furniture of the world, and physical theories are telling us that this basic furniture is remarkably simple. If a theory of consciousness also involves fundamental principles, then we should expect the same. The principles of simplicity, elegance, and even beauty that drive physicists' search for a fundamental theory will also apply to a theory of consciousness.

(A technical note: Some philosophers argue that even though there is a conceptual gap between physical processes and experience, there need be no metaphysical gap, so that experience might in a certain sense still be physical [e.g. Hill 1991; Levine 1983; Loar 1990]. Usually this line of argument is supported by an appeal to the notion of a posteriori necessity [Kripke 1980]. I think that this position rests on a misunderstanding of a posteriori necessity, however, or else requires an entirely new sort of necessity that we have no reason to believe in; see Chalmers 1996 [also Jackson 1994 and Lewis 1994] for details. In any case, this position still concedes an explanatory gap between physical processes and experience. For example, the principles connecting the physical and the experiential will not be derivable from the laws of physics, so such principles must be taken as explanatorily fundamental. So even on this sort of view, the explanatory structure of a theory of consciousness will be much as I have described.)

7: OUTLINE OF A THEORY OF CONSCIOUSNESS

It is not too soon to begin work on a theory. We are already in a position to understand certain key facts about the relationship between physical processes and experience, and about the regularities that connect them. Once reductive explanation is set aside, we can lay those facts on the table so that they can play their proper role as the initial pieces in a nonreductive theory of consciousness, and as constraints on the basic laws that constitute an ultimate theory.

There is an obvious problem that plagues the development of a theory of consciousness, and that is the paucity of objective data. Conscious experience is not directly observable in an experimental context, so we cannot generate data about the relationship between physical processes and experience at will. Nevertheless, we all have access to a rich source of data in our own case. Many important regularities between experience and processing can be inferred from considerations about one's own experience. There are also good indirect sources of data from observable cases, as when one relies on the verbal report of a subject as an indication of experience. These methods have their limitations, but we have more than enough data to get a theory off the ground.

Philosophical analysis is also useful in getting value for money out of the data we have. This sort of analysis can yield a number of principles relating consciousness and cognition, thereby strongly constraining the shape of an ultimate theory. The method of thought-experimentation can also yield significant rewards, as we will see. Finally, the fact that we are searching for a fundamental theory means that we can appeal to such nonempirical constraints as simplicity, homogeneity, and the like in developing a theory. We must seek to systematize the information we have, to extend it as far as possible by careful analysis, and then make the inference to the simplest possible theory that explains the data while remaining a plausible candidate to be part of the fundamental furniture of the world.

Such theories will always retain an element of speculation that is not present in other scientific theories, because of the impossibility of conclusive intersubjective experimental tests. Still, we can certainly construct theories that are compatible with the data that we have, and evaluate them in comparison to each other. Even in the absence of intersubjective observation, there are numerous criteria available for the evaluation of such theories: simplicity, internal coherence, coherence with theories in other domains, the ability to reproduce the properties of experience that are familiar from our own case, and even an overall fit with the dictates of common sense. Perhaps there will be significant indeterminacies remaining even when all these constraints are applied, but we can at least develop plausible candidates. Only when candidate theories have been developed will we be able to evaluate them.

A nonreductive theory of consciousness will consist in a number of psychophysical principles, principles connecting the properties of physical processes to the properties of experience. We can think of these principles as encapsulating the way in which experience arises from the physical. Ultimately, these principles should tell us what sort of physical systems will have associated experiences, and for the systems that do, they should tell us what sort of physical properties are relevant to the emergence of experience, and just what sort of experience we should expect any given physical system to yield. This is a tall order, but there is no reason why we should not get started.

In what follows, I present my own candidates for the psychophysical principles that might go into a theory of consciousness. The first two of these are nonbasic principles—systematic connections between processing and experience at a relatively high level. These principles can play a significant role in developing and constraining a theory of consciousness, but they are not cast at a sufficiently fundamental level to qualify as truly basic laws. The final principle is my candidate for a basic principle that might form the cornerstone of a fundamental theory of consciousness. This final principle is particularly speculative, but it is the kind of speculation that is required if we are ever to have a satisfying theory of consciousness. I can present these principles only briefly here; I argue for them at much greater length in Chalmers (1996).

1. The principle of structural coherence. This is a principle of coherence between the structure of consciousness and the structure of awareness. Recall that "awareness" was used earlier to refer to the various functional phenomena that are associated with consciousness. I am now using it to refer to a somewhat more specific process in the cognitive underpinnings of experience. In particular, the contents of awareness are to be understood as those information contents that are accessible to central systems, and brought to bear in a widespread way in the control of behavior. Briefly put, we can think of awareness as direct availability for global control. To a first approximation, the contents of awareness are the contents that are directly accessible and potentially reportable, at least in a language-using system.

Awareness is a purely functional notion, but it is nevertheless intimately linked to conscious experience. In familiar cases, wherever we find consciousness, we find awareness. Wherever there is conscious experience, there is some corresponding information in the cognitive system that is available in the control of behavior, and available for verbal report. Conversely, it seems that whenever information is available for report and for global control, there is a corresponding conscious experience. Thus, there is a direct correspondence between consciousness and awareness.

The correspondence can be taken further. It is a central fact about experience that it has a complex structure. The visual field has a complex geometry, for instance. There are also relations of similarity and difference between experiences, and relations in such things as relative intensity. Every subject's experience can be at least partly characterized and decomposed in terms of these structural properties: similarity and difference relations, perceived location, relative intensity, geometric structure, and so on. It is also a central fact that to each of these structural features, there is a corresponding feature in the information-processing structure of awareness.

Take color sensations as an example. For every distinction between color experiences, there is a corresponding distinction in processing. The different phenomenal colors that we experience form a complex three-dimensional space, varying in hue, saturation, and intensity. The properties of this space can be recovered from information-processing considerations: examination of the visual systems shows that waveforms of light are discriminated and analyzed along three different axes, and it is this three-dimensional information that is relevant to later processing. The three-dimensional structure of phenomenal color space therefore corresponds directly to the three dimensional structure of visual awareness. This is precisely what we would expect. After all, every color distinction corresponds to some reportable information, and therefore to a distinction that is represented in the structure of processing.

In a more straightforward way, the geometric structure of the visual field is directly reflected in a structure that can be recovered from visual processing. Every geometric relation corresponds to something that can be reported and is therefore cognitively represented. If we were given only the story about information-processing in an agent's visual and cognitive system, we could not directly observe that agent's visual experiences, but we could nevertheless infer those experiences' structural properties.

In general, any information that is consciously experienced will also be cognitively represented. The fine-grained structure of the visual field will correspond to some fine-grained structure in visual processing. The same goes for experiences in other modalities, and even for nonsensory experiences. Internal mental images have geometric properties that are represented in processing. Even emotions have structural properties, such as relative intensity, that correspond directly to a structural property of processing; where there is greater intensity, we find a greater effect on later processes. In general, precisely because the structural properties of experience are accessible and reportable, those properties will be directly represented in the structure of awareness.

It is this isomorphism between the structures of consciousness and awareness that constitutes the principle of structural coherence. This principle reflects the central fact that even though cognitive processes do not conceptually entail facts about conscious experience, consciousness and cognition do not float free of one another but cohere in an intimate way.

This principle has its limits. It allows us to recover structural properties of experience from information-processing properties, but not all properties of experience are structural properties. There are properties of experience, such as the intrinsic nature of a sensation of red, that cannot be fully captured in a structural description. The very intelligibility of inverted spectrum scenarios, where experiences of red and green are inverted but all structural properties remain the same, show that structural properties constrain experience without exhausting it. Nevertheless, the very fact that we feel compelled to leave structural properties unaltered when we imagine experiences inverted between functionally identical systems shows how central the principle of structural coherence is to our conception of our mental lives. It is not a logically necessary principle, as after all we can imagine all the information processing occurring without any experience at all, but it is nevertheless a strong and familiar constraint on the psychophysical connection.

The principle of structural coherence allows for a very useful kind of indirect explanation of experience in terms of physical processes. For example, we can use facts about neural processing of visual information to indirectly explain the structure of color space. The facts about neural processing can entail and explain the structure of awareness; if we take the coherence principle for granted, the structure of experience will also be explained. Empirical investigation might even lead us to better understand the structure of awareness within a bat, shedding indirect light on Nagel's vexing question of what it is like to be a bat. This principle provides a natural interpretation of much existing work on the explanation of consciousness (e.g. Clark 1992 and Hardin 1992 on colors, and Akins 1993 on bats), although it is often appealed to inexplicitly. It is so familiar that it is taken for granted by almost everybody, and is a central plank in the cognitive explanation of consciousness.

The coherence between consciousness and awareness also allows a natural interpretation of work in neuroscience directed at isolating the substrate (or the neural correlate) of consciousness. Various specific hypotheses have been put forward. For example, Crick and Koch (1990) suggest that 40-Hz oscillations may be the neural correlate of consciousness, whereas Libet (1993) suggests that temporally-extended neural activity is central. If we accept the principle of coherence, the most direct physical correlate of consciousness is awareness: the process whereby information is made directly available for global control. The different specific hypotheses can be interpreted as empirical suggestions about how awareness might be achieved. For example, Crick and Koch suggest that 40-Hz oscillations are the gateway by which information is integrated into working memory and thereby made available to later processes. Similarly, it is natural to suppose that Libet's temporally extended activity is relevant precisely because only that sort of activity achieves global availability. The same applies to other suggested correlates such as the "global workspace" of Baars (1988), the "high-quality representations" of Farah (1994), and the "selector inputs to action systems" of Shallice (1972). All these can be seen as hypotheses about the mechanisms of awareness: the mechanisms that perform the function of making information directly available for global control.

Given the coherence between consciousness and awareness, it follows that a mechanism of awareness will itself be a correlate of conscious experience. The question of just which mechanisms in the brain govern global availability is an empirical one; perhaps there are many such mechanisms. But if we accept the coherence principle, we have reason to believe that the processes that explain awareness will at the same time be part of the basis of consciousness.

2. The principle of organizational invariance. This principle states that any two systems with the same fine-grained functional organization will have qualitatively identical experiences. If the causal patterns of neural organization were duplicated in silicon, for example, with a silicon chip for every neuron and the same patterns of interaction, then the same experiences would arise. According to this principle, what matters for the emergence of experience is not the specific physical makeup of a system, but the abstract pattern of causal interaction between its components. This principle is controversial, of course. Some (e.g. Searle 1980) have thought that consciousness is tied to a specific biology, so that a silicon isomorph of a human need not be conscious. I believe that the principle can be given significant support by the analysis of thought-experiments, however.

Very briefly: suppose (for the purposes of a reductio ad absurdum) that the principle is false, and that there could be two functionally isomorphic systems with different experiences. Perhaps only one of the systems is conscious, or perhaps both are conscious but they have different experiences. For the purposes of illustration, let us say that one system is made of neurons and the other of silicon, and that one experiences red where the other experiences blue. The two systems have the same organization, so we can imagine gradually transforming one into the other, perhaps replacing neurons one at a time by silicon chips with the same local function. We thus gain a spectrum of intermediate cases, each with the same organization, but with slightly different physical makeup and slightly different experiences. Along this spectrum, there must be two systems A and B between which we replace less than one tenth of the system, but whose experiences differ. These two systems are physically identical, except that a small neural circuit in A has been replaced by a silicon circuit in B.

The key step in the thought-experiment is to take the relevant neural circuit in A, and install alongside it a causally isomorphic silicon circuit, with a switch between the two. What happens when we flip the switch? By hypothesis, the system's conscious experiences will change; from red to blue, say, for the purposes of illustration. This follows from the fact that the system after the change is essentially a version of B, whereas before the change it is just A.

But given the assumptions, there is no way for the system to notice the changes! Its causal organization stays constant, so that all of its functional states and behavioral dispositions stay fixed. As far as the system is concerned, nothing unusual has happened. There is no room for the thought, "Hmm! Something strange just happened!" In general, the structure of any such thought must be reflected in processing, but the structure of processing remains constant here. If there were to be such a thought it must float entirely free of the system and would be utterly impotent to affect later processing. (If it affected later processing, the systems would be functionally distinct, contrary to hypothesis.) We might even flip the switch a number of times, so that experiences of red and blue dance back and forth before the system's "inner eye". According to hypothesis, the system can never notice these "dancing qualia".

This I take to be a reductio of the original assumption. It is a central fact about experience, very familiar from our own case, that whenever experiences change significantly and we are paying attention, we can notice the change; if this were not to be the case, we would be led to the skeptical possibility that our experiences are dancing before our eyes all the time. This hypothesis has the same status as the possibility that the world was created five minutes ago: perhaps it is logically coherent, but it is not plausible. Given the extremely plausible assumption that changes in experience correspond to changes in processing, we are led to the conclusion that the original hypothesis is impossible, and that any two functionally isomorphic systems must have the same sort of experiences. To put it in technical terms, the philosophical hypotheses of "absent qualia" and "inverted qualia", while logically possible, are empirically and nomologically impossible.

(Some may worry that a silicon isomorph of a neural system might be impossible for technical reasons. That question is open. The invariance principle says only that if an isomorph is possible, then it will have the same sort of conscious experience.)

There is more to be said here, but this gives the basic flavor. Once again, this thought experiment draws on familiar facts about the coherence between consciousness and cognitive processing to yield a strong conclusion about the relation between physical structure and experience. If the argument goes through, we know that the only physical properties directly relevant to the emergence of experience are organizational properties. This acts as a further strong constraint on a theory of consciousness.

3. The double-aspect theory of information. The two preceding principles have been nonbasic principles. They involve high-level notions such as

"awareness" and "organization", and therefore lie at the wrong level to constitute the fundamental laws in a theory of consciousness. Nevertheless, they act as strong constraints. What is further needed are basic principles that fit these constraints and that might ultimately explain them.

The basic principle that I suggest centrally involves the notion of information. I understand information in more or less the sense of Shannon (1948). Where there is information, there are information states embedded in an information space. An information space has a basic structure of difference relations between its elements, characterizing the ways in which different elements in a space are similar or different, possibly in complex ways. An information space is an abstract object, but following Shannon we can see information as physically embodied when there is a space of distinct physical states, the differences between which can be transmitted down some causal pathway. The states that are transmitted can be seen as themselves constituting an information space. To borrow a phrase from Bateson (1972), physical information is a difference that makes a difference.

The double-aspect principle stems from the observation that there is a direct isomorphism between certain physically embodied information spaces and certain phenomenal (or experiential) information spaces. From the same sort of observations that went into the principle of structural coherence, we can note that the differences between phenomenal states have a structure that corresponds directly to the differences embedded in physical processes; in particular, to those differences that make a difference down certain causal pathways implicated in global availability and control. That is, we can find the same abstract information space embedded in physical processing and in conscious experience.

This leads to a natural hypothesis: that information (or at least some information) has two basic aspects, a physical aspect and a phenomenal aspect. This has the status of a basic principle that might underlie and explain the emergence of experience from the physical. Experience arises by virtue of its status as one aspect of information, when the other aspect is found embodied in physical processing.

This principle is lent support by a number of considerations, which I can only outline briefly here. First, consideration of the sort of physical changes that correspond to changes in conscious experience suggests that such changes are always relevant by virtue of their role in constituting informational changes—differences within an abstract space of states that are divided up precisely according to their causal differences along certain causal pathways. Second, if the principle of organizational invariance is to hold, then we need to find some fundamental organizational property for experience to be linked to, and information is an organizational property par excellence. Third, this principle offers some hope of explaining the principle of structural coherence in terms of the structure present within information spaces.

Fourth, analysis of the cognitive explanation of our judgments and claims about conscious experience—judgments that are functionally explainable but nevertheless deeply tied to experience itself—suggests that explanation centrally involves the information states embedded in cognitive processing. It follows that a theory based on information allows a deep coherence between the explanation of experience and the explanation of our judgments and claims about it.

Wheeler (1990) has suggested that information is fundamental to the physics of the universe. According to this "it from bit" doctrine, the laws of physics can be cast in terms of information, postulating different states that give rise to different effects without actually saying what those states are. It is only their position in an information space that counts. If so, then information is a natural candidate to also play a role in a fundamental theory of consciousness. We are led to a conception of the world on which information is truly fundamental, and on which it has two basic aspects, corresponding to the physical and the phenomenal features of the world.

Of course, the double-aspect principle is extremely speculative and is also underdetermined, leaving a number of key questions unanswered. An obvious question is whether all information has a phenomenal aspect. One possibility is that we need a further constraint on the fundamental theory, indicating just what sort of information has a phenomenal aspect. The other possibility is that there is no such constraint. If not, then experience is much more widespread than we might have believed, as information is everywhere. This is counterintuitive at first, but on reflection I think the position gains a certain plausibility and elegance. Where there is simple information processing, there is simple experience, and where there is complex information processing, there is complex experience. A mouse has a simpler information-processing structure than a human, and has correspondingly simpler experience; perhaps a thermostat, a maximally simple information processing structure, might have maximally simple experience? Indeed, if experience is truly a fundamental property, it would be surprising for it to arise only every now and then; most fundamental properties are more evenly spread. In any case, this is very much an open question, but I believe that the position is not as implausible as it is often thought to be.

Once a fundamental link between information and experience is on the table, the door is opened to some grander metaphysical speculation concerning the nature of the world. For example, it is often noted that physics characterizes its basic entities only extrinsically, in terms of their relations to other entities, which are themselves characterized extrinsically, and so on. The intrinsic nature of physical entities is left aside. Some argue that no such intrinsic properties exist, but then one is left with a world that is pure causal flux (a pure flow of information) with no properties for the causation to relate. If one allows that intrinsic properties exist, a natural speculation given the above is that the intrinsic properties of the physical—the properties that causation ultimately relates—are themselves phenomenal properties. We might say that phenomenal properties are the internal aspect of information. This could answer a concern about the causal relevance of experience—a natural worry, given a picture on which the physical domain is causally closed, and on which experience is supplementary to the physical. The informational view allows us to understand how experience might have a subtle kind of causal relevance in virtue of its status as the intrinsic nature of the physical. This metaphysical speculation is probably best ignored for the purposes of developing a scientific theory, but in addressing some philosophical issues it is quite suggestive.

8: CONCLUSION

The theory I have presented is speculative, but it is a candidate theory. I suspect that the principles of structural coherence and organizational invariance will be planks in any satisfactory theory of consciousness; the status of the double-aspect theory of information is less certain. Indeed, right now it is more of an idea than a theory. To have any hope of eventual explanatory success, it will have to be specified more fully and fleshed out into a more powerful form. Still, reflection on just what is plausible and implausible about it, on where it works and where it fails, can only lead to a better theory.

Most existing theories of consciousness either deny the phenomenon, explain something else, or elevate the problem to an eternal mystery. I hope to have shown that it is possible to make progress on the problem even while taking it seriously. To make further progress, we will need further investigation, more refined theories, and more careful analysis. The hard problem is a hard problem, but there is no reason to believe that it will remain permanently unsolved.[*]

NOTES

*[The arguments in this paper are presented in greater depth in my book *The Conscious Mind* (Oxford University Press, 1996). Thanks to Francis Crick, Peggy DesAutels, Matthew Elton, Liane Gabora, Christof Koch, Paul Rhodes, Gregg Rosenberg, and Sharon Wahl for their comments.]

REFERENCES

Akins, K. 1993. What is it like to be boring and myopic? In (B. Dahlbom, ed.) *Dennett and his Critics.* Oxford: Blackwell.

Allport, A. 1988. What concept of consciousness? In (A. Marcel and E. Bisiach, eds.) *Consciousness in Contemporary Science*. Oxford: Oxford University Press.

Baars, B. J. 1988. *A Cognitive Theory of Consciousness*. Cambridge: Cambridge University Press.

Bateson, G. 1972. *Steps to an Ecology of Mind*. Chandler Publishing.

Block, N. 1995. On a confusion about the function of consciousness. *Behavioral and Brain Sciences*.

Block, N, Flanagan, O. & Güzeldere, G, (eds.) 1996. *The Nature of Consciousness: Philosophical and Scientific Debates*. Cambridge, MA: MIT Press.

Chalmers, D. J. 1996. *The Conscious Mind*. New York: Oxford University Press.

Churchland, P. M. 1995. *The Engine of Reason, The Seat of the Soul: A Philosophical Journey into the Brain*. Cambridge, MA: MIT Press.

Clark, A. 1992. *Sensory Qualities*. Oxford: Oxford University Press.

Crick, F. and Koch, C. 1990. Toward a neurobiological theory of consciousness. *Seminars in the Neurosciences* 2:263–275.

Crick, F. 1994. *The Astonishing Hypothesis: The Scientific Search for the Soul*. New York: Scribners.

Dennett, D. C. 1991. *Consciousness Explained*. Boston: Little, Brown.

Dretske, F. I. 1995. *Naturalizing the Mind*. Cambridge, MA: MIT Press.

Edelman, G. 1989. *The Remembered Present: A Biological Theory of Consciousness*. New York: Basic Books.

Farah, M. J. 1994. Visual perception and visual awareness after brain damage: A tutorial overview. In (C. Umilta and M. Moscovitch, eds.) *Consciousness and Unconscious Information Processing: Attention and Performance* 15. Cambridge, MA: MIT Press.

Flohr, H. 1992. Qualia and brain processes. In (A. Beckermann, H. Flohr, and J. Kim, eds.) *Emergence or Reduction?: Prospects for Nonreductive Physicalism*. Berlin: De Gruyter.

Hameroff, S. R. 1994. Quantum coherence in microtubules: A neural basis for emergent consciousness? *Journal of Consciousness Studies* 1:91–118.

Hardin, C. L. 1992. Physiology, phenomenology, and Spinoza's true colors. In (A. Beckermann, H. Flohr, and J. Kim, eds.) *Emergence or Reduction?: Prospects for Nonreductive Physicalism*. Berlin: De Gruyter.

Hill, C. S. 1991. *Sensations: A Defense of Type Materialism*. Cambridge: Cambridge University Press.

Hodgson, D. 1988. *The Mind Matters: Consciousness and Choice in a Quantum World*. Oxford: Oxford University Press.

Humphrey, N. 1992. *A History of the Mind*. New York: Simon and Schuster.

Jackendoff, R. 1987. *Consciousness and the Computational Mind*. Cambridge, MA: MIT Press.

Jackson, F. 1982. Epiphenomenal qualia. *Philosophical Quarterly* 32: 127–36.

Jackson, F. 1994. Finding the mind in the natural world. In (R. Casati, B. Smith, and S. White, eds.) *Philosophy and the Cognitive Sciences*. Vienna: Holder-Pichler-Tempsky.

Kirk, R. 1994. *Raw Feeling: A Philosophical Account of the Essence of Consciousness*. Oxford: Oxford University Press.

Kripke, S. 1980. *Naming and Necessity*. Cambridge, MA: Harvard University Press.

Levine, J. 1983. Materialism and qualia: The explanatory gap. *Pacific Philosophical Quarterly* 64:354–61.

Lewis, D. 1994. Reduction of mind. In (S. Guttenplan, ed.) *A Companion to the Philosophy of Mind*. Oxford: Blackwell.

Libet, B. 1993. The neural time factor in conscious and unconscious events. In (G.R. Block and J. Marsh, eds.) *Experimental and Theoretical Studies of Consciousness* (Ciba Foundation Symposium 174). Chichester: John Wiley and Sons.

Loar, B. 1990. Phenomenal states. *Philosophical Perspectives* 4:81–108.

Lockwood, M. 1989. *Mind, Brain, and the Quantum*. Oxford: Blackwell.

McGinn, C. 1989. Can we solve the mind-body problem? *Mind* 98:349–66.

Metzinger, T. 1995. *Conscious Experience*. Paderborn: Schoningh.

Nagel, T. 1974. What is it like to be a bat? *Philosophical Review* 4:435–50.

Nelkin, N. 1993. What is consciousness? *Philosophy of Science* 60:419–34.

Newell, A. 1990. *Unified Theories of Cognition*. Cambridge, MA: Harvard University Press.

Penrose, R. 1989. *The Emperor's New Mind*. Oxford: Oxford University Press.

Penrose, R. 1994. *Shadows of the Mind*. Oxford: Oxford University Press.

Rosenthal, D. M. 1996. A theory of consciousness. In (N. Block, O. Flanagan, and G. Güzeldere, eds.) *The Nature of Consciousness*. Cambridge, MA: MIT Press.

Seager, W. E. 1991. *Metaphysics of Consciousness*. London: Routledge.

Searle, J. R. 1980. Minds, brains and programs. *Behavioral and Brain Sciences* 3:417–57.

Searle, J. R. 1992. *The Rediscovery of the Mind*. Cambridge, MA: MIT Press.

Shallice, T. 1972. Dual functions of consciousness. *Psychological Review* 79:383–93.

Shannon, C. E. 1948. A mathematical theory of communication. *Bell Systems Technical Journal* 27: 379–423.

Strawson, G. 1994. *Mental Reality*. Cambridge, MA: MIT Press.

Tye, M. 1995. *Ten Problems of Consciousness*. Cambridge, MA: MIT Press.

Velmans, M. 1991. Is human information-processing conscious? *Behavioral and Brain Sciences* 14:651–69.

Wheeler, J. A. 1990. Information, physics, quantum: The search for links. In (W. Zurek, ed.) *Complexity, Entropy, and the Physics of Information*. Redwood City, CA: Addison-Wesley.

Online resources:

David Chalmers Online Papers
http://consc.net/papers.html

21

Rethinking the Mind-Body Problem

Barbara Montero

Is the mind physical? Are mental properties, such as the property of *being in pain* or *thinking about the higher orders of infinity*, actually physical properties? Many philosophers think that they are. For no matter how strange and remarkable consciousness and cognition may be, many hold that they are, nevertheless, entirely physical. While some take this view as a starting point in their discussions about the mind, others, well aware that there are dissenters among the ranks, argue for it strenuously. One wonders, however, just what is being assumed, argued for, or denied. In other words, one wonders: Just what does it mean to be physical? This is the question I call, "the body problem."

As I see it, there is little use in arguing about whether the mind is physical, or whether mental properties are physical properties unless we have at least some understanding of what it means to be physical. In other words, in order to solve the mind-body problem, we must solve the body problem. It strikes me as odd that while bookstores and journals are overflowing with debates about whether consciousness is physical, hardly anyone is concerned with "What counts as physical?" Moreover, it would not be much of an exaggeration to say today, as John Earman did more than twenty years ago, that "attempts to answer this question that have appeared in the philosophical literature are for the most part notable only for their glaring inadequacies."[1] If we want to discuss whether the mind is physical, we should say something about what it means to be physical.

Some may argue that such clarification is unnecessary. They may point out that while we cannot provide necessary and sufficient conditions for *tablehood*, we nonetheless understand the concept, because we can readily identify things that are clearly tables and things that are clearly not. They claim the same is true of our notion of the physical. But the situations are not analogous. While we can identify central cases of being physical—what could be clearer examples of physical than rocks and trees (except, perhaps, quarks and leptons)?—an extra wrinkle is that rocks and trees (as well as quarks and leptons) are clear cases only assuming that idealism is false. In any case, something needs to be said about how to determine what we can place in the category along with rocks and trees. In certain ways, beliefs and desires *are* like rocks and trees, while quarks and leptons are not. For example, talk of beliefs and desires plays a role in our ordinary folk understanding of the world, while talk of quarks and leptons does not. Beliefs and desires also are part of the same macro-level causal network as rocks and trees, while quarks and leptons are not. But few physicalists think that from our central examples of physical objects we should infer that quarks and leptons are nonphysical.

Perhaps these problems could be overlooked if we had clear intuitions regarding the nonphysical. But do we? The stock example of a nonphysical entity is some kind of ghost. For example, Jaegwon Kim defines "ontological physicalism" as the view that "there are no nonphysical residues (e.g. Cartesian souls, entelechies, and the like)."[2] And Jeffrey Poland states that the physicalist's bottom line is really: "There are no ghosts!"[3] But why is a ghost nonphysical? Is it that they can pass through walls without disturbing them? Neutrinos, I am told, can pass right through the earth without disturbing it, yet neutrinos are classified as physical. Is it that they have no mass? Photons have no mass yet are considered physical. Perhaps it is that they supposedly do not take up space. But if taking up no space shows that something is nonphysical, point particles (if they exist) would have to be classified as nonphysical. Yet physicalists, I take it, would not accept this view. So to say that the physical means "no spooky stuff" does not help matters.

Perhaps physicalism at least excludes the possibility of a ghost in a machine, that is, the view that there is some type of mental substance completely different in kind from physical substance. But what does this view amount to, since most physicalists are happy to admit that there is more than one kind of elementary particle? Perhaps the idea is that whether only one basic particle exists, say, strings, or it turns out that in addition to strings there are also Ferris wheels, physicalism holds that everything nonbasic is composed of the same kind, or kinds of basic particles. But this view cannot be right. For example, some evidence indicates that what physicists call "dark matter" is composed entirely of axions, hypothetical new elementary particles.[4] Yet dark matter is no threat to physicalism. So the simple notion of *stuff of a different kind* does not provide us with a notion of nonphysical. But what, then, does?

Philosophers commonly answer this question by deferring to the physicists. The physical is said to be whatever the physicist, or more precisely, the particle physicist, tells us exists (what we might now think of as quarks and leptons, as well as the exchange particles, gluons, gravitons, etc.). And the nonphysical is whatever remains, if there is anything. On this view, physicalists—that is, those who hold that everything is physical—claim that physics provides us with an exhaustive and exclusive line to all reality. Here is a straightforward answer to the body problem, but one that is too simple, since most philosophers believe that things like rocks, tables, and chairs are just as physical as quarks, leptons, and gluons.

Granted, whether to say that the physical is only what the physicists take as fundamental is partially a terminological issue. But while the question whether to reserve the name "physical" for just the fundamental constituents of reality or to use it more broadly *is* terminological, the question of how many layers of reality to countenance is not. Because most physicalists allow for not only the smallest stuff, but also for atoms, molecules, rocks and galaxies, the leave-it-to-the-physicists approach is usually amended to the view that the physical world is the world of the fundamental particles, forces, laws and such *as well as* whatever depends on this physical stuff. As such, we can allow for the possibility that rocks may be physical.

My concern, however, is not with the dependence relation *per se* but with what everything is being related to: the lower level dependence base or what is often referred to as "the microphysical." One thinks of microphysical phenomena as described by the most recent microphysics. But if the physical is defined in terms of current microphysics, and a new particle is discovered next week, the particle will not be physical—a consequence most philosophers want to avoid. But if not current microphysics, what else could the microphysical be?

Carl Hempel posed a dilemma for those attempting to define the physical in reference to microphysics.[5] On the one hand, we cannot define the physical in terms of current microphysics since today's microphysics is probably neither entirely true (some of our theories may look as wrong-headed to future generations as phlogiston theory looks to us now) nor complete (more remains to be explained). On the other hand, if we take microphysics to be some future unspecified theory, the claim that the mind is physical is vague, since we currently have no idea of that theory. Faced with this dilemma, what is a physicalist to do?

Some try to take the middle road, explaining the "microphysical" by referring to "something like current microphysics—but just improved."[6] But in what respect is this future microphysics like current microphysics? And in what respect will it be improved? Since these questions are usually not addressed (save, of course, for the implication that it is similar enough to be intelligible yet different enough to be true) it seems that Hempel's dilemma recurs for these compromise views. For the theory in question will be false if it is significantly similar to current physics, and if not, we are left with no clear notion of the physical.

Taking the first horn of Hempel's dilemma, that is, defining the physical in terms of current microphysics, does not provide us with a comfortable solution to the body problem. For it is rather awkward to hold a theory that one knows is false.[7] But does taking the second horn fare any better? David Armstrong thinks so. He explicitly tells us that when he says "physical properties" he is not talking about the properties specified by current physics, but rather "whatever set of properties the physicist in the end will appeal to."[8] Similarly, Frank Jackson holds that the physical facts encompass "everything in a completed physics, chemistry, and neurophysiology, and all there is to know about the causal and relational facts consequent upon all this."[9] As Barry Loewer puts it, "what many have on their minds when they speak of fundamental physical properties is that they are the properties expressed by simple predicates of the true comprehensive fundamental physical theory."[10] So for Armstrong and others the physical is to be defined over a completed physics, a physics in the end. But what is this final physics? The answer, as Hempel has pointed out, is unknown.

Basing one's notion of the physical on an unfathomable theory seems to be a serious enough problem to discourage defining the physical over a final theory. But most philosophers ignore this problem and charge ahead to the more juicy questions, such as whether knowledge of all the physical facts, (whatever they may be) enables us to know what it is like to see colors. So consider that another consequence of using the notion of a completed physics to explain the physical is that, at least under one interpretation, it trivially excludes the possibility that the mind is not physical. For on one understanding of it, a completed physics amounts to a physics that explains *everything*. So if mentality is a feature of the world, a completed physics, on this definition, will explain it too. While there is nothing wrong with trivial truth *per se*, this is not the solution to the mind-body problem most philosophers would accept. For neither physicalists nor their foes think that we already know by definition that the mind is physical.

Chomsky has identified a related problem for those who define the physical in terms of a final physics. His point is that since we cannot predict the course of physics, we cannot be sure that a final physics will not include mental properties, qua mental, as fundamental properties.[11] Yet if final physics takes the mental realm to be fundamental, the difference dissolves between physicalists who claim that mental properties will be accounted for in final physics and dualists who claim that mental properties are fundamental.

A solution to the body problem is not forthcoming. Perhaps, we should focus on questions other than the question "Is the mind physical?" So let me conclude with a suggestion. Physicalism is, at least partly, motivated by the belief that the mental is ultimately non-mental, that is, that mental properties are not fundamental properties, whereas dualism holds, precisely, that they are. So a crucial question is whether the mental is ultimately nonmental. Of course, the notion of the non-mental is also open-ended. And, for this reason, it may be just as difficult to see what sort of considerations are relevant in determining what counts as non-mental as it is to see what sort of considerations are relevant in determining what counts as physical. However, we do have a grasp of one side of the divide—that is, the mental. So, rather than worrying about whether the mind is physical, we should be concerned with whether it is non-mental. And this question has little to do with what current physics, future physics, or a final physics says about the world.

NOTES

1. John Earman, "What is Physicalism?" *Journal of Philosophy* 72 (1975), p. 566.
2. Jaegwon Kim, "Supervenience, Emergence, Realization in Philosophy of Mind," in M. Carrier and P. Machamer (eds.), *Mindscapes: Philosophy, Science, and the Mind*, Pittsburgh, University of Pittsburgh Press, 1997.
3. Jeffery Poland, *Physicalism: The Philosophical Foundations*, Oxford: Oxford University Press, 1994, p. 15. He emphasizes this point again later: "ghosts, gods, and the paranormal are genuine threats to physicalism" (p. 228). That is, according to Poland, if ghosts were to exist, physicalism would be false.
4. See Leslie Rosenberg, "The Search for Dark Matter Axions," *Particle World* 4 (1995), pp. 3–10.
5. See Carl Hempel, "Comments on Goodman's Ways of Worldmaking," *Synthese* 45 (1980), pp. 193–9. Also see Hempel, "Reduction: Ontological and Linguistic Facets," in S. Morgenbesser, P. Suppes and M. Whit (eds.), *Philosophy, Science and Method: Essays in Honor of Ernest Nagel,* New York: St. Martin's Press, 1969. I am using different terminology from Hempel, and my emphasis is on the question of whether the mind is physical rather than the question of physicalism in general, but the point is essentially the same.
6. See for example, David Lewis, "New Work for a Theory of Universals," *Australasian Journal of Philosophy* 61 (1983), pp. 343–77 and Robert Kirk, *Raw Feeling: A Philosophical Account of the Essence of Consciousness*, New York: Oxford University Press, 1994.
7. For further discussion of this point see Barbara Montero, "The Body Problem," *Nous* 33 (1999), pp. 183–200.
8. David Armstrong, "The Causal Theory of Mind," in D. Rosenthal (ed.) *The Nature of Mind*, New York: Oxford University Press, 1991, p. 186. Of course, not all properties the physicist appeals to are relevant: when a physicist is explaining a proposed budget in a grant application or explaining to her supervisor why she was late to work, she may be appealing to very different properties than when she is applying her mathematical skills in computing a wave function. But perhaps this distinction is intuitive enough.

9. Frank Jackson, "What Mary Didn't Know," in D. Rosenthal (ed.), *The Nature of Mind*, New York: Oxford University Press, 1991, p. 291.

10. Barry Loewer, "Humean Supervenience," *Philosophical Topics* 24 (1996), p. 103.

11. See Noam Chomsky, "Language and Nature," *Mind* 104 (1995), pp. 1–61 and *Language and Thought*, Rhode Island: Moyer Bell, 1993.

Online resources:

Barbara Montero
http://barbara.antinomies.org/

Glossary

Anti-reductionist: A position in philosophy of mind that the mind and mental states are complex phenomena and cannot be wholly reduced to and wholly explained by more basic entities such as the brain and brain states or even more basic material states.

Artificial Intelligence: The scientific research project of designing computer programs and machines that model or simulate human intelligence.

Asymmetry: A lack of a relationship of correspondence, equivalence, or identity between something's parts or between different things.

Begging the question (Question-begging): A fallacy or logical mistake in reasoning in which an argument assumes as a true premise the conclusion that is supposed to be proven.

Category mistake: A mistake regarding the kind or type of entity under discussion in which this entity is described in terms that do not apply to it but to entities of a different kind.

Causally quiescent: "Quiescence" is a state of rest or stillness. When something is causally quiescent it is not causally interacting with any other things such that they would be affected by it and, in turn, cause other effects.

Central State Identity/Type Identity: The view that types of mental states are identical to types of brain states.

Cogito, ergo sum: Latin phrase meaning, "I think, therefore I am."

Contingent: A condition that is likely or possible but is not necessarily determined. A state of affairs that could be otherwise.

Disposition: A tendency toward a state that results from the constitution of an entity. Dispositions, such as the *solubility* of sugar in liquids, are qualities that are activated or realized only under certain conditions (e.g., the sugar is placed in water), although the physical constitution determines these tendencies.

Dualism: The metaphysical view that there are two different fundamental or basic substances, mental substance and physical substance.

Eliminative Materialism/eliminativism: The view that our everyday, commonsense terms that regard mental states can be eliminated by more precise and accurate neuro-scientific terminology.

257

Epiphenomenal: A secondary phenomenon accompanying a primary phenomenon. In philosophy of mind, epiphenomenalism holds that mental states are the products accompanying the activity of the brain, but these secondary products do not have further causal powers.

Evil Genius: In the first of Descartes' *Meditations*, he describes an all-powerful "Evil Genius" whose sole intent is to deceive a thinker into believing that the world and the body are real when they are illusions.

Extended Thing (*Latin: Res Extensa*): Physical entities that take up space (are extended in space) and can be measured and quantified.

Folk-psychology: The psychological explanation of people's behavior implied in ordinary language through ascribing beliefs, desires, and other mental states to persons. It is a "folk theory" in that it is not a theory that has been subject to rigorous scientific testing but is an explanatory tool in place in everyday circumstances.

Functional description: A description of a system's inputs, outputs, and internal state changes.

Functionalist/Functionalism: In philosophy of mind, functionalism is the view that mental states are defined by their causes, effects, and relations to other mental states. A functionalist (in philosophy of mind) is someone who holds this viewpoint.

Homunculi (plural): A *homunculus* (singular) is a miniature human being.

Hyperbolic doubt: Descartes' method of destroying his earlier beliefs found in the first of his *Mediations*. Hyperbolic doubt is exaggerated doubt in which Descartes treats any belief that can possibly be doubted as if it was a false belief.

Intentional: In philosophy of mind, an intentional state regards the manner in which a mental state relates to some kind of entity or is "about" something. Beliefs and desires are considered good examples of intentional states. Intentional states are sometimes referred to as propositional attitudes.

Intentional stance: An attitude of attributing beliefs and desires to people and even to other kinds of entities.

Introspection: Looking in upon or reflecting upon one's own mental states. Observing how things seem to oneself.

Intuition: Insight or understanding that is pretheoretical; coming prior to scientific or other kinds of explanations.

Knowing how: Skills or abilities that, once acquired, do not require one to think through each step of a process. Riding a bicycle is an example of such a skill.

Knowing that: Propositional knowledge; knowledge of rules and/or facts.

Leibniz' Law: Entities A and B are identical if and only if A and B possess all of the same qualities.

Logical Behaviorism (also known as Analytical Behaviorism): The view in philosophy of mind that mental states are behavioral dispositions or tendencies to act in certain ways under certain conditions.

Machine Functionalism: The type of functionalism attributed frequently to Alan Turing in which mental processes are defined as analogues to computer programs.

Materialist/materialism: Materialism is the view that all that exists is made of matter (is material). A materialist is someone who holds this viewpoint.

Mental causation: Our commonsense explanations of people's behavior indicate that mental states cause physical states (and vice-versa). Mental causation is often considered a sharp criticism of the dualist position on the nature of the mind.

Mentalist: The view that some mental phenomena cannot be explained through scientific investigation.

Multiple realization: The idea that mental states or mental properties can be realized in different kinds of physical systems.

Naturalistic/naturalism: Naturalism in philosophy is the view that all phenomena can be explained and accounted for through scientific investigation and the laws of nature. A naturalistic perspective holds that science will eventually explain all phenomena.

Objective: The quality of being observable and having a factual basis.

Ockham's Razor: The principle that "Entities should not be multiplied beyond necessity." It is desirable in forming theories that we choose the simplest theories in which the unknown entities we seek to explain are explained by way of entities we do know.

Phenomenon: An event or occurrence.

Phenomenological: The way in which things seem or appear to be from the perspective of one's own experience.

Physicalist/Physicalism: A view that, like materialism, holds that what is factually real is physical stuff. A physicalist holds that our knowledge of the world can only regard physical, observable entities and causes.

Primitive term: A simple or basic term that is undefined and from which other terms are derived.

Property dualism: The view that at least some mental qualities are not reducible to physical qualities. The physical entity—the brain—has both qualities and physical qualities; but unlike the dualist, the property dualist does not need to hold that the mind as a whole is a completely different substance than that of the body.

Psychofunctionalism: The view that the mind is explained scientifically by way of its organizational structure (as in a computer program) and not through its biological structure.

Psycho-physical/Psychophysical: Regarding the interrelations of the mental (psychological) and the physical.

Qualia: The feeling or sensation of "what it is like" to experience something.

Reductionism: The explanation of a complex set of facts by way of a simpler set of facts.

Representational Theory of the Mind: A view of the mind that holds that our intentional states such as beliefs and desires involve a relation between the believer or desirer and a symbolic mental representation of the belief or desire. The meaning of a symbolic representation in the mind may remain the same, while there can be a change in one's intentional state (propositional attitude) toward this representation.

Scientific hypothesis: A conditional of the form If H (hypothesis) then O (observational consequence). The observational consequence of the hypothesis confirms the hypothesis, if it occurs. If the observational consequence fails to occur, the hypothesis is falsified.

Semantics: The study of the meanings in language.

Skeptic/Skepticism: Skepticism is the view that knowledge is not possible either as a whole or in a specific area. A skeptic is someone who doubts that knowledge exists as a whole or within an area.

Stance: An attitude toward someone or something; a point of view.

Strict identity: See Leibniz' Law

Syntactical operations: Manipulation of a syntactic or grammatical structure; following the rules of syntax or the formation of proper sentences.

Subjective: Something particular to an individual's perspective or point of view.

Substance Dualism: See Dualism

Thinking thing (*Latin: Res Cogitans*): Mental substance, which for Descartes is not extended in space and cannot be observed, but is the substance that engages in mental activity (thinking, doubting, perceiving, willing . . .).

Thought experiment: An experiment carried out only in thought. Thought experiments are used in philosophy to test ideas and theories.

Token identity (also known as Functionalism): The view that an individual mental state is a token (particular instance) of a general type of mental state. There are many different tokens of any one mental state type. For instance, different people and animals, when they each experience a pain, experience a token of a general type of mental state—pain. Each individual pain token is said to be identical to the material that realizes that token (a human brain, a dog brain) but, importantly, this identity between a token and the material is contingent. Different materials can realize token instances of pain.

Turing Test: A phrase that refers to Alan Turing's "Imitation Game" in which a human interrogator must ask questions of a computer (hidden from view) and then must try to gauge from its replies whether the computer is human or not. Turing believed that a computer could eventually pass this test and be found intelligent.

Type Identity/Central State Identity: The view that types of mental states are identical to types of brain states.

Index

261

About the Author

Maureen Eckert is an assistant professor of philosophy at the University of Massachusetts, Dartmouth. Her interests include ancient Greek philosophy, philosophy of mind, and metaphysics. Textbooks that she has co-edited include *Knowledge and Reality: Classic and Contemporary Readings*, with Steven M. Cahn and Robert Buckley (2003), and *Philosophical Horizons: Introductory Readings*, with Steven M. Cahn (2005). She lives in Providence, Rhode Island, where she enjoys creating and collecting art in her spare time.

About the Contributors

PART I

René Descartes (1596–1650) was a philosopher, mathematician, and scientist, widely considered a founder of modern philosophy. His most famous work, *Meditations on First Philosophy* (1641), sought to integrate all of the sciences and provide a foundation for all knowledge. Other works of his include his *Optics, Meteorology, and Geometry* and its preface, "Discourse on the Method of Rightly Conducting the Reason and Seeking Truth in the Sciences" (1637) and *Principles of Philosophy* (1644) from which our selections are taken.

Gilbert Ryle (1900–1976), British philosopher, principally known for his critique of Cartesian dualism, for which he coined the phrase "the ghost in the machine." He referred to some of his ideas as "behaviourism." A capable linguist, he was recruited to intelligence work during World War II, after which he became Wayneflete Professor of Metaphysical Philosophy at Oxford and published his principal work, *The Concept of Mind* in 1949. Other books include *Plato's Progress* and *Dilemmas*, a collection of shorter pieces. He was editor of the philosophical journal *Mind* from 1947 to 1971.

Jerry A. Fodor is a professor of philosophy at Rutgers University. He has published numerous articles on the philosophy of mind and cognitive science. Some important books he has written include *The Modularity of Mind: An Essay on Faculty Psychology* (1983), *The Mind Doesn't Work That Way; The Scope and Limits of Computational Psychology* (2000), and *The Language of Thought* (1975) from which our selection comes.
   See also, chapter 7, The Mind Body Problem.

PART II

J. J. C. Smart is Emeritus Professor of Philosophy at the Australian National University and Honorary Research Fellow at Monash University. His works include papers on physicalism as well as other areas of philosophical inquiry such as ethics and philosophy of religion. A published collection of his articles is *Essays Metaphysical and Moral* (1987).

Alan M. Turing (1912–1954), British mathematician, logician, and cryptographer, is considered one of the fathers of modern computer science. His Turing Test contributed to the debate regarding artificial intelligence— whether it will ever be possible to say that a machine is conscious and can think. During World War II, Turing worked at Bletchley Park, Britain's codebreaking center and was for a time responsible for German Naval cryptanalysis. He devised techniques for breaking German codes, including the Enigma code. After the war, at the University of Manchester he worked largely on software, on the Manchester Mark I, then emerging as one of the world's earliest true computers.

David Lewis (1941–2001) was a professor of philosophy at Princeton University. He worked in many areas of philosophy, including philosophy of mind, language, and metaphysics. Famous works of his include, *Counterfactuals* (1973), *On the Plurality of Worlds* (1986), and several volumes of collected papers including *Philosophical Papers*, Vol. 1 (1983).

Ned Block is Silver Professor of Philosophy and Psychology at New York University. He is the author of numerous papers in the areas of philosophy of mind and consciousness, psychology, and cognitive science. He is one of the editors of *The Nature of Consciousness: Philosophical Debates* (1997).

Frank Jackson is Distinguished Professor at the Australian National University. His research includes the areas of Philosophical Logic, Cognitive Science, Epistemology and Metaphysics, and Meta-Ethics. His works include *Perception: A Representative Theory* (1977) and his collected papers are reprinted in *Mind, Method, and Conditionals: Selected Essays* (1998).

Paul Churchland is professor of philosophy at the University of California, San Diego. His research spans the areas of philosophy of mind, artificial intelligence and cognitive neurobiology, epistemology, and perception. His books include *The Engine of Reason, The Seat of the Soul: A Philosophical Journey into the Brain* (1995) and *A Neurocomputational Perspective: The Nature of Mind and the Structure of Science* (1989), as well as *Matter and*

Consciousness (1984; second edition 1988) which provides us with our reading selection.

Daniel Dennett is University Professor of Philosophy, Austin B. Fletcher Professor and Director of the Center for Cognitive Studies at Tufts University. He is author of numerous papers in the areas of philosophy of mind, consciousness, and cognitive science and major works include *The Intentional Stance* (1989), *Consciousness Explained* (1991), and *Freedom Evolves* (2003).

Andy Clark is professor of philosophy and director of the Cognitive Science Program at Indiana University, Bloomington. His books include *Being There: Putting Brain, Body and World Together Again* (1997) and *Mindware: An Introduction to the Philosophy of Cognitive Science* (2000).

PART III

John Searle is Mills Professor of the Philosophy of Mind and Language at the University of California, Berkeley. His works include *Minds, Brains and Science* (1985), *The Rediscovery of the Mind* (1992), *The Construction of Social Reality* (1995), and *Mind* (2004).

Patricia Churchland is University Professor of Philosophy at the University of California, San Diego. Her works include *Neurophilosophy: Toward a Unified Science of the Mind-Brain* (1986), *The Computational Brain*, with T. J. Sejnowski (1992), and *On the Contrary*, with Paul M. Churchland (1998).

PART IV

Thomas Nagel is Fiorello La Guardia Professor of Law, University Professor, and professor of philosophy at New York University. His works include *Mortal Questions* (1979), *The View From Nowhere* (1986), and *What Does It All Mean?* (1987).

Keith Gunderson is professor of philosophy at the University of Minnesota. He is the author of *Mentality and Machines*, 2nd ed. (1985).

David M. Armstrong is Emeritus Professor of Philosophy, University of Sydney, 1992–present. He is the author of numerous papers and books on the philosophy of mind and metaphysics, including *The Nature of Mind* (1981) and *Universals: an Opinionated Introduction* (1989).

David Chalmers is professor of philosophy, director of the Centre for Consciousness, and an ARC Federation Fellow at the Australian National University. He is author of the book, *The Conscious Mind: In Search of a Fundamental Theory* (1996).

Barbara Montero is assistant professor of philosophy at the College of Staten Island of the City University of New York. Her research includes the metaphysics of the mind and proprioception.